Library of
Davidson College

# Economic Theory of
# Regulatory Constraint

# Economic Theory of Regulatory Constraint

Elizabeth E. Bailey
Bell Telephone Laboratories
and
New York University

**Lexington Books**
D.C. Heath and Company
Lexington, Massachusetts
Toronto     London

338.4
B154e

**Library of Congress Cataloging in Publication Data**

Bailey, Elizabeth E.
  Economic theory of regulatory constraint.

  Includes bibliographical references.
  1. Public utilities—Rate of return—Mathematical models. 2. Monopolies—Mathematical models. I. Title II. Title: Regulatory constraint.
HD2763.B24     338.4'3     73-11313
ISBN 0-669-87114-1

*Copyright © 1973 by D.C. Heath and Company.*

All rights reserved. No part of this publication may be reproduced or transmitted in any form or by any means, electronic or mechanical, including photocopy, recording, or any information storage or retrieval system, without permission in writing from the publisher.

Published simultaneously in Canada.

Printed in the United States of America.  75-6525

International Standard Book Number: 0-669-87114-1

Library of Congress Catalog Card Number: 73-11313

To William who wants to be first and
to James that he may one day be so.

# Contents

| | | |
|---|---|---|
| | List of Tables and Figures | xi |
| | Notation | xv |
| | Preface | xvii |
| | *Introduction* | 1 |
| Chapter 1 | An Analytic Approach to Regulation | 3 |
| | *Part I: A Regulatory Model* | 7 |
| Chapter 2 | Formulation of Model and Method of Solution | 9 |
| | Introduction and Summary | 9 |
| | Description of the Model | 9 |
| | Kuhn-Tucker Conditions | 15 |
| Chapter 3 | Operation off the Production Frontier | 23 |
| | Introduction and Summary | 23 |
| | The Regulatory Model | 24 |
| | Single Productive Variable Case | 28 |
| | Regulation Limiting Return on Total Costs | 35 |
| Chapter 4 | Symmetric and Asymmetric Constraints | 41 |
| | Introduction and Summary | 41 |
| | Symmetric Constraint | 43 |

|  |  |  |
|---|---|---|
|  | Asymmetric Constraint | 52 |
|  | Related Regulatory Models | 58 |
|  |  |  |
|  | **Part II: Rate of Return Regulation** | 63 |
|  |  |  |
| Chapter 5 | **Averch-Johnson Model** | 65 |
|  | Introduction and Summary | 65 |
|  | Components of Model | 66 |
|  | Major Theoretical Results | 72 |
|  | Two-Output Version of Model | 84 |
|  |  |  |
| Chapter 6 | **Fair Rate of Return** | 87 |
|  | Introduction and Summary | 87 |
|  | Regulatory Expansion Path | 88 |
|  | Invariance Property of Path | 97 |
|  | Optimal Fair Return | 104 |
|  |  |  |
| Chapter 7 | **Effect of Lagged Regulation** | 111 |
|  | Introduction and Summary | 111 |
|  | Effect of Lag when $s > r$ | 111 |
|  | Two Graphical Examples | 118 |
|  | Zero-Profit Constraint | 122 |
|  |  |  |
| Chapter 8 | **Comparative Statics Analysis of AJ Model** | 125 |
|  | Introduction and Summary | 125 |
|  | Changes in the Market Cost of Capital | 127 |
|  | Increase in the Acquisition Cost of Capital | 132 |
|  | Changes in the Wage Rate | 135 |
|  | Changes in Tax Parameters | 137 |

| | | |
|---|---|---|
| Chapter 9 | **Rising Cost of Capital** | 139 |
| | Introduction and Summary | 139 |
| | Components of the Model | 139 |
| | Graphical Analysis | 143 |
| | Mathematical Analysis | 149 |
| Chapter 10 | **Peak-Load Pricing under Regulatory Constraint** | 155 |
| | Introduction and Summary | 155 |
| | Traditional Approach to Peak-Load Pricing | 155 |
| | Peak-Load Pricing under Profit Objective | 162 |
| | *Summary* | 169 |
| Chapter 11 | **Some Theorems about Regulatory Constraint** | 171 |
| | Notes | 175 |
| | References | 181 |
| | Index | 193 |
| | About the Author | 201 |

# List of Tables and Figures

**Tables**

| | | |
|---|---|---|
| 6-1 | Comparative Statics Results of a Change in Fair Rate of Return | 89 |
| 8-1 | Comparative Statics Properties of Monopoly versus Regulated Firm | 126 |
| 9-1 | Rising Cost of Capital Theorems | 149 |
| 10-1 | Peak and Off-peak Pricing Rules | 161 |

**Figures**

| | | |
|---|---|---|
| 2-1 | Misallocation versus Operation off the Production Frontier | 12 |
| 2-2 | Stationary Points and Corner Optima | 17 |
| 2-3 | Typical Profit Hill and Constraint Curve for Single-Variable Model | 19 |
| 2-4 | Nonconcave Profit Hill with a Binding but Inactive Constraint | 20 |
| 2-5 | Nonstandard Configurations for Constraint | 21 |
| 3-1 | Size of Lagrangian Multiplier | 27 |
| 3-2 | Monopoly and Regulated Outputs | 29 |
| 3-3 | Marginal Revenue Associated with Productive and Wasteful Activity | 32 |
| 3-4 | Optimal Fair Return under a Return-on-Cost Constraint | 36 |
| 4-1 | Profit Hill for Two-Variable Model | 46 |
| 4-2 | Symmetric Constraint Surface | 47 |

| 4-3 | Symmetric Regulation | 48 |
| 4-4 | Expansion Path under Symmetric Regulation | 49 |
| 4-5 | Expansion Path in Two-Input Model | 52 |
| 4-6 | Asymmetric Constraint Surface | 54 |
| 4-7 | Asymmetric Regulation | 55 |
| 4-8 | Asymmetric Expansion Path | 56 |
| 4-9 | Asymmetric Regulation with Independent Markets | 57 |
| 4-10 | Expansion Path under Operating-Ratio Regulation | 60 |
| 5-1 | Rate-of-Return Regulation | 70 |
| 5-2 | Isorate of Return and Isoprofit Contours | 71 |
| 5-3 | Theorem on Use of Overly Capital-Intensive Technology | 79 |
| 5-4 | Nonconvexity of Feasible Region | 81 |
| 5-5 | Theorem on Use of Overly Labor-Intensive Technology | 82 |
| 6-1 | Capital and Profit Response to Changes in Fair Return | 90 |
| 6-2 | Factor Inferiority and the Capital-Labor Ratio | 94 |
| 6-3 | AJ and Efficient Expansion Path | 96 |
| 6-4 | End Points of *AJP* and *EEP* | 97 |
| 6-5 | Graduated Fair Return | 98 |

| | | |
|---|---|---|
| 6-6 | Corporate Income Tax | 100 |
| 6-7 | Corporate Property Tax | 102 |
| 6-8 | True Investment Model | 104 |
| 6-9 | Optimal Fair Return in Partial Equilibrium Model | 106 |
| 6-10 | Optimal Fair Return in General Equilibrium Model | 109 |
| 7-1 | Lagged Regulation and the Incentive to Misallocate | 112 |
| 7-2 | Effect of Lag on Discounted Profit Stream | 114 |
| 7-3 | Minimum Cost versus Enlargement | 119 |
| 7-4 | Optimal Level of Capital Usage for Particular Example | 121 |
| 7-5 | Efficient Operation under Zero-Profit Regulation | 122 |
| 8-1 | Cost of Capital versus Fair Return | 128 |
| 8-2 | Inefficiency Worsens with Increase in Cost of Capital | 131 |
| 8-3 | Profit Goes down with Increase in Acquisition Cost of Capital | 133 |
| 8-4 | Increases in Wage Rate and Technical Change | 136 |
| 9-1 | Rising Cost of Capital Leads to Hill-Shaped Constraint Curves | 142 |
| 9-2 | Indeterminacy in Labor Usage and Output Level | 144 |

| | | |
|---|---|---|
| 9-3 | Profit Hill and Constraint Surface for Rising Cost of Capital Model | 146 |
| 9-4 | Possibility of Waste when Fair Return Equals Marginal Cost of Capital | 147 |
| 9-5 | Comparative Statics for the Fair Return Parameter | 148 |
| 10-1 | Typical Load Curve with Peak and Off-Peak Periods | 156 |
| 10-2 | Peak and Off-Peak Pricing in a Two-Period Model | 161 |
| 10-3 | Peak-Load Pricing and Rate-of-Return Regulation | 164 |

# Notation

$\alpha$ : fractional allocation of costs between markets; also degree of homogeneity in homogeneous production function

$AC_{AJ}$ : average cost of production in Averch-Johnson (AJ) model

$b$ : turnover period for circulating capital; also parameter in capacity constraint

$c$ : acquisition cost per physical unit of capital (constant)

$C(L,K) = wL + rcK$ : total costs in a two-input model

$C(q)$ : cost of producing $q$ units of output

$C(z,y,x)$ : total costs including those associated with the productive variables, $z$ and $y$, and those associated with operation off the production frontier, $x$

$d$ : discount rate

$D$ : bordered Hessian determinant

$e$ : demand elasticity of price

$E$ : customer charge in a two-part tariff model

$\epsilon$ : a small number

$g$ : markup over cost

$G(z,y,x)$ : ceiling level of profit permitted by the regulator

$h$ : degree of Hicks-neutral technological change

$H(q,K)$ : minimum labor requirement to produce output $q$ when there are $K$ units of capital

$H(q_1,\ldots,q_n)$ : operating expenses to produce output $q_1,\ldots,q_n$.

$i$ : actual rate of return earned by the firm; or index of an off-peak period

$I$ : social indifference curve

$j$ : index of a peak period

$k$ : transfer price for multi-stage firm; also corporate property tax rate

$K$ : physical units of capital

$K^*$ : wasteful units of capital

$L$ : physical units of labor

$L^*$ : wasteful units of labor

$\lambda$ : Lagrange multiplier associated with regulatory constraint

$m$ : unit cost of managerial emoluments; also markup permitted by regulator; also turnover period for fixed

capital; also multiple in a homogeneous production function; also slope of production curve
$MC_{AJ}$ : marginal cost of production in AJ model
$MC_K$ : marginal cost of capital
$MR$ : marginal revenue
$\mu$ : Lagrange multiplier associated with internal profit constraint; also Lagrange multiplier associated with capacity constraint
$p(q)$ : inverse demand function giving price as a function of quantity, $p' < 0$
$\phi$ : Lagrangian function
$\pi$ : net profit after all costs have been subtracted from revenue
$q$ : output
$q(L,K)$ : production function which translates the labor and capital inputs into an output $q$
$q_K$ : marginal physical product of capital
$q_L$ : marginal physical product of labor
$r$ : market cost of capital (constant)
$r(K)$ : market cost of capital (rising, $r' > 0$)
$R(L,K) = p(q)q(L,K)$ : revenues in a two-input model as determined by the firm's demand and production functions
$R(q_1, \ldots, q_n)$ : revenue from output $q_1, \ldots, q_n$
$R(z,y)$ : revenue generated by the productive variables $z$ and $y$
$R'$ : marginal revenue
$R_K = R'q_K$ : marginal revenue product of capital
$R_L = R'q_L$ : marginal revenue product of labor
$s$ : fair rate of return on investment set by regulator (constant)
$t$ : corporate income tax rate
$T$ : lag interval
$U(q,K,L)$ : social welfare function
$U(x)$ : utility of waste
$V$ : total present value of the firm
$W$ : welfare
$w$ : unit cost of labor or wage rate (constant)
$x$ : a measure of the degree to which the firm is operating off its production frontier
$y$ : productive variable, either input or output quantity
$z$ : productive variable, either input or output quantity; also expenditure on managerial staff

# Preface

Many of the articles that have recently been published on the subject of regulation have been theoretically oriented. However, this orientation has not been reflected in the books on regulation, which are institutional in approach. This text constitutes an attempt to fill the gap.

In the first part, a general structural framework is presented to accommodate a number of interesting models of regulatory constraint. The second part treats in some detail the most theoretically intriguing interpretation of the general structure, which is the Averch-Johnson model of rate-of-return regulation. Some ways of altering the model to include issues such as regulatory lag, peak-load pricing, and a rising cost of capital are also discussed.

An attempt has been made to make the Averch-Johnson material self-contained, so that a reader can restrict his attention to this part of the book if that is desired. Wherever possible the results are described using both graphical and mathematical methods so that a reader who has difficulty with one or the other of the approaches to the analysis can nevertheless come to an understanding of the properties of regulatory models.

I have received superlative guidance from William Baumol, who was my dissertation advisor at Princeton University and who carefully reread the revised manuscript as my friend and colleague at New York University. I shall always be indebted to him for teaching me standards of scholarly and of literary excellence that are a joy for me to try to achieve. Charles Berry, Gregory Chow, Dwight Jaffee, Uwe Reinhardt, and Lawrence White, of Princeton University also commented helpfully at various stages in my thinking, as did Philip Commins, Allan Zelenitz, and Donald Fry.

A number of my students at Bell Laboratories and at New York University have made contributions of a specific and significant nature. In this regard, I am especially grateful to Charles McCallum, Philip Unger, Craig Bender, Frank Gratzer, Alan Tedesco, David Dayan, Eric Lindenberg, Robert Dansby, Kyu Lie, and John Chu. Kyu Lie contributed the very thorough index.

In addition, I have relied on advice and counsel from Gerald Faulhaber, Vincent Mowery, and Edward Zajac, at Bell Laboratories, and on extensive written comments by Richard Schmalensee of the University of California, San Diego. Others who have given me suggestions for improvements are Leland Johnson, Eric Davis, William Jordan, Paul Joskow, Paul W. MacAvoy, David McNicol, James Rosse, S.C. Chu, and Robert Spann.

Bell Laboratories financed my initial research through their Doctoral Support Program, and provided drafting and typing support. The excellence of the graphics is attributable to the tireless efforts of Sam Bennett. I also wish to thank Sally Daino and Patti Plewa for outstanding typing jobs on the manuscript, and Leigh Tripoli for her editorial suggestions.

Roger Coleman and Austin Finch kindly consented to let me use as Chapters 7 and 9 respectively the material from Bailey and Coleman[1] and Bailey and Finch.[2] William Baumol, Perry Shapiro, and Edward Zajac gave me access to some especially helpful items of personal correspondence. Chapter 10 is taken for the most part from Bailey.[3]

# Introduction

# 1
# An Analytic Approach to Regulation

Averch and Johnson[1] were the first authors to extend the traditional economic theory of the firm to include a regulatory constraint on the firm's behavior. Our methodology builds upon theirs, and like theirs is focused for the most part on regulatory models that are static, deterministic, and in a partial equilibrium setting. Nevertheless, using the mathematical and graphical tools of microeconomic theory, we are able to illustrate why regulation can have economic consequences that were not intended and why the gloomy view that regulation is a "dead hand"[2] can have some validity. The models also indicate aspects of regulation and types of constraints that are likely to achieve positive economic goals.

An analytic approach to studying the behavior of the regulated monopoly thus turns out to be more than an exercise in "arcane mathematical skills."[3] It illuminates many of the issues usually treated only descriptively, and lends credence to the view that often "common sense recognizes itself only under the search-light of mathematics."[4] It helps to separate fact from fancy in the regulatory folklore, and enhances substantially our understanding of the economic implications of regulation on the behavior of a monopoly firm.

Throughout the discussion, it is supposed that entry into regulated industries, such as public utilities and telecommunications, is closed or severely limited. Monopolistic behavior on the part of the firm is restricted by a regulatory agency that imposes a constraint on earnings. The constraint is intended to ensure that monopoly profit is passed on to the consumer in the form of lower price. However, instead of achieving this objective, the constraint may instead offer the firm incentives to introduce nonminimum cost behavior.

Rather than discuss such incentives on an a priori or intuitive basis, we use mathematical models to derive rules which indicate when the regulated profit-maximizing firm prefers one of the available alternatives to another. We explain in a rigorous manner why regulation can sometimes lead to padding the staff or the rate base, or to behavior consistent with a revenue rather than a profit objective, even though the sort of behavior in question is not assumed to have any utility in itself.

The regulatory process is assumed to be costless, so that we avoid the question of whether regulation costs more than the benefits it brings.[a] We do, however, investigate conditions under which gains to society arising from larger output or higher quality under regulation are counteracted by losses to society arising from inefficiencies caused by the regulatory constraint. Thus, the direct

---
[a]See MacAvoy (1970) and Jordan (1972).

costs of regulation are ignored, although the indirect costs are often accounted for.

In order to emphasize the structural similarity of a variety of models of regulatory constraint, the initial chapters describe a general model that is flexible both as to the form of the functions it can accommodate and as to the interpretation of the variables. In this way, we characterize with one calculation a very broad range of models, and can understand more clearly the differences in their solutions. We can also see which conclusions depend upon a particular symmetry or asymmetry present in the method of constraint, or upon a particular interpretation of the decision variables or their interrelationships, and which conclusions do not.

The most interesting theorem derived in the first part of the book shows that when the profit ceiling under regulation increases by the same amount if an added dollar is spent on any decision variable (symmetric constraint), then operation off the production frontier will never prove optimal in the elastic region of the revenue curve. Instead, the regulated profit-maximizing firm chooses precisely the same product line and the same quantities of each product as are produced by a revenue-maximizing firm subject to its own minimum-profit constraint. The optimal response to regulation thus differs from the usual allegations that ceiling profit constraints are always accompanied by inefficiencies, and that averaging profit over many markets causes anomalous cross-subsidizations.

The chapters in Part II are primarily devoted to the most important specialized interpretation of the regulatory model, namely the Averch-Johnson (AJ) model of rate-of-return regulation. In this model, the constraint is of an asymmetric variety. The standard result is that the firm has an incentive to misallocate resources by substituting capital for labor in production, and that this misallocation is strictly preferred by the firm to any padding of the rate base. We show further that the misallocation is ordinarily not so severe that it prevents output from increasing as the constraint is tightened, but is strong enough to prevent operation in the inelastic region of the revenue curve. This latter result can be used to test the appropriateness of the rate-of-return model as a description of the regulated firm's behavior.

An important policy issue confronting the regulator is whether the fair rate of return should be set larger than the market cost of capital or equal to it. We argue that it is not possible a priori to advocate one rather than the other of these possible solutions. Instead, the appropriate choice in a particular situation depends both on the social valuation of the regulated good relative to the valuation of other goods, and on the extent of the increase in productive inefficiency as the fair return is lowered.

Another result reported here is that changes in the market cost of capital do not, when the fair rate is held fixed, alter the demand for capital or the output of the regulated firm. Because this result differs from that arising when the firm is unconstrained, it may be possible to empirically test the effectiveness of the rate-of-return constraint.

Also interesting, and largely contrary to recent thinking, is our finding that as long as the marginal physical product of capital is positive, it will not be profitable for the regulated firm to collude with the suppliers of its capital inputs. Any increase in the price of capital equipment or in the wage rate is detrimental not only to the firm (lower profits at the new equilibrium) but also to consumers (higher prices).

A new extension of the model portrays a per unit cost of capital that rises as more capital is used by the firm. We find that while capital and profit remain uniquely determined, there exists a range of fair returns over which the labor, output, and waste levels are indeterminate. The firm thus has some slack which can be used in a wasteful fashion, or in increasing output, thereby perhaps expanding operation to the inelastic region of demand. Over this same range of fair returns, the firm's most profitable policy is to reduce capital usage as the fair rate is lowered; as a consequence, the regulated firm may eventually switch from an overly capital-intensive to an overly labor-intensive operation.

Two models of rate-of-return regulation that do not lie completely within the confines of the general regulatory model are also described. One of these models reflects in at least a rudimentary fashion the delays in the adjustment of prices that ordinarily characterize regulatory proceedings. The other recognizes that the demands actually facing the typical regulated utility or telecommunications firm exhibit peaks and hollows.

The chapters in Part II thus serve to illustrate the richness of result that is available by studying not only the particularization of a model but also its general form. In addition, they show that it is often necessary to depart from a given framework in order to better represent some specific reality.

**Part I:**
**A Regulatory Model**

# 2

## Formulation of Model and Method of Solution

**Introduction and Summary**

The model we investigate in this and the following chapters is simple yet sufficiently flexible to characterize a variety of regulatory situations. It includes three variables, two of which contribute in some way to the firm's output, while the third reflects the possibility of operating off the production frontier. The firm is assumed to maximize profit subject to a regulatory constraint that limits profit to a ceiling level, where the ceiling is ordinarily portrayed as increasing in at least one of the firm's decision variables. The model assumes that there is a differential between the profit that can be achieved by the unregulated firm and the profit that is permitted under regulation. The constraint thus effectively reduces profit from the monopoly level to some lower, but still positive, level.

A number of different analytical methods can be used to study a constrained system such as the one described here. Since the methods using Lagrangian or Kuhn-Tucker conditions are the most familiar to economists, they are the ones we adopt. In this chapter, we present a detailed statement of the Kuhn-Tucker theorem as it applies to the regulatory model. Both mathematical methods and graphics are used to clarify various aspects of this theorem.

**Description of the Model**

In the regulatory model, the firm is assumed to

$$\text{Maximize} \quad \pi(z,y,x) = R(z,y) - C(z,y,x) \quad (2.1)$$
$$\underset{z,y,x}{} $$
Subject to $\quad \pi(z,y,x) \leqq G(z,y,x),$

where

$z$ and $y$ = productive variables, either input or output quantities
$x$ = a measure of the degree to which the firm is operating off its production frontier
$R(z,y)$ = revenue generated by the productive variables $z$ and $y$
$C(z,y,x)$ = total costs, including those of both a productive and a wasteful nature
$\pi(z,y,x)$ = net profit after all costs have been subtracted from revenue
$G(z,y,x)$ = ceiling level of profit permitted by the regulator.

*Productive Variables*

The most standard interpretation of the productive variables takes them to represent the quantities of the capital and labor inputs. The profit function can then be written as

$$\pi = p(q)q(L,K) - w(L+L^*) - r(K+K^*), \qquad (2.2)$$

where

$L = z$ = labor used by the firm
$K = y$ = capital used by the firm
$q(L,K)$ = production function which translates the labor and capital inputs into an output $q$
$p(q)$ = inverse demand function which is downward sloping since the firm is a monopolist
$w$ = unit cost of labor or wage rate (constant)
$r$ = unit cost of capital (constant)
$x = wL^* + rK^*$ = dollar cost of any padding of the staff or of the rate base.

An equivalent formulation which is sometimes used for the two-input model is

$$\pi = p(q)q - wH(q,K) - rK - x, \qquad (2.3)$$

where

$H(q,K)$ = minimum labor requirement to produce output $q$ when there are $K$ units of capital.[a]

In this formulation the production function is embedded in the cost term so that revenues reflect only demand conditions rather than both demand and technological considerations [as happens in (2.2)].

The model becomes a special case of Williamson's expense preference theory of the firm[1] if the objective function is written as

$$\pi = R(q,z) - C(q) - z + mx, \qquad (2.4)$$

where

---
[a] Klevorick (1971) introduced the "labor requirements" function into the regulatory literature, but his analysis did not include the possibility of operating off the production frontier.

$q$ = quantity of output
$z$ = expenditure on managerial staff
$m$ = unit cost of managerial emoluments
$x$ = number of units of managerial emoluments
$C(q)$ = cost of production.

Still other interpretations of the productive variables take them to be two products, or two variables that represent the quality and quantity of some commodity, or two variables that represent the quantity of some commodity and the advertising expenditure devoted to it.

The use of two productive variables in Model (2.1) is intended as a simplification and should not be thought of as a restriction. The two-variable case enables us to capture the essence of various productive interrelationships without having to adopt a cumbersome notation. Almost without exception, the theorems we derive for the two-variable case can be generalized to an $n$-variable model.

*Operation off the Production Frontier*

The inclusion of the possibility of operation off the production frontier is not widespread in models of firm behavior. This is because such models ordinarily deal with the unregulated profit-maximizing firm, and such a firm chooses not to pad its staff or its capital expenditures. For example, the necessary conditions for profit maximization in (2.2) are

$$\pi_L: \qquad R'q_L = w \qquad (2.5)$$

$$\pi_K: \qquad R'q_K = r \qquad (2.6)$$

$$\pi_{L^*}: \qquad -w \leqq 0, \; wL^* = 0 \qquad (2.7)$$

$$\pi_{K^*}: \qquad -r \leqq 0, \; rK^* = 0, \qquad (2.8)$$

where

$R'$ = marginal revenue = $p + qp'$

$q_L$ = marginal physical product of labor, $q_L > 0$

$q_K$ = marginal physical product of capital, $q_K > 0$.

Equations (2.5) and (2.6) assert that a slight increase in either factor, holding the other factor constant, changes revenue just enough to compensate for the cost of increasing that factor. Equations (2.7) and (2.8) are only satisfied if

$L^* = K^* = 0$, since any operation off the production frontier entails an uncompensated cost. Hence, it is not optimal for an unregulated profit maximizer to operate off its production frontier.

When a regulatory constraint is imposed, however, it seems intuitively clear that "extravagant or unnecessary"[2] expenses may be a real possibility. Garfield and Lovejoy write that the problem of "a management whose attitude is complacent" instead of "anxious to lower costs in any way possible" is "inherent whenever there is price regulation on a cost-plus basis."[3] Furubotn and Pejovich assert that regulated firms may "capture the benefits of higher profits and conceal the true profits from the regulatory agency by reporting higher costs of doing business."[4]

In order to evaluate such statements in the framework of theoretical analysis, it is essential to include in the model the possibility of nonminimum cost activity. Operation off the production frontier is certainly one form which such activity can take, and this is why the variable $x$ (or its surrogates $L^*$ and $K^*$) is introduced into the analysis.[b] A positive level of $x$ means that managers and/or workers are working less hard and/or that units of capital are less fully utilized than they would be under profit maximization. Stated differently, output could be increased by utilizing in a different manner the inputs already employed.

An example is given in Figure 2-1 which displays two of the firm's isoquants; curves giving those combinations of labor and capital that can be combined to

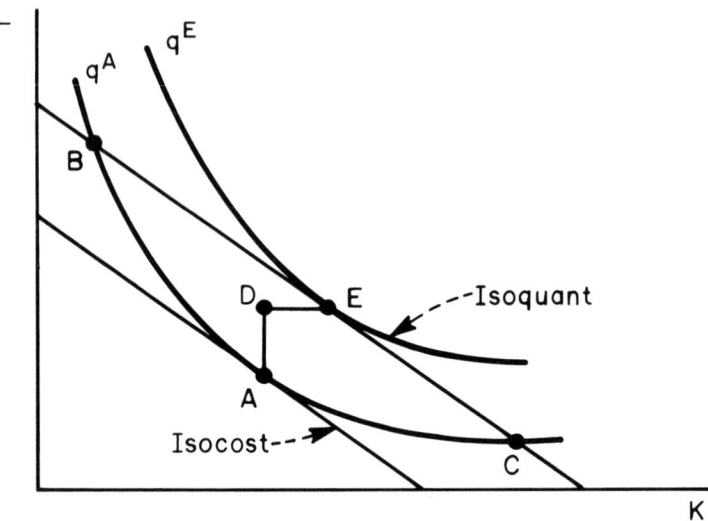

**Figure 2-1.** Misallocation versus Operation off the Production Frontier.

---

[b]See also Rees (1973), who classifies various forms of nonminimum cost behavior in a manner very similar to our own.

produce the same output. Operation off the production frontier takes place at a point such as $E$ if the firm produces only output $q^A$ instead of the larger output $q^E$. The firm is not transforming the labor and capital on hand into the largest attainable output. There is a waste of $DA$ worth of labor and $DE$ worth of capital. In terms of familiar theoretical models, the firm is adopting managerial emoluments of the Williamson variety of an amount $DA$, and it is padding the rate base by an amount $DE$.[5]

The distinguishing feature of the waste variable in Model (2.1) is that revenue is determined completely from production and demand conditions, with operation off the production frontier reflected only in the cost term. The ability to separate analytically the wasteful activity in this way is a convenient property in the model, but it can unfortunately be rather misleading in a practical sense. There is no reason to suppose that the regulator is always able in the real situation to detect the unnecessary expenditure that can be isolated in the theory, for such expenditure would presumably take a subtle rather than a blatant form.

Operation off the production frontier is not the only form of inefficiency that can arise within Model (2.1). It is possible that the firm is operating on its production boundary but is reacting to imputed relative prices different from those prevailing in the market. In this case, too much of one or the other factor is being used, yet output cannot be increased unless there is an increase in the quantity of labor and/or capital employed. If the variables are defined as in (2.2), this form of inefficiency is called a misallocation of inputs in which too much (too little) capital is being used relative to labor at the output produced. The inefficiency is similar to operation off the production frontier in that costs are not minimized at the output produced, but it is different in that the largest output is forthcoming given the specified levels of labor and capital.

In terms of Figure 2-1, the points $B$ and $C$ represent labor-capital combinations at which the firm is misallocating its inputs by being overly labor intensive and overly capital intensive, respectively. Both points lie on the $q^A$ isoquant, but they are not points at which costs are minimized at current factor prices. The diagonal isocost lines (lines such that $wL + rK$ = constant) indicate that point $A$ offers the lowest cost combination of labor and capital in producing $q^A$, and that at the expenditure level required to operate at $B$ or $C$, the firm could instead produce the larger output $q^E > q^A$. Yet, points $B$ and $C$ render the largest output that can be achieved with their respective combinations of inputs.

A third form of nonminimum cost behavior occurs if the firm uses a minimum-cost technology at all outputs, but increases the amount it spends on quality or advertising. It is not altogether clear that such forms of activity should always be termed inefficient. For example, the unconstrained monopolist will choose quality to equate marginal revenue with marginal cost, but society may prefer equating the marginal value to society of the quality improvement (as measured by price) to marginal cost. Hence, increases in quality brought about by regulation may increase rather than diminish welfare.

The profit function $\pi(z,y,x)$ differs slightly from minimum-cost profit because it includes the cost of any wasteful practice. It is thus a net profit which, if $x > 0$, is less than the maximal attainable profit at the particular values of the productive variables. Because the word profit covers both its usual meaning and the net profit if there is operation off the production frontier, one must exercise care to avoid confusion.

*Constraint Ceiling*

The profit ceiling is perhaps the most difficult concept in the model, probably because it is the least familiar. The constraint is taken to limit profit to a level not exceeding a particular dollar amount, the amount depending on the values of the variables. Since the aim of regulation is to encourage the firm to increase its usage of the productive variables from the unconstrained monopoly level, it is ordinarily supposed that the profit ceiling increases with increases in at least one of the productive variables, $G_z > 0$, $G_y \geqq 0$ and $G_x \geqq 0$. The interpretation of $G_z = \partial G/\partial z > 0$ is that the increase in the profit ceiling when $z$ is increased by one unit, $y$ and $x$ being held constant, is positive.

The assumption $G_x \geqq 0$ requires some justification, for this states that the regulator may permit the firm to increase profit as it increases waste. Presumably, if the regulator is perfectly able to detect wasteful practice, he will set $G_x = 0$, so that wasteful expenditures will be completely disallowed in the cost base. If $G_x > 0$, the regulator lacks information about the firm's costs, and treats at least a part of the expense connected with operation off the production frontier as if it were productive.

The precise functional form of the profit ceiling is often far less important in determining the firm's behavior than the ceiling's symmetry (or asymmetry). The best-known example of an asymmetry in the profit ceiling arises under rate-of-return regulation. The constraint takes the form

$$\pi \leqq (s-r)K$$

where $s$ = fair rate of return set by regulator, with $s > r$. In this constraint, the per-unit profit permitted on capital investment is a constant $(s-r)$, and the total profit ceiling increases linearly with increases in capital investment. Translating to the more general notation, the preceding relationship falls under a class of constraints of the form

$$\pi \leqq G(K) \text{ with } G_K > 0.$$

The asymmetry is obvious since constrained profit increases with increases in capital investment, but it is not affected by changes in the labor variable or the waste variable.

The profit ceiling can be rewritten to reflect the degree of tightness in the constraint. In the preceding illustration, a higher level of fair return permits larger constrained profit at each value of $K$, and a lower fair return keeps the firm more tightly constrained. In general, the constraint ceiling can take on the form

$$gG(z,y,x)$$

where $g$ = fair return or markup set by regulator.

## Kuhn-Tucker Conditions

To further analyze Model (2.1), we examine the Kuhn-Tucker conditions. Since these conditions will be used in a number of places in the analysis, the theorem will be carefully stated.

*Kuhn-Tucker Theorem for Regulatory Models*

Suppose that $(\bar{z},\bar{y},\bar{x})$ maximizes $\pi(z,y,x)$ subject to the constraint $\pi(z,y,x) \leq G(z,y,x)$. Suppose also that $\pi$ and $G$ are differentiable functions and that a constraint qualification holds at $(\bar{z},\bar{y},\bar{x})$. Let a Lagranian function $\phi$ be defined as

$$\phi(z,y,x,\lambda) \equiv \pi(z,y,x) + \lambda[G(z,y,x) - \pi(z,y,x)]. \qquad (2.10)$$

Then in order that $(\bar{z},\bar{y},\bar{x})$ be a solution of the maximum problem, it is necessary that there exist a $\bar{\lambda}$ such that

$$\phi_{\bar{z}} \leq 0, \quad \bar{z}\phi_{\bar{z}} = 0, \quad \bar{z} \geq 0 \qquad (2.11)$$

$$\phi_{\bar{y}} \leq 0, \quad \bar{y}\phi_{\bar{y}} = 0, \quad \bar{y} \geq 0 \qquad (2.12)$$

$$\phi_{\bar{x}} \leq 0, \quad \bar{x}\phi_{\bar{x}} = 0, \quad \bar{x} \geq 0 \qquad (2.13)$$

$$\phi_{\bar{\lambda}} \leq 0, \quad \bar{\lambda}\phi_{\bar{\lambda}} = 0, \quad \bar{\lambda} \geq 0 \qquad (2.14)$$

The constraint qualification states that for any $(z^*,y^*,x^*)$ which satisfies $\pi(z^*,y^*,x^*) = G(z^*,y^*,x^*)$, there must exist a $(z,y,x)$ such that

$$\psi = z\left\{\left(\frac{\partial \pi}{\partial z} - \frac{\partial G}{\partial z}\right)\bigg|_{z^*,y^*,x^*}\right\} + y\left\{\left(\frac{\partial \pi}{\partial y} - \frac{\partial G}{\partial y}\right)\bigg|_{z^*,y^*,x^*}\right\}$$

$$+ x\left\{\left(\frac{\partial \pi}{\partial x} - \frac{\partial G}{\partial x}\right)\bigg|_{z^*,y^*,x^*}\right\} > 0$$

*if* $\pi - G$ *is concave at* ( $z^*,y^*,x^*$ ), *and such that* $\psi \geq 0$ *if* $\pi - G$ *is not concave at* ( $z^*,y^*,x^*$ ).

*End of Theorem*

The symbol $\phi_{\bar{z}}$ represents the partial derivative of the Lagrangian function $\phi$ with respect to $z$ evaluated at the optimal value $\bar{z}$. The constraint qualification is Mangasarian's version of that given in Arrow-Hurwicz-Uzawa.[c]

*Explanation of the Theorem*[d]

The theorem is a statement of existence. If there is no quadruple ($\bar{z},\bar{y},\bar{x},\bar{\lambda}$) which simultaneously satisfies the necessary conditions, then the problem as stated has no solution. The necessary conditions are a natural generalization of the calculus requirements that stationary points of an expression (maxima, minima, and points of inflexion) occur where all partial derivatives of the expression are zero. Figure 2-2 portrays the necessary conditions on a variable $z$.

If the partial derivative, $\phi_{\bar{z}}$, is zero, then the stationary point can occur either at the boundary of the feasible region (the $\phi$ axis in Figure 2-2) or in the interior. If the stationary point is on the boundary, such as at point $B$, the necessary conditions are $\phi_{\bar{z}} = 0, \bar{z} = 0$. If there is an interior maximum such as at point $A$, then the necessary conditions are $\phi_{\bar{z}} = 0, \bar{z} \geq 0$. Therefore, when there is a stationary point solution,

$$\phi_{\bar{z}} = 0, \bar{z} \geq 0.$$

It is possible that the function has no maximum in the stationary point sense, but nevertheless takes on a highest value in the region $z \geq 0$. This must occur at a boundary point such as $C$ in Figure 2-2. Thus, there is a corner solution, but since it is nonstationary, the necessary conditions are

$$\phi_{\bar{z}} < 0, \bar{z} = 0.$$

A last variant of the necessary conditions arises when there is a corner minimum of the nonstationary point variety. This is illustrated by the point $D$ in

---

[c]See Kuhn-Tucker (1950), Mangasarian (1969) and Arrow-Hurwicz-Uzawa (1961).

[d]See Baumol (1972), Chapter 7, for an explanation of the Kuhn-Tucker conditions for the general case.

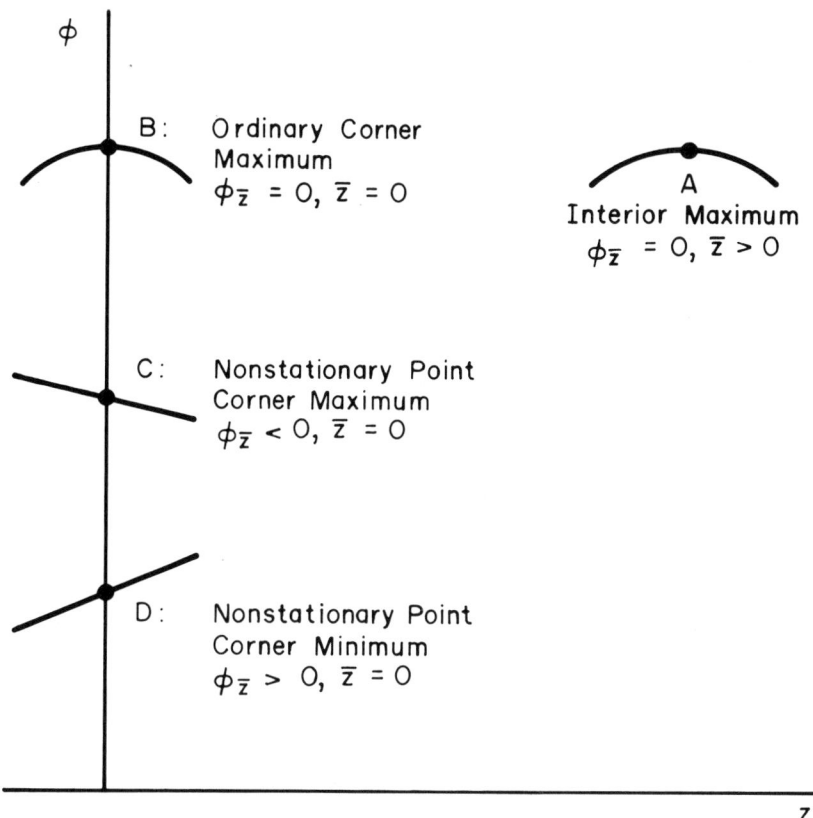

**Figure 2-2.** Stationary Points and Corner Optima.

Figure 2-2, and here
$$\phi_{\bar{z}} > 0, \bar{z} = 0.$$

In sum, the form of the necessary conditions for any particular variable enables us to tell whether a corner or an interior solution has been found, and whether the solution is a maximum or a minimum (points of inflexion are ignored).

Since $z$ must satisfy $\phi_{\bar{z}} \leq 0$, the Lagrangian taken as a function of $z$ for fixed $(\bar{y}, \bar{x}, \bar{\lambda})$ is being maximized. A similar argument holds for $y$ and $x$. The Lagrangian taken as a function of $\lambda$ for fixed $(\bar{z}, \bar{y}, \bar{x})$ is being minimized, however, since the $\lambda$ must satisfy $\phi_{\bar{\lambda}} \geq 0$. Thus, optimization of the Lagrangian expression $\phi$ entails the solution of a saddle value problem (by definition, a saddle value problem is one in which the function in question is maximized with respect to some variables while simultaneously being minimized with respect to other variables). In effect, the problem of finding a saddle point of a function $\phi$, which involves no constraints other than nonnegativity requirements on all the variables, has been substituted for the original problem. The Kuhn-Tucker theorem can then be interpreted as asserting that the optimal solution of the saddle value problem is also the optimal solution to the original problem.

The Lagrangian expression $\phi$ is obtained by writing down the objective that is being maximized, and then adding to this the constraints, each of which is multiplied by a Lagrangian variable (here just the $\lambda$). Since the saddle value problem minimizes all of the multipliers, the original constraint enters $\phi$ as $\lambda(G - \pi)$, so that $\phi_{\overline{\lambda}} \geq 0$ gives back $\pi \leq G$.

An interpretation of the optimal value of the multiplier is

$$\overline{\lambda} = \frac{d\phi}{dG}\bigg|_{(\overline{z}, \overline{y}, \overline{x})}, \qquad (2.15)$$

which states that $\overline{\lambda}$ measures the change in the equilibrium value of the Lagrangian function as the regulatory constraint ceiling is relaxed. We also know, by substituting (2.14) into (2.10) at ($\overline{x,y,z,\lambda}$), that the Lagrangian function evaluated at the optimal point equals the profit at the optimal point. Thus $\overline{\lambda}$ can be interpreted as the change in the equilibrium value of constrained profit. If the constraint is relaxed by a marginal amount such as one dollar, $\overline{\lambda}$ measures whether the change in profit between the new equilibrium and the old is less than, or more than, or equal to one dollar. If the change is zero, then the firm was not constrained, for the relaxation in the constraint does not alter profit. The higher the value of $\overline{\lambda}$, the tighter is the constraint (the more profit the firm can obtain if the regulator loosens the constraint).

An important point to remember about $\overline{\lambda}$ is that its value is determined by the analysis. If the constraint is active ($\phi_{\overline{\lambda}} = 0$), all that is really implied by the Kuhn-Tucker condition $\overline{\lambda}\phi_{\overline{\lambda}} = 0$ is that $\overline{\lambda}$ is nonnegative. To guarantee that $\overline{\lambda}$ is positive, other assumptions may have to be imposed on the model.

The Kuhn-Tucker theorem, as it has been stated, rests on the assumption that the "constraint qualification" is satisfied. The simplest constraint qualifications require, as Takayama[6] has pointed out, that both the profit function and $G - \pi$ be concave.[e] Under these circumstances, the Kuhn-Tucker theorem yields necessary and sufficient conditions for a maximum. Unfortunately, in regulatory models $G - \pi$ is likely to be a convex function due to the concavity of profit. Hence, we resorted to the more complicated constraint qualification of Arrow-Hurwicz-Uzawa. This qualification requires that at every ($z^*, y^*, x^*$) on the boundary region $\pi = G$, there exist some other ($z, y, x$) which makes a nonnegative inner product with the gradient vector at that boundary point. If

---

[e]A function is concave if a line segment drawn to join any two points on the graph of the function all lie on or below the graph of the function. Convexity of a function requires that the points on the line segment lie on or above the graph of the function. Convexity of a set means that a line segment joining any two points in the set never lies outside the set.

this condition is satisfied, then even if $G - \pi$ is nonconcave, the necessity of the Kuhn-Tucker conditions for a constrained maximum is guaranteed. The sufficiency, however, need no longer follow.

*Graphical Representation*

To understand better what is going in in the regulatory model, it is convenient to graphically portray the various possibilities. We at first restrict the discussion to the case of a single productive variable, $z$, which is thought of as output.

Figure 2-3 shows a typical configuration of the profit function $\pi(z)$ and the ceiling constraint $G(z)$. The profit hill is the locus of points $z^A BMEz^D$. It represents the largest attainable profit for each value of output between $z^A$ and $z^D$; for instance, choosing the output $z^B$ amounts to choice of point $B$ on the hill. The profit hill is ordinarily assumed to be concave and to attain a single maximum at point $M$. The constraint $G(z)$ is assumed to increase monotonically in the variable $z$ and to cut the profit hill below its maximum. The profit permitted under the regulatory constraint is thus traced out by the curve $z^A BEz^D$. The set of feasible $z$ which satisfy the constrained system is made up of two disjoint sets of points $z^A \leqq z \leqq z^B$ and $z^E \leqq z \leqq z^D$. Since the sets are not even connected (and hence the feasible region cannot be), it is clear that the sufficiency portion of the Kuhn-Tucker theorem may not be satisfied. It is possible, however, to analyze each region separately and to pick out the respective local maximums (point $B$ yields a higher profit than that attainable with any smaller output, and point $E$ is more profitable than any point with

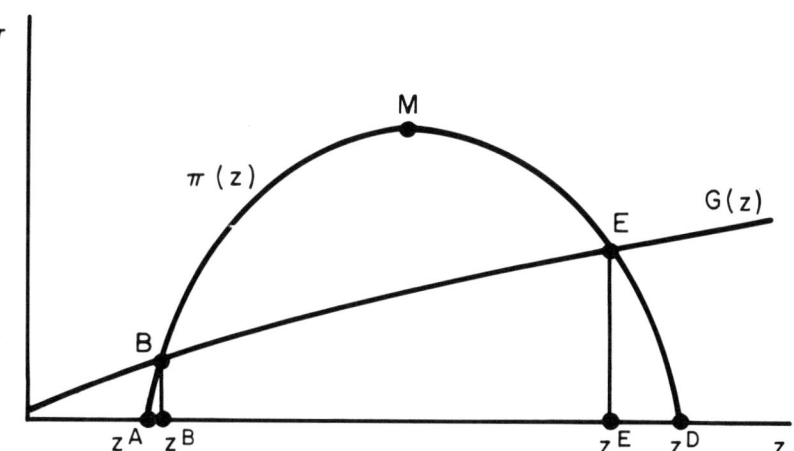

**Figure 2-3.** Typical Profit Hill and Constraint Curve for Single-Variable Model.

larger output). Of the two points, each of which satisfies the Kuhn-Tucker conditions, the right-most point $E$ is the global profit maximum since the constraint is rising in the variable $z$.

Point $E$ also has the property that the constraint is active, that is, profit exactly equals the ceiling permitted, $\pi(z) = G(z)$ at point $E$. Thus, in the usual case shown in Figure 2-3, the intuitive economic interpretation of an active constraint—one which binds the firm away from maximum profit—does correspond exactly to the Kuhn-Tucker definition of an active constraint. Such an identity between the two concepts normally follows when the profit function is concave, but need not follow otherwise as Figure 2-4 makes clear. In Figure 2-4, the Kuhn-Tucker conditions are satisfied at points $A$, $B$, and $E$, since all are local maxima of the constrained system. The global optimum among these points is $E$, but the constraint is not active here since $\pi(z) < G(z)$ at point $E$. Thus, in Figure 2-4, the constraint binds the firm away from the unconstrained optimum (point $M$), but the constraint is not active at the global optimum of the constrained system.

Figure 2-5 depicts some situations that are not considered standard in the analysis of Model (2.1), although they may occur in special cases. Figure 2-5a illustrates a constraint that is not effective. The Kuhn-Tucker conditions are satisfied at points $B$ and $M$, and the constraint is active at points $B$ and $D$. The solution to the constrained system occurs at point $M$, where the constraint is neither active nor binding, and where the firm is earning the full amount of profit that it does if unconstrained.

In Figure 2-5b the level of the constraint ceiling decreases monotonically as output increases. Clearly, this type of constraint gives the firm an incentive to

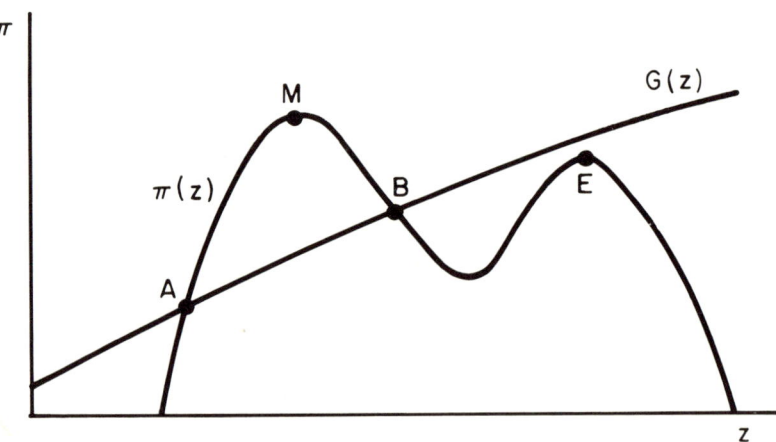

**Figure 2-4.** Nonconcave Profit Hill with a Binding but Inactive Constraint.

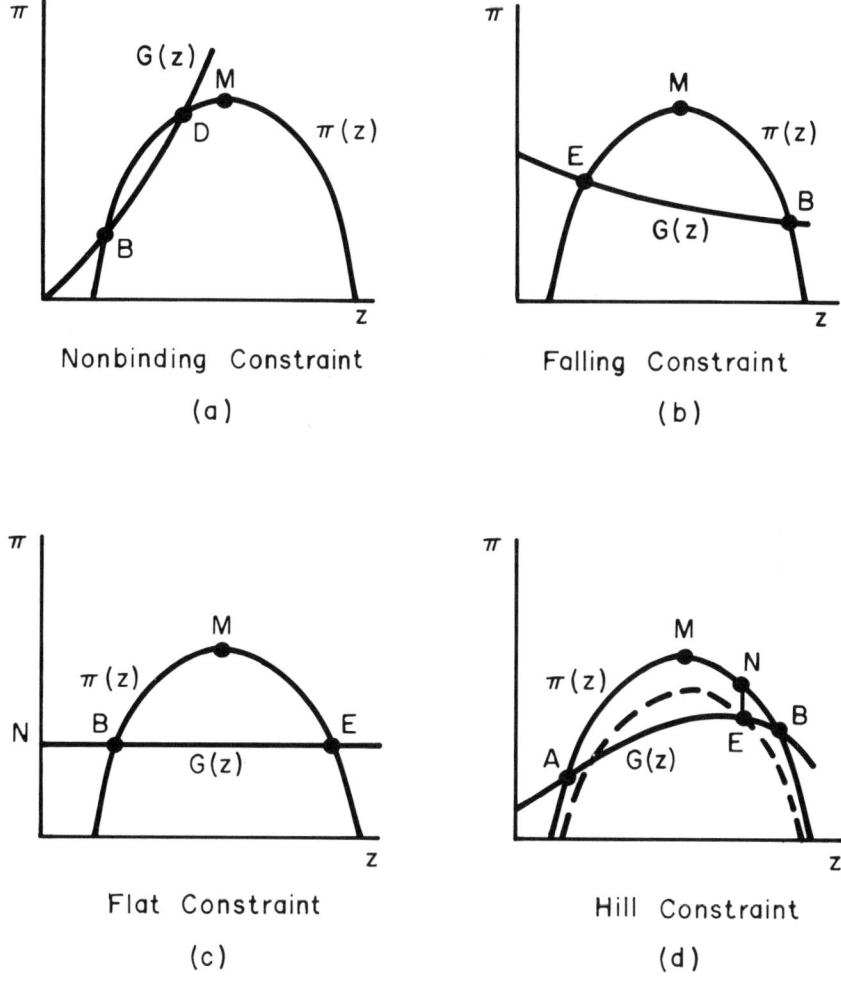

**Figure 2-5.** Nonstandard Configurations for Constraint.

reduce the $z$ variable below the monopoly level and to operate at intersection point $E$. Since one of the economic motivations for regulation is to increase usage of the productive variables beyond the monopoly level, this method is ordinarily not included in the analysis. There are cases, however, such as in the operating ratio method of regulation, in which a variant of this type of constraint can occur (see Chapter 4).

Figure 2-5c depicts a constraint that limits profit to a fixed dollar amount. To the extent that the regulator is interested in influencing the final operating point of the firm, this constraint form is disadvantageous in that the firm is indifferent between the points $E$ and $B$. Therefore, the break-even or $N$-dollar profit constraint (which is so often used in models in which the objective is taken to be maximization of Pareto optimality or of a social welfare objective) does not result in a unique optimum in regulatory models in which the firm's objective is profit maximization.

It sometimes happens that there is at least one variable for which the constraint is flat, $G_z = 0$, while there is another variable for which the constraint is rising, $G_y > 0$. The equilibrium rule for the variable with a flat constraint is identical in form with that of the profit-maximizing firm. Intuitively, this happens because at a point such as $M$ for variable $z$, the differential between the attainable and permitted profit is the greatest, so that the largest amount of profit can be transferred to encourage increases in the preferred variable. This tendency to maximize the use of any factor which is included in the profit ceiling is plausible intuitively since increases in such factors increase the permitted level of profit. In the Averch-Johnson model (Chapter 5), this means that the labor variable has the same equilibrium condition as that in the unconstrained monopoly. In the peak-load pricing model (Chapter 10) where the profit ceiling increases with increases in peak capacity, the equilibrium rule for setting off-peak prices is unaltered. Thus, a condition $G_z = 0$ that causes indeterminacy in the level of $z$ when there is only one variable, specifies $z$ quite precisely, if, for some other variable in the system, the constraint is rising.

Figure 2-5d shows that the profit ceiling can sometimes have a maximum just as the profit hill does. The solution in Figure 2-5d is that the firm operates at point $E$ and absorbs the differential $EN$. More specifically, by operating off the production frontier by an amount $EN$ dollars, the firm shrinks the profit possibility curve by $EN$ dollars at each level of output, yielding the dashed net profit curve. The equilibrium for $(z,x)$ is then an active one in which $\pi = G$, but where the $\pi$ in question is not the solid curve shown in Figure 2-5d, but is rather the hill lowered throughout by the $EN$ dollars of excess expenditure. The constraint in Figure 2-5d proves important in the rising cost of capital model described in Chapter 9.

For the two-variable model, the $\pi(z,y) = G(z,y)$ boundary is a closed curve in the $zy$-plane, and the feasible region consists of all points outside this boundary. In Chapter 5, we derive such a feasible region in the model of rate-of-return regulation and illustrate it in Figure 5-4. Since a straight line joining points in the region does not always lie everywhere within the region, it is clear that the feasible region is not convex. Therefore, for the two-variable as well as for the one-variable illustration, we cannot assume convexity as a way of guaranteeing sufficiency in the regulatory model. We will see in Chapter 5, however, that the sufficiency can sometimes be established by other means.

# 3

## Operation off the Production Frontier

**Introduction and Summary**

Wilcox has suggested that a regulatory constraint

cannot compel or even induce efficiency; it offers no incentive to good administration, imposes no penalty on incompetence[1]

and Kahn has asserted that

regulation as such contains no built-in mechanism for assuring efficiency. To the extent that it effectively restrains public utility companies from fully exploiting their potential monopoly power, it tends to take away any supernormal returns they might earn as a result of improvement in efficiency, thereby diminishing their incentive to try.[2]

The theory described in this chapter provides some propositions that are somewhat different from these standard views.

We show that the regulated firm is not neutral about a decision between operation off the production frontier and expansion of production using a minimum-cost technology. Instead, the minimum-cost alternative is distinctly the preferred one if output remains in the elastic region of the revenue curve. Operation off the production frontier can constitute an optimal solution in the constrained system, but does so only after regulation has become so tight that the revenue-maximizing output has been reached.

This proposition can be explained by a simple and intuitive rule. For any level of costs, the firm adopts that decision (productive or wasteful) which causes revenue to be as large as possible. If demand is elastic, productive expenditure is always preferable, since the increase in output contributes to revenue, whereas operation off the production frontier does not. However, at the revenue-maximizing output, waste becomes preferable since it prevents movement into the inelastic region of the revenue curve, a region where increases in output are associated with decreases in revenue.

A second result derived in this chapter is that whenever operation off the production frontier is included as a possibility in a regulatory model, a proof that the Lagrangian multiplier does not exceed one follows immediately from the necessary conditions. Thus, the waste variable provides a very natural means of limiting the range of values possible for the multiplier, which itself plays a crucial role in the solution and economic interpretation of the model.

## The Regulatory Model

The regulatory model, as presented in the last chapter, portrays the firm as

$$\text{Maximize } \pi(z, y, x) = R(z, y) - C(z, y, x) \tag{3.1}$$
$$z, y, x$$
$$\text{Subject to } \pi(z, y, x) \leqq G(z, y, x)$$

where

$z, y$ = productive variables
$x$ = waste variable indicating the extent to which the firm is operating off its production frontier
$\pi(z, y, x)$ = net profit
$R(z, y)$ = revenue from productive activities
$C(z, y, x)$ = cost of all activities
$G(z, y, x)$ = constraint ceiling which is rising in the variable $z$, $G_z > 0$, and non-decreasing in the other variables $G_y \geqq 0, G_x \geqq 0$.

When regulation is effective, the firm actually attains the maximum level of profit permitted by the constraint ceiling, that is, $\pi(z, y, x) = G(z, y, x)$.

*Necessary Conditions*

The Lagrangian function for Model (3.1) is

$$\phi(z, y, x) = (1 - \lambda)[R(z, y) - C(z, y, x)] + \lambda G(z, y, x). \tag{3.2}$$

When equality is taken to hold in the constraint, it is tempting to think that Lagrangian rather than Kuhn-Tucker conditions may be all that are required. However, we do need the pair of Kuhn-Tucker conditions for the waste variable, $x$, since the firm can decide to operate on or inside the production frontier. We can also permit the variable $y$ to take on a zero or a positive value.

The Kuhn-Tucker conditions for a maximum are then

$$\phi_z: \quad (1 - \lambda)(R_z - C_z) + \lambda G_z = 0 \tag{3.3}$$

$$\phi_y: \quad (1 - \lambda)(R_y - C_y) + \lambda G_y \leqq 0 \tag{3.4a}$$

$$y[(1 - \lambda)(R_y - C_y) + \lambda G_y] = 0 \tag{3.4b}$$

$$\phi_x: \quad \lambda - \frac{C_x}{C_x + G_x} \leqq 0 \tag{3.5a}$$

$$x[\lambda(C_x + G_x) - C_x] = 0 \qquad (3.5b)$$

$$\phi_\lambda: \quad \pi(z,y,x) \leqq G(z,y,x)] \qquad (3.6a)$$

$$\lambda[G(z,y,x) - \pi(z,y,x)] = 0 \qquad (3.6b)$$

$$z > 0, \; y \geqq 0, \; x \geqq 0, \; \lambda \geqq 0. \qquad (3.7)$$

Equation (3.3) follows from the assumption that at least one of the productive variables, $z$, has a positive optimal value so that the firm is engaged in production. Conditions (3.4a) and (3.4b) show that the other productive variable need not be assumed positive. Conditions (3.5a) and (3.5b) permit either positive or zero waste. Condition (3.6a) is normally taken to be satisfied as an equality, so that the optimal solution occurs where the constraint is active. For simplicity of notation, we have dropped the upper bars which denoted the optimal values of the variables (see Chapter 2). It should be understood that these are the equilibria that we shall be discussing.

*Range of Lagrangian Multiplier*

The interpretation of Conditions (3.3) and (3.4) obviously depends on the size of the Lagrangian multiplier $\lambda$. Discussions of various ways of limiting the range of values for $\lambda$ have appeared frequently in the literature on regulatory modeling. In the usual models, such as that of Averch and Johnson, information sufficient to limit the range of $\lambda$ is not readily obtainable from the first-order conditions. The interesting result that we can now derive is that this is only because the standard models of regulatory constraint have failed to include operation off the production frontier as a possibility. If a slack variable for rate base padding had been included in the Averch-Johnson model, then a bound on $\lambda$ would have been obtained automatically.

*Proposition 3.1: The value of the Lagrangian multiplier $\lambda$ at an optimal solution lies in the region*

$$0 \leqq \lambda \leqq 1$$

*in any model of regulatory constraint which is of the general form (3.1).*

*Proof:* From (3.7), $\lambda \geqq 0$. Since $G_x \geqq 0$ and $C_x > 0$, condition (3.5a) limits $\lambda$ to $\lambda \leqq 1$.

*End of Proof*

It should be emphasized that this method of proof is valid only if $G_x \geq 0$. If the regulator not only detects and disallows wasteful endeavors, but actually penalizes the firm for them so that $G_x < 0$, an alternative method must be used[a] to limit the range of $\lambda$.

It is natural to inquire whether the bound on the range of $\lambda$ appears reasonable in economic terms. Various possibilities are illustrated in Figure 3-1. Figure 3-1a depicts a horizontal constraint. An upward shift in the constraint of one dollar permits the firm to move from point $E$ to point $B$ at which constrained profit is a full dollar larger. In this case, $\lambda = 1$, the new equilibrium profit is one dollar higher than the previous level. In Figure 3-1b, the one-dollar increase in the constraint ceiling ($BD$) is larger than the increase actually obtained by the firm ($AB$). Thus, in Figure 3-1b, $\lambda < 1$.

A second theorem restricting the value of $\lambda$ is readily established.

*Proposition 3.2: If the profit ceiling increases in either productive variable, then $\lambda < 1$ at the optimal solution of a model of general form (3.1).*

*Proof:* Assume $G_z > 0$. Then Equation (3.3) requires $\lambda \neq 1$. Proposition 3.1 then establishes that $0 \leq \lambda < 1$.

*End of Proof*

The result is counterintuitive at first glance, since it would seem that the firm can somehow take full advantage of any relaxation in the constraint. If it is permitted to earn an additional dollar, it will always find some way to do so. Indeed, the increase in profit ($BD$ in Figure 3-1b) is precisely one dollar over what it would have been if production had been at this comparatively low level before the shifting of the constraint ceiling. Because of the reduction in output when the firm moves from $E$ to $B$, however, the resulting increase in equilibrium profit is less than the full dollar.

An intuitively appealing proof that $\lambda < 1$ in Figure 3-1b can be obtained by noting that the right-most intersection between the constraint and the profit hill must occur at a point where the slope of the constraint is larger than that of the objective function. This follows trivially because the slope of the profit hill is negative while that of the constraint is positive. The symbolic representation is

$$\frac{d\pi}{dz} < \frac{dG}{dz} \text{ or dividing by } \frac{dG}{dz} \text{ which is positive}$$

$$\frac{d\pi/dz}{dG/dz} = \frac{d\pi}{dG} = \lambda < 1.$$

---

[a]Zajac's (1972a) method is perhaps the best alternative. It has many of the same advantageous features as the technique adopted here in that it permits us to limit the range of $\lambda$ for a general form of more than just the one constraint, and it avoids the use of Hessians of second derivatives. Other methods can be used to determine the bounds of the value of $\lambda$, most of them applicable only to the Averch-Johnson model: Baumol and Klevorick (1970) have an elegant proof using second-order conditions; see also, Takayama (1969), Bailey and Malone (1970), Dayan (1972), and El Hodiri and Takayama (1973).

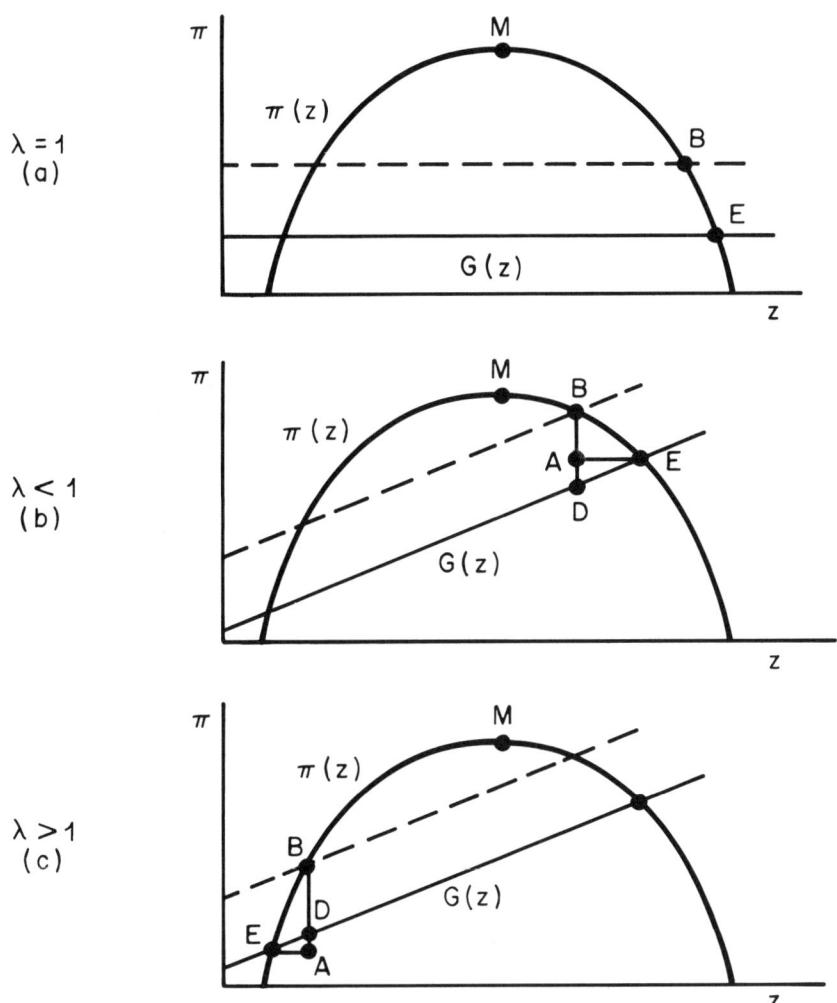

**Figure 3-1.** Size of Lagrangian Multiplier.

Thus, the value of the multiplier must be less than one whenever tightening of the regulatory constraint serves to increase output.

Proposition 3.2 eliminates the possibility that the effect of regulation could be to move the firm to a new equilibrium point below the monopoly output. To see this, consider the points $E$, $D$, and $B$ in Figure 3-1c. It is obvious from the graph that the one dollar increase in the profit ceiling ($DB$) increases the profitability at the new intersection point $B$ by more than one dollar ($AB$). Alternatively, since at such intersection points the slope of the profit hill is steeper than that of the constraint, $\dfrac{d\pi}{dz} > \dfrac{dG}{dz}$ or,

$$\frac{d\pi/dz}{dG/dz} = \lambda > 1.$$

Finally, we must consider the possibility that $\lambda$ will equal zero. The usual approach taken in the literature is just to assume that $\lambda$ will not be zero at the optimal solution to a constrained system. However, this is not a legitimate argument since (3.7) says merely that $\lambda \geq 0$, not that $\lambda > 0$. If the profit function is concave, however, it can be proved that $\lambda > 0$.

*Proposition 3.3: If profit attains a maximum and is concave, and if the constraint cuts the profit hill below its maximum, then $\lambda > 0$ at the optimal point.*

*Proof:* If $\lambda = 0$, then (3.3) gives the same set of candidate solutions as those of an unconstrained profit maximizer. Conditions (3.3) and (3.6) will not be jointly consistent unless the constraint curve is either tangent to or above the profit hill at solutions where (3.3) is satisfied. The assumption that the constraint curve cuts below the profit hill rules out the tangency possibility; the assumption that the profit hill attains a maximum and is concave rules out the possibility (illustrated at point $E$ in Figure 2-4) that the local optimum lies below the constraint curve.

*End of Proof*

We will generally assume concavity, and hence will consider only the $\lambda > 0$ case. The necessary condition (3.3) for the productive variable $z$ will therefore differ from that which occurs for the monopoly firm that is not regulated.

**Single Productive Variable Case**

Our first step in analyzing Model (3.1) is to study the single variable case ($z > 0, y = 0$). There will then be only two possible ways of responding to regulation: increasing the value of the productive variable (which we are thinking of as output), or moving off the production frontier. We will return in the next chapter to the case where both $z > 0$ and $y > 0$.

It is convenient to rewrite Conditions (3.3) and (3.5a) in some equivalent forms

$$R_z = C_z - \frac{\lambda}{1-\lambda} G_z, \quad \frac{R_z}{C_z} + \frac{\lambda}{1-\lambda} \frac{G_z}{C_z} = 1 \qquad (3.8, 3.9)$$

$$0 \leq C_x - \frac{\lambda}{1-\lambda} G_x, \quad \frac{\lambda}{1-\lambda} \frac{G_x}{C_x} \leq 1. \qquad (3.10, 3.11)$$

The division by $(1 - \lambda)$ is legitimate by Proposition 3.2, and the division by $C_z$ causes no difficulty since $C_z > 0$ by assumption. Equation (3.8) makes it clear that the equilibrium rule for the variable $z$ is not the usual rule of the unregulated monopoly firm that marginal revenue equals marginal cost. Instead, marginal revenue is equated to something less than marginal cost. This is depicted in Figure 3-2 where the monopoly price and output are ($p^M$, $z^M$) and the regulated price and output are ($p^E$, $z^E$).

The number, one, on the right-hand side of Equation (3.9) represents an additional unit of expenditure. To interpret the left-hand side of Equation (3.9), it helps to use an example. Suppose that the cost of increasing $z$ by one unit, holding everything else constant, is $50 and that the marginal revenue associated with the added cost is $34. Then $R_z/C_z = 34/50 = .68$. Thus, if the firm has an additional unit of money to spend and chooses to spend it on variable $z$, then it gets .68 of the unit back in the form of revenue. An unregulated monopolist will spend the added unit only if it can recover the full unit in revenues. The regulated firm spends an additional unit if the added revenue plus the increase in the constraint ceiling times a regulatory multiplier together add up to the unit.

Equations (3.10) and (3.11) give similar rules for operation off the production frontier. Comparing Equations (3.8) and (3.10), wasteful practice increases costs without altering revenue, that is, the marginal revenue of waste equals zero on the left-hand side of (3.10). Note that if the strict inequality is in force in (3.10), then from (3.5b) there can be no operation off the production frontier.

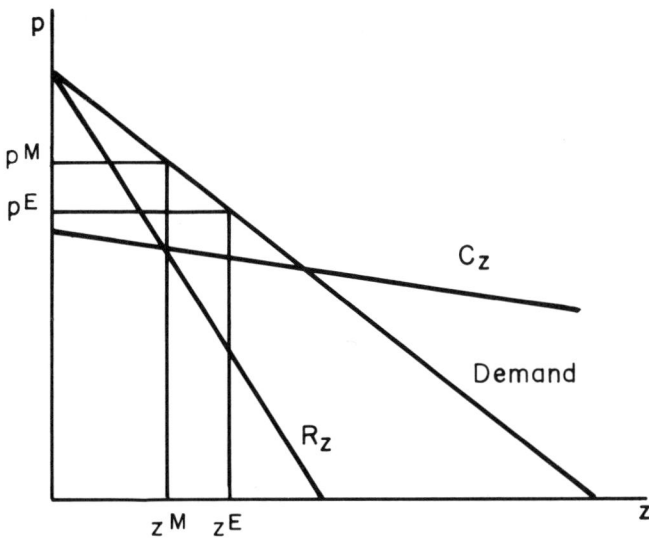

**Figure 3-2.** Monopoly and Regulated Outputs.

*Increase in Output under Regulation*

*Proposition 3.4:* If the firm is permitted larger profit for a larger scale of operation, then output is larger and price is lower under a regulatory constraint than it is for the unregulated monopoly. This is true even if the regulator does not in any way distinguish productive endeavors from operation off the production frontier.

*Proof:* Assume $G_z > 0$. Proposition 3.2 gives $\lambda < 1$, so that $R_z < C_z$ by Equation (3.3). We know that the monopolist determines output according to the rule $R_z = C_z$. The regulated output is thus larger than the monopoly output as long as the marginal revenue curve is downward sloping, and the marginal cost curve cuts the marginal revenue curve from below (which is required if the solution is to be stable). Thus, as Figure 3-2 shows, $z^E > z^M$ with $p^E < p^M$.

*End of Proof*

In the case of two productive variables, Proposition 3.4 cannot necessarily be established for both of them. This is because Figure 3-2 is drawn under the assumption that all other variables in the system are held fixed. But if $y > 0$ and the $y$ and $z$ are interrelated (through cross-elasticities or joint costs), then the value of the other variables may change when $z$ does. A rule similar to Proposition 3.4 can be established for some important special cases, however. If both the revenues and costs of $y$ and $z$ are separable, and if both $G_z > 0$ and $G_y > 0$, then both variables are larger under regulation than in the unregulated situation. Similarly, if the second activity is advertising expenditure or a quality improvement, which serves always to increase the amount demanded of the $z$ variable at any given price, then both quality and quantity will increase under an effective regulatory constraint.[b]

*The Marginal Revenue Rule*

One important implication of our model is that the regulated firm will take utmost advantage of any revenue effects. To explore this notion more thoroughly, consider the case in which it is equally profitable, in terms of the effect upon the profit ceiling, to spend an added dollar productively as wastefully. Mathematically,

$$\frac{G_z}{C_z} = \frac{G_x}{C_x}, \tag{3.12}$$

---

[b]This result agrees with that derived by Rosse (1972) for rate-of-return regulation. But see his paper for a more thorough treatment of this and related issues.

so that the regulator allows any expenditure whatsoever to be included in the base used to calculate ceiling profit.

*Proposition 3.5:* In the elastic region of the revenue curve, the regulated firm finds it more profitable to expand output using minimum-cost techniques than to operate off the production frontier. This is true even if the regulator does not distinguish wasteful from productive expenditure. Production at the revenue-maximizing output, however, may be consistent with operation off the production frontier.

*Proof:* By (3.12)

$$\left(\frac{\lambda}{1-\lambda}\right)\frac{G_z}{C_z} = \left(\frac{\lambda}{1-\lambda}\right)\frac{G_x}{C_x}. \tag{3.13}$$

There are three possible cases, $R_z > 0$, $R_z = 0$ and $R_z < 0$. If $R_z > 0$ so that $\frac{R_z}{C_z} > 0$, then (3.13) can be used to show that the only case in which necessary conditions (3.9) and (3.11) are compatible is when (3.11) is a strict inequality. But then, by (3.5b), $x$ is zero, so that we have by implication

$$R_z > 0 \rightarrow x = 0. \tag{3.14}$$

When $R_z = 0$, Equation (3.9) becomes $\frac{\lambda}{1-\lambda}\frac{G_z}{C_z} = 1$. Using (3.13), the equality must hold in (3.11), which together with (3.5b) and (3.7) yields

$$R_z = 0 \rightarrow x \geq 0 \tag{3.15}$$

If $R_z < 0$, then by (3.9), $\frac{\lambda}{1-\lambda}\frac{G_z}{C_z} > 1$. But then, by (3.13), $\frac{\lambda}{1-\lambda}\frac{G_x}{C_x} > 1$, which contradicts (3.11). Therefore, a negative marginal revenue is impossible at a solution to the constrained system.

*End of Proof*[c]

Proposition 3.5 asserts that if the marginal revenue is positive at the point at which the profit hill and constraint curve intersect, the firm's optimal policy is to increase output to this point, and not to waste at all. If the marginal revenue at the intersection of the profit hill and constraint curve is negative, then the optimal policy is to increase output to the point where marginal revenue is zero,

---
[c]For alternative derivations of essentially the same theorem, see Bailey and Malone (1970) and Zajac (1972).

and thereafter to absorb any remaining slack by increasing the amount by which the firm is operating off its production frontier.

Figure 3-3 gives a graphical interpretation of Proposition 3.5. Since the increase in the profit ceiling is the same whether the additional dollar is spent on waste or on output [Equation (3.13) holds], the comparison between (3.9) and (3.11) reduces to one in which the marginal revenue from increased output is compared with the marginal revenue obtained when waste is increased. As Figure 3-3 indicates, the marginal revenue associated with increased output starts out positive at the profit-maximizing output $z^M$, becomes zero at the revenue-maximizing level $z^S$, and thereafter is negative. For all levels of the waste variable, marginal revenue is zero.

The optimal policy is to select that path along which the greatest marginal revenue is obtained. This will be the productive path until $z^S$ is reached, and thereafter will be the wasteful path as is clearly shown. In intuitive terms, the firm is trying to increase the constraint ceiling, and hence $z$ and $x$, as much as possible. When cost effects are the same, the alternative with the largest revenue is preferred, because this revenue can be used in turn to increase the values of the variables, and hence the magnitude of constrained profits still further.

The standard literature on regulation ignores for the most part the role of demand elasticity in determining whether efficient or inefficient operation is the

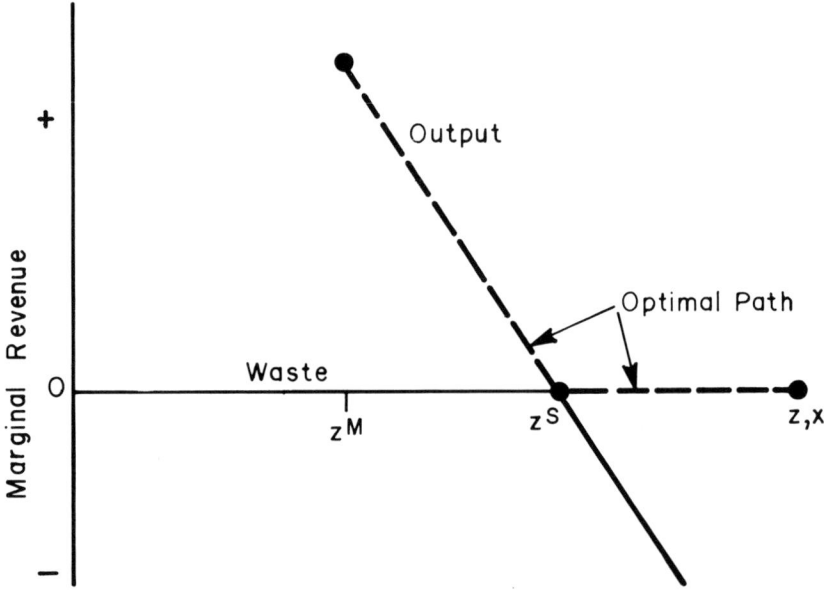

**Figure 3-3.** Marginal Revenue Associated with Productive and Wasteful Activity.

firm's most profitable alternative. Yet our Proposition 3.5 shows that the regulated firm definitely prefers minimum-cost to inefficient production when demand is elastic. A careful study of the model thus reveals behavioral incentives consistent with regulatory goals but which have not been recognized or understood.

A second novel observation that derives from the theory is the significance of the revenue-maximizing output level in regulatory models. Once this level of output has been reached, the regulatory agency may worsen rather than improve matters if it attempts to tighten the constraint still further.

In order to judge the importance of this revenue effect for any particular industry, we would need some further information about production and demand conditions in the industry. If these conditions are such that profit becomes negative before the revenue-maximizing point is reached, then minimum-cost production would always be the firm's most profitable policy. If there are opportunities for price discrimination among various customers (such as commercial, industrial, and residential), or for imposing multi-part tariffs, the minimum-cost production result might also hold, since these opportunities tend to make marginal revenue remain positive.[d]

*Detection of Waste*

It seems clear that in the real situation regulators try to be on the alert for wasteful practice and that they respond by disallowing such expenditures from the rate base. In such a case, another theorem is appropriate.[e]

*Proposition 3.6:* *If a portion of any operation off the production frontier is detected and not entered into the base used to calculate ceiling profit, then minimum-cost production may be profitable even in the inelastic region of demand. In the limiting case where all wasteful expense is excluded from the rate base, the profit-maximizing firm never finds operation off the production frontier to be an optimal policy, no matter how inelastic the demand.*

*Proof:* The assumption is that

$$0 \leq \frac{G_x}{C_x} < \frac{G_z}{C_z} \tag{3.16}$$

so that one dollar spent on $z$ increases the profit ceiling more than does one dollar spent on $x$. If marginal revenue is positive, the same argument used in the proof of

---

[d]See Oi (1971), Bailey and White (1974), MacAvoy and Noll (1973) or Feldstein (1972).

[e]If by some quirk, the regulator were to reward the firm more for wasteful than for productive expenditures, then the point at which operation off the production frontier becomes worthwhile is moved inside the region where demand is elastic. The proof is similar to that for Proposition 3.6.

Proposition 3.5 shows that waste will be zero. If marginal revenue is zero, then an equality in (3.9) combined with (3.16) requires the inequality in (3.11). Hence, by (3.5b), $x = 0$ in this case as well. Operation off the production frontier will be possible if at some point $\dfrac{R_z}{C_z} + \dfrac{\lambda}{1-\lambda}\dfrac{G_z}{C_z} = \dfrac{\lambda}{1-\lambda}\dfrac{G_x}{C_x}$ or, equivalently, if

$$\frac{(1-\lambda)}{\lambda}\frac{R_z}{C_z} = \left(\frac{G_x}{C_x} - \frac{G_z}{C_z}\right). \tag{3.17}$$

Substituting from (3.16) into the right-hand side of (3.17), we see that (3.17) cannot hold unless $\dfrac{R_z}{C_z}$ is negative. In the limiting case where all waste is detected and disallowed, $\dfrac{G_x}{C_x} = 0$, (3.11) is always an inequality, and by (3.5b), $x = 0$.

*End of Proof*

Proposition 3.6 asserts that there are conditions under which a regulatory constraint can succeed in getting the firm to operate in the inelastic region of the revenue curve. The proposition thus seems exceptionally strong, for in almost all familiar models of profit-maximizing behavior, operation in the inelastic region cannot occur. The proposition suggests as well that as long as inputs can be lumped into one category and as long as the constraining agency has a reasonably good ability to detect and disallow waste, regulation can result in efficient operation and in an output that is well beyond the monopoly and perhaps even the revenue-maximizing level.

*Regulatory Methods*

There are at least two regulatory methods discussed in the literature which fit the model that has just been described. One method limits the firm's profits to a fixed amount per unit of output, $\pi \leq mz$, where $m =$ markup permitted by the regulator. Since under this constraint the regulator automatically disallows waste (the ceiling rises only with output), this method is one to which Proposition 3.6 applies.

The method is ideal in a theoretical sense, since the regulator is able to obtain any level of profit reduction and output increase that is deemed fair. Unfortunately, the method is not operational since no unambiguous measure of output is ordinarily available in the service industries. Another serious problem is that without other information at our disposal (such as total profit or rate of return obtained), it is impossible to say whether a ceiling of 0.1 cent per kilowatt hour in an electric firm is more reasonable than a ceiling of 0.001 cent, or to compare either of these with a ceiling of 0.00001 cent per message-minute-mile in a telecommunications firm.

A second model of regulation which requires only the single variable, $z$, is one under which the profit ceiling increases with increases in all costs. Because of the significance of this method, we will describe it in some detail.

## Regulation Limiting Return on Total Cost[f]

Under the markup method of regulation, the constraint becomes

$$\pi \lesseqgtr g[C(z) + x] , \qquad (3.18)$$

where $g$ = markup over cost. The markup method includes in the regulatory base all rather than only some of the firm's costs. Thus, this method of regulation does not avoid the problem of rate-base determination. The capital costs as well as all other costs must be calculated and included in the base.

Return-on-cost regulation is described by Cross[g] as a method in which price $p$ is set at a markup over the average cost of production

$$p \lesseqgtr (1+g)\left(\frac{C(z)+x}{z}\right) \qquad (3.19)$$

The equivalence is immediately evident if we multiply (3.19) through $z$ and rearrange it into the form given in (3.18). Our conclusions for the return on cost model are, however, more specific than those Cross was able to reach. He remained satisfied with the statement:

The general relationship between $W$ [waste] and $\pi$ is not obvious from [his] equation (2), nor is it particularly simple to derive.[3]

In constrast, Proposition 3.5 pinpoints quite precisely the conditions under which operation of the production frontier constitutes an optimal policy.

The markup over average cost interpretation of the constraint brings out a

---

[f]Most of this section is taken from Bailey (1972).

[g]See Cross (1970). The constraint is the same as that implicitly assumed by Kafoglis (1971), when he includes fair return as a part of the cost term. The method is not equivalent to what is known as operating ratio regulation (see Chapter 4) which entails a markup over the firm's expenses (excluding capital costs). The constraint is also not equivalent to a cost-plus arrangement that is standard in government contracts [see McCall (1970)]. That method works by guaranteeing the firm a fixed percentage markup over an initial target cost with the possibility that the markup will be paid as well if costs exceed their estimated levels.

striking parallel between markup regulation and the markup rule that is adopted by firms engaging in "full cost pricing." Unfortunately, this parallel can easily mislead, for as we have seen, the profit-maximizing firm whose price is regulated by Cross' average cost ceiling does not adopt a pattern of pricing and input and output choices based on average yields but, since it is a maximizer, it must, as usual, base its decisions on marginal principles.

*Optimal Fair Return*

Our results suggest that the markup method has economic properties that are far more desirable than those usually attributed to it. In particular, we can arrive at some unambiguous welfare implications for return-on-cost regulation. If the profit ceiling has the form (3.18), then as $g$ is varied from its profit-maximizing level to the level $g^0$ at which revenues are maximized, the response of the firm is to increase output and not to operate off the production frontier. Thereafter, as $g$ is lowered still further, output remains at the revenue-maximizing level, whereas the amount of waste increases. This is depicted in Figure 3-4, which shows the output-waste combinations chosen by the firm for different levels of the fair return.

The optimal value of the fair return is seen to be the one that maximizes the benefits to society in terms of larger output, while at the same time entailing no social loss through operation off the production frontier. If profit

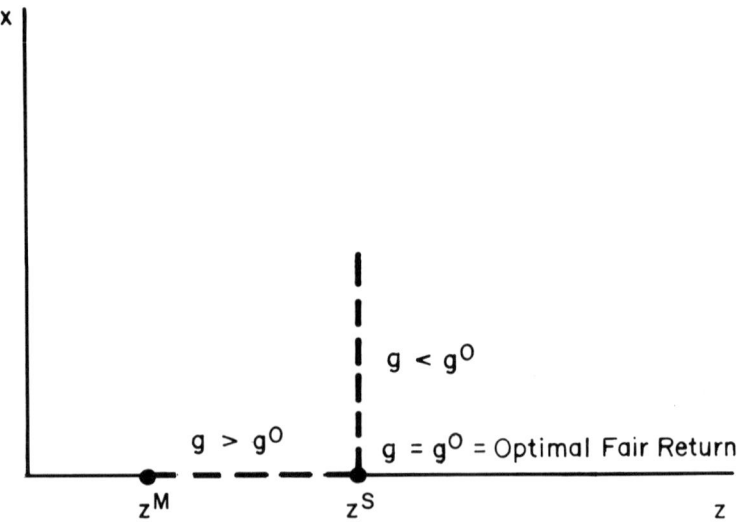

**Figure 3-4.** Optimal Fair Return Under a Return-on-Cost Constraint.

is positive at the revenue-maximizing point, then the optimal $g$ is obtained by solving $R(z^S) = (1+g) C(z^S)$ for $g$, that is

$$g^0 = \frac{R(z^S)}{C(z^S)} - 1. \tag{3.20}$$

If profit is negative at the revenue-maximizing output, then the optimal $g$ is one which is just detectably different from zero (at $g = 0$, profit is zero and a profit-maximizing firm is presumably indifferent among any of the zero-profit output versus waste possibilities).

Unfortunately, the level of the optimal fair rate, as given by (3.20), depends on the particular demand and production function in the industry in question. For firms that earn a large profit at the revenue-maximizing output, a large fair rate is dictated; for firms with small profit at $z^S$, a small fair rate is deemed best. Such a policy seems rather unsatisfactory, but is the only one that is available when a ceiling profit constraint is the method of regulation employed. It simply does not improve matters in the slightest to lower the fair return below $g^0$, even when profit seems excessive, for such a lowering merely serves to make operation off the production frontier attractive.

*Relation to Expense Preference Theory*

Propositions 3.5 and 3.6 together describe how nonminimum-cost behavior can arise in a regulatory model. They show that when regulation is based on total costs and demand is inelastic, the firm may have an incentive to operate off its production frontier. In the elastic region of demand, however, there is no incentive for such wasteful practice.

The motivation for minimum-cost behavior in the elastic region of demand may be weakened, however, if the objectives of the firm include considerations other than profit. A number of economists have felt that the typical monopoly or regulated firm is not exposed to the usual competitive pressures, and that without these pressures the profit objective is no longer forced upon the firm. As Leibenstein puts it in his description of x-inefficiency

In situations where competitive pressure is light, many people will trade the disutility of greater effort, of search, and the control of other peoples' activities for the utility of feeling less pressure and of better interpersonal relations ... [thus] they actually work on a production surface that is well within that outer bound.[4]h

Williamson describes the phenomenon as one entailing discretionary expenditures. Management may indulge its preferences for additional staff, esthetically

---
hSee also Alchian and Kessel (1962), Harberger (1954), and Stigler (1971).

appealing buildings, expense accounts, lush carpets, or an easier life.[5] The conclusions drawn from a regulatory model change dramatically when such incentives are included in the firm's objective function.

For example, suppose the markup on the total costs model had the form

$$\text{Maximize } \pi + U(x) \qquad (3.21)$$
$$z, x$$

$$\text{Subject to } \pi \leqq g(C(z) + x),$$

where $U(x)$ is the utility of waste. Then it is easy to show that the locus of operating points for different values of $g$ is similar to that drawn in Figure 3-4, except that some output intermediate between $z^M$ and $z^S$ will be the level at which waste commences rather than $z^S$. The larger the marginal utility of waste to the firm, the nearer to the profit-maximizing point the firm will produce. Thus, if the models of regulation and expense preference theory are combined, the output of the firm will be much less responsive to regulation.

## Two-Part Tariffs Under a Return on Cost Constraint

An interesting contrast to the preceding conclusion is provided by a model combining two-part tariffs and return-on-cost regulation. Here, if all customers had identical demand curves,[i] and if the firm could levy a customer charge as well as a usage charge, the model would be

$$\text{Maximize} \quad \pi = E + p(z)z - C(z) - x$$
$$E, z, x$$

$$\text{Subject to} \quad E \leqq \int_0^z p(\bar{z}) d\bar{z} - p(z)z \qquad (3.22)$$

$$\pi \leqq g(C(z) + x)$$

where the entrance fee, $E$, cannot exceed the area below the demand curve and above the usage charge, $p$ (that is, $E$ cannot exceed the consumer's surplus), and where regulation is on rate-of-return but not on the firm's price structure.

In Model (3.22) the firm's best policy is to set the customer charge so as to absorb all of the consumer's surplus, and to set the usage charge sufficiently below marginal cost so that the regulatory constraint is satisfied. It does not pay the firm to waste resources until the usage charge is driven down to zero.

The model perhaps raises more questions than it answers. It suggests that public utility firms might find it in their best interests to levy fairly high customer charges. But, in practice, these charges tend to be rather low, probably

---

[i]See Oi (1971) for a discussion of the nonidentical demand curve case; see Feldstein (1972) for distributional aspects; see Bailey and White (1974) for an application to a return-on-investment model.

because regulatory agencies monitor customers charges fairly closely to ensure that they are used as a method of covering fixed costs rather than as a method under which a firm can extract an excessive amount of surplus.

# 4 Symmetric and Asymmetric Constraints

**Introduction and Summary**

When two productive variables are included in the analysis, the treatment of these two variables in the regulatory profit ceiling proves to be exceedingly important. We shall call the constraint symmetric in the productive variables if marginal increases in expenditure on each such variable result in identical changes in the profit ceiling; otherwise, the constraint is asymmetric.

A comparison of symmetric and asymmetric constraints suggests strongly that symmetric constraints, such as a markup over total costs, are preferred on grounds of allocative efficiency to asymmetric constraints, such as rate-of-return regulation. The reason is simply that under the symmetric constraint, the firm gains by minimizing its costs as long as output level is between that which maximizes profit and that which maximizes revenue. In contrast, under an asymmetric constraint, the firm may, at virtually every output level, find it profitable to use its inputs in proportions that do not minimize its costs.

More specifically, we will show in this chapter that there is a one-to-one correspondence between the behavior of a profit-maximizing firm subject to a symmetric regulatory constraint and that of a revenue (sales) maximizer subject to its own internal profit constraint. The correspondence holds when there is a single input or when there are several. Therefore, a constraint limiting average profit does not lead, as might have been expected, to various sorts of perverse behavior on the part of the regulated firm. The theorem derived here states that while such behavior is possible, it is not optimal. In the elastic region of demand, there is no incentive to misallocate resources between the productive variables, nor is there any incentive to operate off the productive frontier.

When the constraint is not symmetric in the productive variables, however, a misallocation of resources between the productive variables may prove optimal. Such a policy may be adopted even when demand is elastic. In responding to regulation, the firm can be shown to have an incentive to increase that variable which is most effective in raising the profit ceiling.

*The Regulatory Model*

The regulatory model is

$$\text{Maximize } \pi(z,y,x) = R(z,y) - C(z,y,x)$$
$$z,y,x$$
$$\text{Subject to } \pi(z,y,x) = G(z,y,x).$$

The Lagrangian function for model (4.1) is

$$\phi(z,y,x) = (1-\lambda)[R(z,y) - C(z,y,x)] + \lambda G(z,y,x). \qquad (4.2)$$

If the values of both productive variables are positive, then the Kuhn-Tucker conditions are

$$\frac{R_z}{C_z} + \frac{\lambda}{1-\lambda}\frac{G_z}{C_z} = 1 \qquad (4.3)$$

$$\frac{R_y}{C_y} + \frac{\lambda}{1-\lambda}\frac{G_y}{C_y} = 1 \qquad (4.4)$$

$$\frac{\lambda}{1-\lambda}\frac{G_x}{C_x} \leq 1 \qquad (4.5a)$$

$$x\left[\lambda - \left(\frac{1}{1+G_x/C_x}\right)\right] = 0 \qquad (4.5b)$$

$$G(z,y,x) - R(z,y) + C(z,y,x) = 0 \qquad (4.6)$$

$$z > 0, \; y > 0, \; x \geq 0, \; \lambda \geq 0. \qquad (4.7)$$

To facilitate comparison, the numbering of the equations is the same as that in the last chapter.

### Wasteful Use of Resources

The theorem concerning operation off the production frontier is easily stated, and is seen to be a direct extension of Propositions 3.5 and 3.6.

*Proposition 4.1: In the region between the profit- and revenue-maximizing points, the most profitable response to regulation does not entail operation off the production frontier.*

*Proof:* Since by assumption the firm is operating between the profit- and revenue-maximizing points, $R_z > 0$ and $R_y > 0$. Assume that for either variable $z$ or $y$, say $z$, that $\frac{G_z}{C_z} \geq \frac{G_x}{C_x}$. Then, a marginal increase in productive endeavor contributes at least as much toward an increase in the profit ceiling as does a marginal increase in wasteful expense. This assumption, together with $\frac{R_z}{C_z} > 0$

establishes that conditions (4.3) and (4.5a) are compatible only if (4.5a) is a strict inequality. But then by (4.5b), $x = 0$.

*End of Proof*

Proposition 4.1 can be elaborated to show that operation off the production frontier can be part of an optimal solution only if the marginal revenue associated with all productive endeavors is nonpositive. Furthermore, operation off the frontier can never be the most profitable alternative unless it contributes in some way to an increase in the profit ceiling.

In order to determine the extent to which other departures from cost minimization might prove attractive, there is a new set of interactions which must be explored. We do this now by undertaking a separate analysis for the two pertinent cases—that in which the constraint ceiling is symmetric in the productive variables and that in which it is asymmetric.[a]

**Symmetric Constraint**

*Revenue-Maximizing Expansion Path*

A constraint is symmetric in its treatment of the productive variables if a marginal increase in expenditure on one variable results in the same increase in the ceiling level of profit as a marginal increase in expenditure on the other:

$$\frac{G_z}{C_z} = \frac{G_y}{C_y}. \tag{4.8}$$

A type of constraint that fits Equation (4.8) is regulation which limits return on total costs. If the variables are labor and capital inputs, for instance, then (4.8) says that the profit ceiling increases when total costs are increased, quite independently of whether these costs are generated by labor or capital inputs.

The important characteristic of the constraint that is symmetric in the firm's

---

[a]Zajac (1972b) has devised a way of re-expressing model (4.1) in terms of vector analysis. He is then able to derive the same sets of theorems as we do—on operation off the production frontier, on symmetric constraints, and on asymmetric constraints—without ever having to use the Lagrange multiplier technique. His terminology is somewhat different than ours, however. For example the asymmetric constraint $\frac{G_z}{C_z} > 0, \frac{G_y}{C_y} = 0$ is described as the requirement that the gradient of the cost vector be nowhere colinear with the gradient of the profit-ceiling vector. See also Edelson (1971) and Westfield (1965) for some other approaches to the allocation-waste issue.

decision variables is that the equilibrium rules are all altered from their usual form of marginal revenue equals marginal cost by precisely the same proportion.

*Proposition 4.2: In the case of a symmetric regulatory constraint, the regulated firm's most profitable alternative is to adopt the ratio rule used by a profit-maximizing firm, or by a revenue-maximizing firm subject to a minimum-profit constraint. Thus, the regulated firm expands production along the revenue-maximizing expansion path. Furthermore, since profit decreases monotonically along this path, the regulated firm earning N dollars in profit operates with precisely the same mix of inputs (outputs) as the revenue maximizer earning N dollars in profit.*

*Proof:* The unconstrained profit maximizer has as first-order conditions $R_z = C_z$ and $R_y = C_y$, so that

$$\frac{R_z}{C_z} = \frac{R_y}{C_y}. \qquad (4.9)$$

The revenue (sales) maximizer with profits constrained to be at least $N$ dollars operates according to the model[b]

Maximize $R(z,y)$
$z, y$

Subject to $R(z,y) - C(z,y) \geqq N$.

The Lagrangian is

$$\phi(z,y,\mu) = R(z,y) + \mu(R(z,y) - C(z,y) - N)$$

and the necessary conditions for $z > 0$ and $y > 0$ are

$$(1+\mu)R_z = \mu C_z \text{ and } (1+\mu)R_y = \mu C_y$$

so that, as before, (4.9) holds.

The regulated monopoly has a constraint of the form

$$\pi \leqq gG(z,y,x).$$

In order to trace out the expansion path, we first set $g$ so high that the firm behaves as an unconstrained profit maximizer, and then lower it progressively. For large $g$, marginal revenue is positive for both variables, so that the firm has

---

[b]See Baumol (1967).

an incentive to continue to employ both inputs (outputs) as the constraint is tightened. To show that the firm uses the ratio rule under symmetric regulation, we need only substitute (4.8) in (4.3) and (4.4) to obtain (4.9). To show that profit decreases monotonically as the regulatory constraint is tightened, we must first establish that $\frac{d}{dg}[gG(z,y,x)] > 0$. For then as $g$ goes down, constrained profit which equals $gG(z,y,x)$ goes down also. First, we perform the indicated differentiation obtaining

$$\frac{d}{dg}[gG(z,y,x)] = g\left[G_z \frac{dz}{dg} + G_y \frac{dy}{dg} + G_x \frac{dx}{dg}\right] + G. \qquad (4.10)$$

We also differentiate Equation (4.6) totally substituting $gG(z,y,x)$ for $G(z,y,x)$ to obtain

$$(\pi_z - gG_z)\frac{dz}{dg} + (\pi_y - gG_y)\frac{dy}{dg} + (-C_x - gG_x)\frac{dx}{dg} = G. \qquad (4.11)$$

The necessary conditions (4.3) and (4.4) can be written $\pi_z = \frac{-\lambda g G_z}{1-\lambda}$ and $\pi_y = \frac{-\lambda g}{1-\lambda}$ which can be substituted into (4.11), yielding

$$gG_z \frac{dz}{dg} + gG_y \frac{dy}{dg} = (1-\lambda)(-C_x - gG_x)\frac{dx}{dg} - (1-\lambda)G.$$

Substitution back into (4.10) yields

$$\frac{d}{dg}[gG(z,y,x)] = \lambda G + \left\{(1-\lambda)[-C_x - gG_x] + gG_x\right\}\frac{dx}{dg}. \qquad (4.12)$$

It has already been established by Proposition 4.1 that over the entire range of $g$ where marginal revenue is positive, $x = 0$, so that $\frac{dx}{dg} = 0$, and (4.12) is then positive as was asserted. There is thus only one $g$ and one point on the expansion path which corresponds to any specified level of profit. We then have the result that any two firms which operate on the same expansion path and attain the same profit must be using the same input (output) levels.

*End of Proof*

Although the preceding proof assumes that both $y > 0$ and $z > 0$, the argument can be extended to the case in which a formerly zero-valued variable might be introduced at some level of constraint both under regulation and by a revenue maximizer. Such a variable could be an improvement in quality or a service that does not bring in enough revenue to compensate for the expense incurred. As the regulatory constraint is tightened, less and less additional revenue is required in order for such a service to appear advantageous to the firm. All that is necessary is that at some point this variable offers the largest additional revenue per dollar of expense, that is, that the marginal revenues of other variables be forced down to the level offered by this one.

*Graphical Interpretation*

Proposition 4.2 is in some ways the most remarkable proposition we have arrived at so far, and it is well to examine its rationale. A graphic depiction of the profit hill appears in Figure 4-1, which shows a joint profit function for the two variables $z$ and $y$. The curves drawn are isoprofit contours, ($z,y$) pairs for which

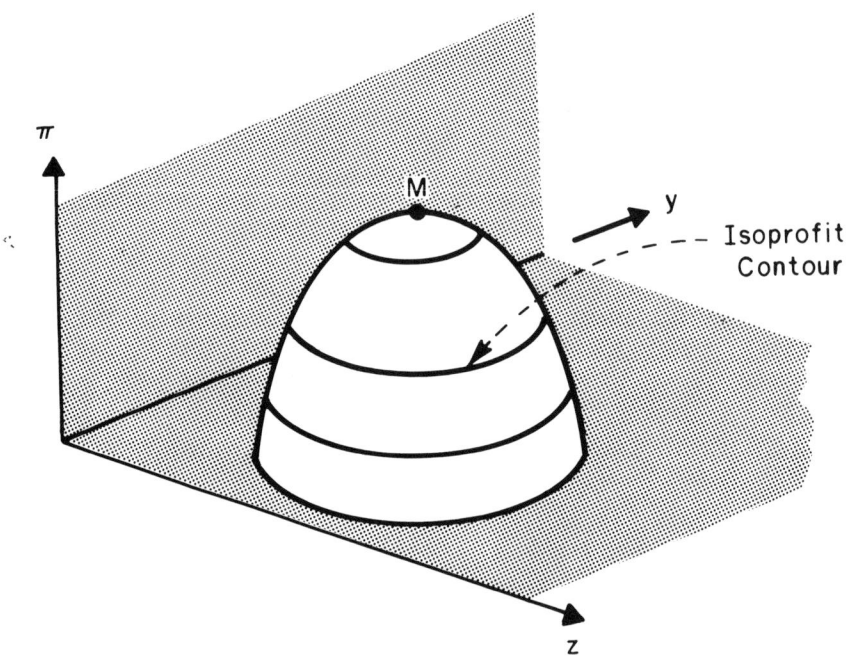

**Figure 4-1.** Profit Hill for Two-Variable Model.

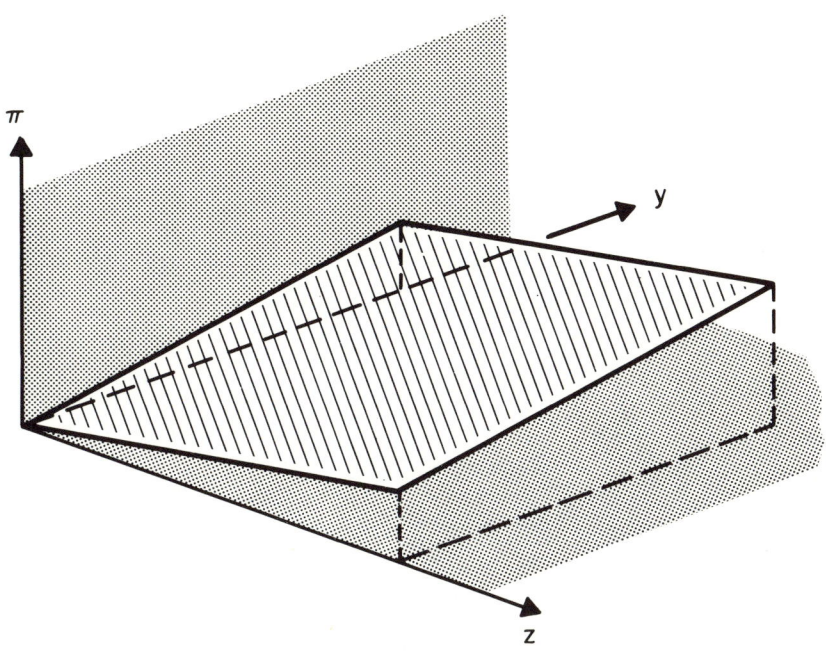

**Figure 4-2.** Symmetric Constraint Surface.

profit is the same. They are constructed by passing horizontal planes parallel to the $zy$-plane through the profit hill. A single point of maximum profit is attained at the point $M$ (the monopolist's ($z,y$) pair).

Figure 4-2 shows a regulatory constraint surface of the symmetric variety. As is indicated, the ceiling profit increases with increases in either of the productive variables. If the parameter $g$ were zero, then the constraint surface would lie on the floor of the $zy$-plane. Positive values of $g$ cause the surface to tilt upward, with greater angles of tilt being associated with larger values of $g$.

Figure 4-3 combines the firm's profit hill with the symmetric constraint surface. The solution to the constrained maximization problem is the point where profit is as large as possible given that it must lie on or below the constraint surface. As is evident, this point occurs somewhere on the back side of the profit hill (where $y$ and $z$ are larger than the monopoly levels) and entails less profit than the monopoly level.

Figure 4-4 shows the projection of the isoprofit contours onto the $zy$-plane. They are seen to be concentric contours emanating from the point $M$ with contours that are farther from $M$ having smaller profit associated with them. The contours are displayed as circles since the profit hill of Figure 4-1 is perfectly symmetric. The shaded area is a set of points that yield "at least as much profit as."

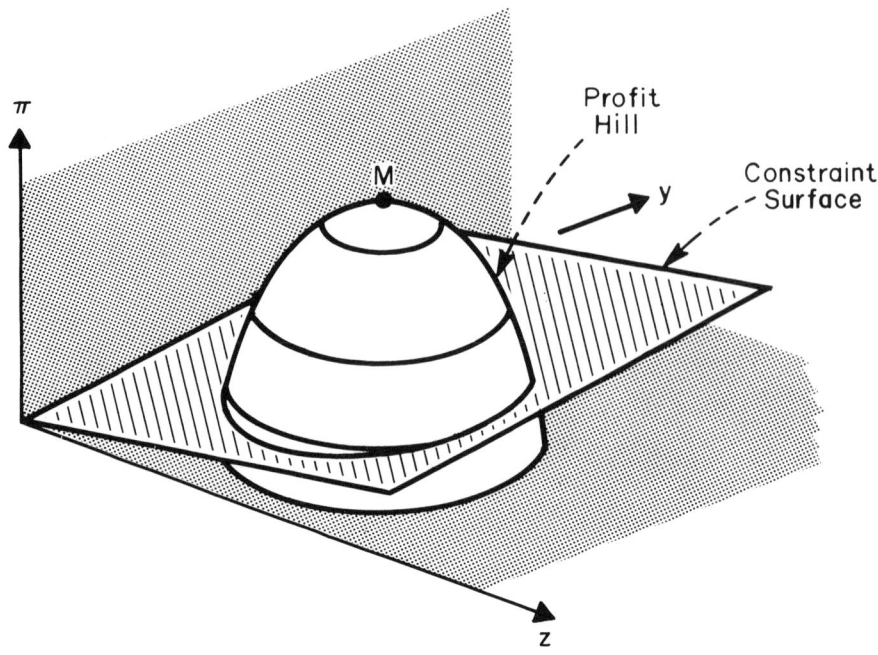

**Figure 4-3.** Symmetric Regulation.

Figure 4-4 also illustrates a curve that is tangent to one of the isoprofit contours. This is an isorevenue curve; that is, it gives combinations of $z$ and $y$ for which the firm's total revenue remains at the same level. Larger revenues are associated with curves that are located farther from the origin, at least out to the point $S$ where revenue is maximized. The locus of points ($MS$) in Figure 4-4 traces out the expansion path of the revenue-maximizing firm as the internal profit requirement is varied between the profit-maximizing level and that at which revenues are maximized.

Proposition 4.2 has asserted that, under a symmetric constraint, this locus is also the regulatory expansion path. To see this, it is convenient to derive algebraically what the tangency condition is. Start with an isorevenue line $R(z,y) = R^*$, for $R^*$ a constant, and differentiate totally to obtain

$$-\frac{dy}{dz} = \frac{R_z}{R_y}. \tag{4.13}$$

By (4.8) and (4.9)

$$\frac{R_z}{R_y} = \frac{C_z}{C_y} = \frac{G_z}{G_y}.$$

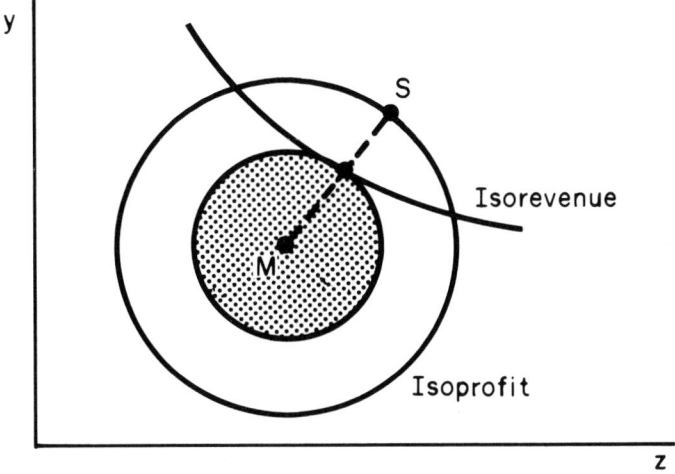

**Figure 4-4.** Expansion Path Under Symmetric Regulation.

The slope along an isoprofit contour is given by

$$-\frac{dy}{dz} = \frac{\pi_z}{\pi_y} = \frac{R_z - C_z}{R_y - C_y}. \qquad (4.14)$$

Equilibrium conditions (4.3) and (4.4) can be rewritten as $R_z - C_z = -\frac{\lambda}{1-\lambda} G_z$ and $R_y - C_y = -\frac{\lambda}{1-\lambda} G_y$ which can be substituted into (4.14) to yield $-\frac{dy}{dz} = \frac{G_z}{G_y}$. Thus, the expansion paths are indeed the same since at the intersection points

$$\frac{R_z}{R_y} = \frac{\pi_z}{\pi_y} = \frac{G_z}{G_y} = \frac{C_z}{C_y}. \qquad (4.15)$$

For a symmetric constraint then, the marginal revenue of $z$ relative to $y$ equals the marginal profit of $z$ relative to $y$ and also equals the marginal cost and the contribution to the profit ceiling of $z$ relative to $y$.

*Significance of the Revenue-Maximization Result*

Proposition 4.2 establishes that it is not optimal for the firm to produce one service in the inelastic region of demand while another is produced in the elastic region. This is evident from (4.15) (4.9) since the equality cannot hold if one of the products has a negative marginal revenue while the other has a positive marginal revenue. This result clearly has implications that can be tested, for if a firm is found to have some variables which yield positive marginal revenue and others which yield negative marginal revenue, then it follows that the firm is not behaving in accordance with this model of regulatory constraint.

Proposition 4.2 has interesting implications with respect to the possible cross-subsidization[c] of one product or service by another, and with respect to the firm's desire to

expand into other regulated markets even if it operates at a (long run) loss in these markets.[1]

On both of these issues the preceding analysis has stated that the regulated firm has an incentive to engage in such activities only if its counterpart, the unregulated revenue maximizer, also would find them advantageous.

For example, consider the case cited in Kafoglis,[2,d] in which it is supposed that business customers, who have the more inelastic demand, are providing the firm with profits sufficient to expand the services to residential customers, perhaps even beyond the point at which price to the residential users equals their marginal cost. Our results say that if this behavior is a solution to the constrained system, the solution is not anomalous: rather, given the same opportunities for price discrimination, the revenue-maximizing firm subject to an internal profit constraint would behave in the same way. The theory has indicated that, at the margin, each of the decision variables controlled by the regulated firm will be set in accordance with the familiar ratio rule relating marginal revenues to marginal costs.

In sum, Proposition 4.2 has shown that because the constraint treats all productive variables symmetrically, the optimal solution also treats all variables symmetrically, and hence they are utilized according to the usual ratio rule. As long as the firm operates in the region between the profit- and revenue-maximizing points, the firm will find it optimal to introduce services in the same way as the revenue-maximizing firm. Thus it has not been necessary to assume a revenue objective in order to get revenue-maximizing behavior;[e] such behavior emerges as a natural outcome of the analysis.

---

[c]See Baumol, Eckstein and Kahn (1970) for a description of a way to test that, at any given set of prices, a service is not a burden on other services. Although they use a break-even constraint, a markup on total costs constraint can be substituted without difficulty into their analysis. Some implications of this and other tests are discussed in Zajac (1972c), and Faulhaber (1972a). Posner (1971) suggests that internal cross-subsidization may, in some cases, be a deliberate policy objective on the part of the regulator. See also Loehman and Whinston (1971). Baumol and Walton (1973) summarize the current status of regulator's views on these matters.

[d]For other multi-product analyses, see Rees (1968), Manne (1952), and Bergson (1972).

[e]This was done in Kafoglis (1969) and Bailey and Malone (1970).

Combining Propositions 4.1 and 4.2, we can assert that if regulation is symmetric in the production variables, then the uneasiness expressed by Baumol is justified only if regulation results in operation beyond the revenue-maximizing point. Under these circumstances, it may indeed be true that

when [the regulator] imposes a ceiling on company profit he is left with the uncomfortable feeling that this limitation still leaves management with too much room for maneuver. He still suspects that somehow, even within the limits imposed on profit, the company may end up setting some prices too high and some too low.³ᶠ

*Interpretations of the Variables*

If the variables are two outputs, then since the firm has no choice in input quantities, the point $S$ in Figure 4-4 is a unique joint-revenue-maximizing point. There is no other point in the plane (no other combination of $z$ and of $y$) that attains this revenue. If regulation tightens, the firm commences to operate off the production frontier, since the quantities of its inputs are fixed by hypothesis.

If the variables are labor and capital inputs to production, then the isorevenue curve tangent to $S$ is not a point as it was in the preceding discussion. Rather, it is an entire isoquant. In this case there are many pairs of ($K,L$) values, having different costs associated with them, which can produce the same revenue (as, for example, points $A$, $S$, and $B$ in Figure 4-5). For the situation depicted in Figure 4-5, movement into the inelastic region of demand (the shaded region) will not be so profitable a policy as operation off the production frontier or as substitution of labor for capital, $A$, (or capital for labor, $B$) in production.

A third interpretation of the variables is as a quality-quantity pair for a particular commodity. An increase in quality or advertising is normally supposed to add not only to costs but also to the revenues of the firm, for at any given price, it increases the quantity demanded.ᵍ Price and quality can thus be viewed as two variables that together determine output. Under regulation, if expenditures on quality improvement always bring in added revenue $\frac{R_z}{C_z} > 0$, then there is, in effect, no maximum to the revenue curve in the range where profits are positive. In this case the firm has no incentive to operate off the production frontier; instead, it finds it optimal to lower price and improve product quality.ʰ

As a last example the two variables can be taken to represent quantity and excess managerial staff. At the regulatory equilibrium this staff, or general

---
ᶠThe statement may also hold true if the firm is constrained to just break-even in its operations, or as mentioned in Chapter 3, if the firm has objectives other than profit.

ᵍSee Baumol (1967), Dorfman and Steiner (1954), or Schmalensee (1972).

ʰSee also Rosse (1972), White (1972), and Levhari and Peles (1973).

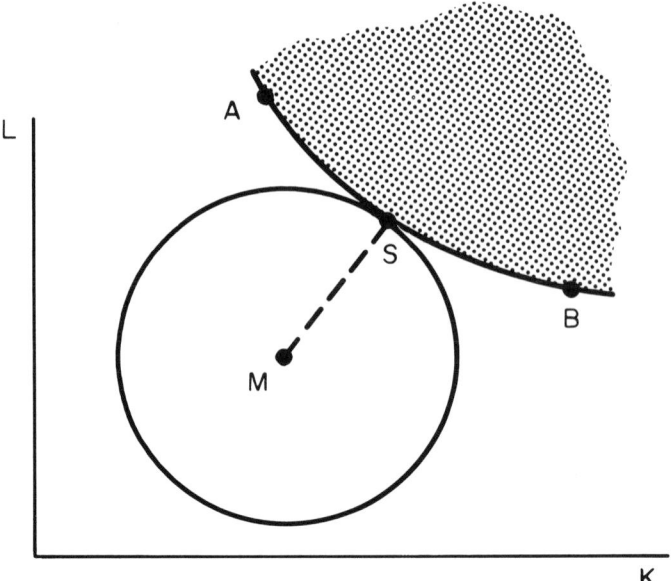

**Figure 4-5.** Expansion Path in Two-Input Model.

administrative expense, exceeds the most profitable level (it is expanded beyond the point at which an extra dollar's worth of selling expenses brings in as much as a dollar's worth of revenue). The reason that the firm will find the additional expenses attractive is different from the usual one given by Williamson.[i] In his work, the managers derive positive utility from having the additional staff report to them; in the regulatory model, the added staff offers a way to respond to the regulatory constraint that is more profitable than pure waste.

## Asymmetric Constraint

*Definition and Graphical Interpretation*

Any constraint for which $\frac{G_z}{C_z} > \frac{G_y}{C_y} \geq 0$ can be called asymmetric, and it yields an equilibrium rule for the ($z,y$) pair of the form

---

[i]See Williamson (1964, 1970); see also Machlup (1967) and Rees (1973).

$$\frac{R_z}{R_y} = \frac{C_z}{C_y} \frac{\left[1 - \frac{\lambda}{1-\lambda} \frac{G_z}{C_z}\right]}{\left[1 - \frac{\lambda}{1-\lambda} \frac{G_y}{C_y}\right]} < \frac{C_z}{C_y}. \qquad (4.16)$$

that requires a distortion in resource allocation making for a large value of the $z$ variable relative to that of the $y$ variable. Any such asymmetric constraint also has the property that as long as the firm is operating in a rising part of the revenue curve, operation off the production frontier is not the firm's most profitable policy.

Of the various possible asymmetries in the constraint ceiling, our attention will be confined for the most part to the form of asymmetry in which

$$\frac{G_z}{C_z} > 0 \text{ and } \frac{G_y}{C_y} = 0, \qquad (4.17)$$

that is, one of the productive variables is excluded entirely from the constraint ceiling. The asymmetric constraint (4.17) is of particular interest since the Averch-Johnson model of rate-of-return regulation is of this form.

Figure 4-6 illustrates an asymmetric constraint. The constraint surface is hinged on the $y$ axis. Each line drawn on the surface indicates the height of the ceiling, measured in terms of profit. This height is the same for all values of $y$, given that a particular value of $z$ has been selected; the height of the ceiling changes, however, as $z$ is changed.

Figure 4-7 shows the intersection between the asymmetric constraint curve and the profit hill. It is clear that the point at which constrained profit is the largest will be a point of tangency between the profit hill and a $z$ = constant line on the constraint surface. The economic implications of this tangency condition will become apparent as we proceed somewhat further with the mathematical analysis.

*Misallocation of Resources*

*Proposition 4.3: The equilibrium rule for the ( z,y ) pair under asymmetric regulation represents a distortion from the usual ratio rule. The misallocation is such that the firm uses too much of the variable z whose value enters in the profit ceiling relative to its use of the variable y which does not.*

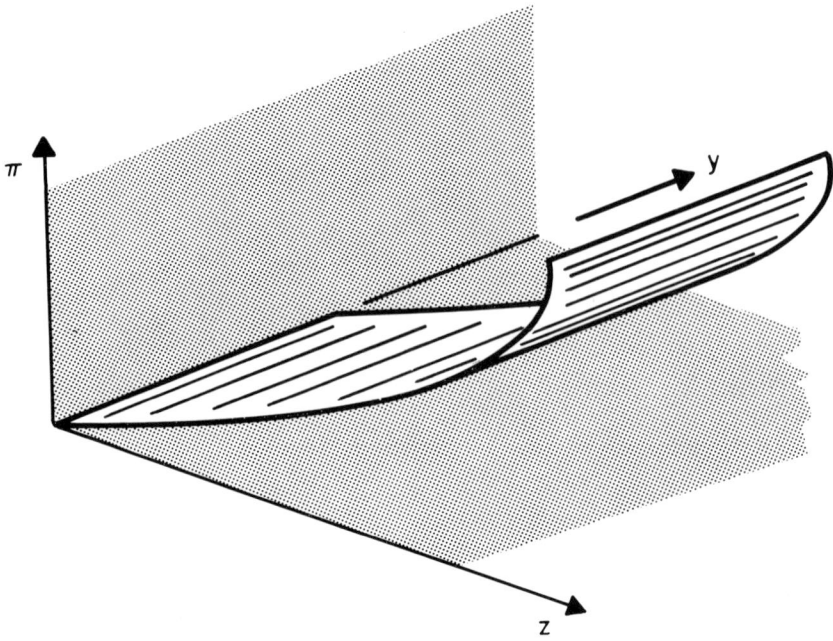

**Figure 4-6.** Asymmetric Constraint Surface.

*Proof*: When $G_y = 0$, the first-order condition on $y$ becomes $(1 - \lambda)(R_y - C_y) = 0$. The first-order condition on $z$ is $(1 - \lambda)(R_z - C_z) = -\lambda G_z$. Since $\lambda < 1$ by Proposition 3.2, we can divide to obtain

$$\frac{R_z}{R_y} = \frac{C_z}{C_y} - \frac{\lambda}{1-\lambda} \frac{G_z}{C_y}. \tag{4.18}$$

*End of Proof*

The proof of Proposition 4.3 utilizes the equilibrium rules for $z$ and $y$. For variable $y$, we notice that since $\lambda < 1$, the necessary condition reduces to

$$R_y = C_y, \tag{4.19}$$

which is precisely the same rule as that used by the profit-maximizing firm. The amount of the variable $y$ that is used, however, may well be changed from its monopoly level. The reason, of course, is that the values of the variables are determined by all the Kuhn-Tucker conditions simultaneously. Since the equilibrium condition for the $z$ variable as given by (4.3) is not the monopoly

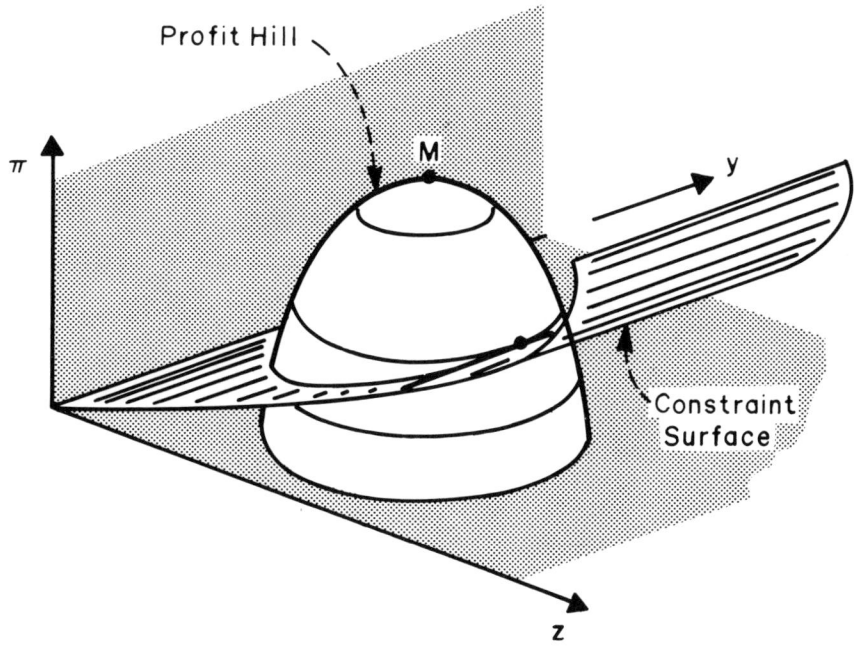

**Figure 4-7.** Asymmetric Regulation.

rule, cross-effects between the productive elements may produce changes in the levels of employment of both factors.

A closely related theorem concerns the expansion path under asymmetric regulation.

*Proposition 4.4: The expansion path under asymmetric regulation is invariant to changes in the particular functional form of the profit ceiling, although the equilibrium operating point on the expansion path does depend upon the form of the constraint.*

*Proof:* The isoprofit contour is specified by Equation (4.14). Substituting (4.19) and (4.3) into (4.14) we have

$$\frac{-dy}{dz} = \frac{\pi_z}{\pi_y} = \frac{-\frac{\lambda}{1-\lambda}G_z}{0} = -\infty \qquad (4.20)$$

so that the solution point in the $zy$-plane is at the intersection of the isoprofit contour with a line parallel to the $y$-axis.

*End of Proof*

Proposition 4.4 says that under an asymmetric constraint, the regulatory expansion path traces out the intersection of the isoprofit contours with vertical lines parallel to the $y$-axis. This is illustrated graphically in Figure 4-8. Intuitively, of all points yielding the same profit, the firm prefers that point at which the usage of $z$ is largest, since the constraint ceiling is always larger for this $z$ than for any other.

Proposition 4.4 is at first unexpected for it seems as though different functional forms for the ceiling constraint $G(z)$ might be able to shift the path to make it lie somewhere between the regulated and revenue-maximizing paths shown in Figure 4-8. But, as we have shown, so long as $G_z > 0$ and $G_y = 0$, the regulated path is traced by vertical tangencies, and this path is then quite independent of the functional form of the ceiling constraint. In Chapter 6, this theorem will clarify considerably why it is that the "graduated return" method of regulation is not successful in moving the firm off the Averch-Johnson expansion path. Proposition 4.4 also has important practical implications because it says that many changes in decision procedures that arise in the course of applying an asymmetric method of regulation do not in any way alter the expansion path which the firm selects. They may, however, determine where on this expansion path the firm ends up.

The misallocation of resources under asymmetric regulation is shown by the divergence of the regulated path in Figure 4-8 from the revenue maximizer's path in the figure. It should be noticed, however, that the term "misallocation" seems less a propos under some interpretations of the productive variables than

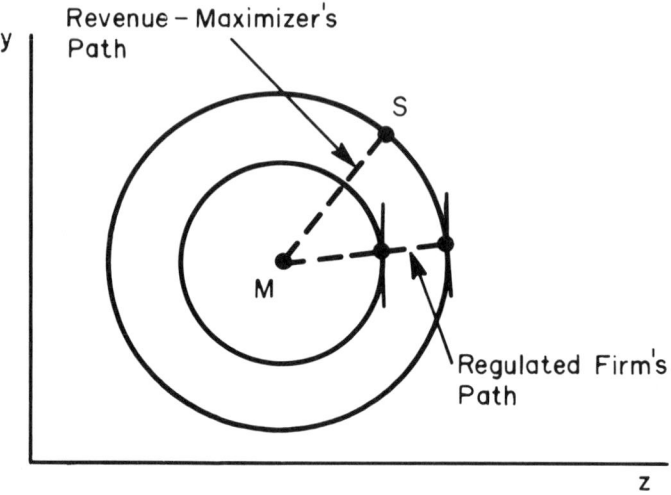

**Figure 4-8.** Asymmetric Expansion Path.

it is under others. For example, in a quantity-quality interpretation of the model, the asymmetric constraint might limit profit on the basis of quantity but not of quality. In that case, the firm will automatically be induced to maximize the contribution of quality to total profits, and use the profit obtained in this way to expand output as much as possible. Alternatively, if an asymmetric constraint calls for a profit limitation based on one output but not the other (the luxury service $y$ is exluded from the rate base, but the basic service is included), then the volume of basic services would be maximized. This may be a misallocation or an improvement, depending on the welfare implications of the revenue maximizer's expansion path.

Figure 4-9 illustrates what can happen when the two variables are independent. An example might be a model which combines price discrimination and peak-load pricing; that is, business demand for electricity results in a daytime peak with residential demand occurring largely during off-peak evening hours. A ceiling constraint based on capacity rises with increases in peak but not with increases in off-peak service. Since the outputs are independent, the $R_y = C_y$ rule can be used to solve for the level of profit from the off-peak users, which can then be superimposed upon the profit hill for the peak users as is done in Figure 4-9. The point $E$ at which the joint profit $\pi(z) + \pi(y)$ intersects with the $G(z)$ curve is the point at which the firm will operate. It is clear that such a point could entail a negative profit on the peak service $z$.[j] In sum, by leaving a variable out of the ceiling constraint, the regulator can deliberately or unwittingly encourage the firm to distort the use of the one activity relative to the other.

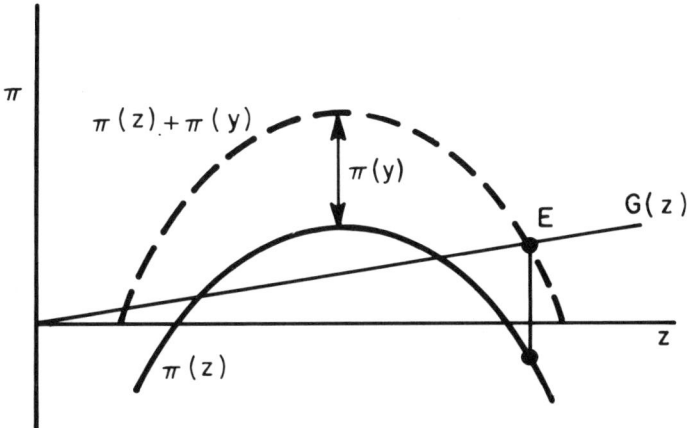

**Figure 4-9.** Asymmetric Regulation with Independent Markets.

---

[j]See Bailey and White (1973). Notice that the above discussion only holds if there is no switching to a joint peak as prices to peak users are lowered. See also Chapter 10.

**Related Regulatory Models**

Some regulatory constraint situations that are of interest do not strictly adhere to regulatory Model (4.1). One of these, entailing two-part tariffs, was described briefly at the end of Chapter 3. To offer some additional examples of what can arise, we now describe several other classes of problems, and outline why it is that they must be treated separately. Chapters 7 and 9 go into more detail on still other variations.

*Regulation of One Market Only*

Consider the gas industry in which a firm's total profit is sometimes determined by sales to both commercial, $y$, and residential, $z$, users, but profit is only regulated in the residential market. MacAvoy and Nell have modeled the process as one in which the firm seeks to

$$\text{Maximize } \pi(z,y) = R(z) + R(y) - C(z,y) \quad (4.21)$$
$$z, y$$

$$\text{Subject to } R(z) \leqq g\alpha C(z,y),$$

where $\alpha$ is the proportion of total costs that are attributed to service $z$ and $g$ is the markup permitted by the regulator, $g > 1$.[k] When $\alpha$ is determined on an arbitrary basis, Model (4.21) has first-order conditions that differ from those discussed previously in this chapter.

If the cost attribution is accomplished on the basis of revenues, however, so that

$$\alpha = \frac{R(z)}{R(z) + R(y)} \quad (4.22)$$

then the constraint in (4.21) reduces to

$$R(z) + R(y) \leqq gC(z,y)$$

which is a symmetric constraint of precisely the usual sort. It is possible to find, therefore, an allocation of joint costs between the commercial and residential users which permits regulation of the single market to result in the usual rules for a symmetric constraint.

A third possibility is that there is no joint cost problem so that the model becomes

---

[k]This is actually a somewhat simplified version of the MacAvoy and Noll (1973) model. See also Breyer and MacAvoy (1972). I am grateful to Kyu Lie for pointing out the implications of defining $a$ in accordance with (4.22).

Maximize $\pi(z,y) = R(z) + R(y) - C(z) - C(y)$ (4.23)
$z, y$

Subject to $R(z) \leqq gC(z)$.

In this case, the first-order condition for $y$ is $\pi_y = 0$, which is the profit maximizer's rule; the first-order condition for the residential user is $(1-\lambda)\pi_z + \lambda gC_z = 0$. Thus, the firm charges as high a price as is compatible with competitive conditions in the commercial market and transfers any proceeds into the residential market. The regulatory constraint has distorted the firm's operations from the revenue-maximizing path to the path which offers the greatest amount of service to the residential users.

## Operating Ratio Method of Regulation

The operating ratio method of regulation provides a second example of a constraint which may not adhere to regulatory Model (4.1). Under this method, the firm will

Maximize $R(z,y) - C(y) - C(z)$ (4.24)
$z, y$

Subject to $R(z,y) \leqq (1+g)C(y)$,

where $z$ = capital, $y$ = labor, and $g > 0$ is the markup permitted over operating expenses (excluding capital costs).[1] This method of regulation is sometimes used in industries in which the capital-labor ratio is low, such as trucking or postal service or bus transportation. For such firms even a small change in circumstances can prevent the earning of a fair return under rate-of-return regulation.

If (4.24) is rewritten into the usual constraint form, we obtain

$$\pi \leqq gC(y) - C(z).$$ (4.25)

It is apparent from (4.25) that $G_z = -C_z < 0$, that is, the firm has a disincentive to use $z$. The derivation of the expansion path is not difficult. We merely note that the isoprofit curve has slope $\dfrac{dy}{dz} = -\dfrac{R_z - C_z}{R_y - C_y}$ and that the isoconstraint curve has slope $\dfrac{dy}{dz} = \dfrac{-R_z}{R_y - (1+g)C_y}$. The two are tangent at a solution to the constrained system, so that $\dfrac{R_z - C_z}{R_y - C_y} = \dfrac{R_z}{R_y - (1+g)C_y}$. Upon multiplying and

---
[1]See Kahn (1971), p. 54, and Wilson (1972).

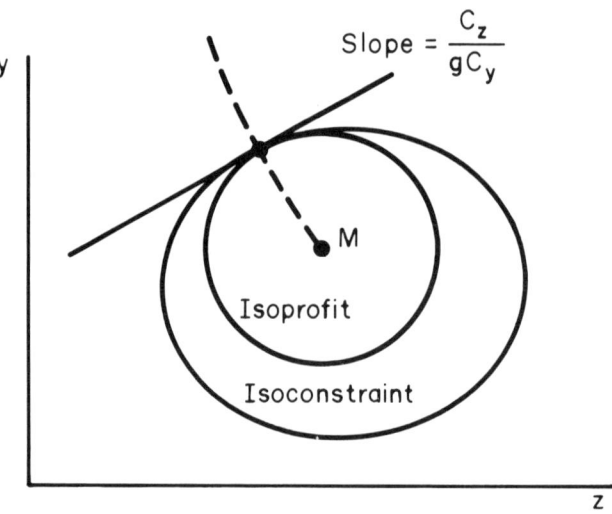

**Figure 4-10.** Expansion Path under Operating-Ratio Regulation.

rearranging, this yields $\dfrac{dy}{dz} = \dfrac{C_z}{gC_y}$. Thus, the tangency occurs at intersections such as those depicted in Figure 4-10. As $g$ is lowered, the firm moves out from the monopoly point $M$ along the dotted line; hence, it always uses less than the monopolist's quantity of capital, and for many classes of production functions, output declines. The expansion path may therefore more correctly be termed a contraction path.

This last argument has relied on the fact that the solution to any regulatory model is nothing more than the intersection between an iso-objective (isoprofit) contour and an isoconstraint contour. By remembering this, we can often investigate a property of the regulatory model that is of interest to us without having to resort to the Kuhn-Tucker or Lagrangian method. This is not surprising since the Lagrangian method after all serves mainly as a convenient way of arriving at the optimal solution. If the original model can be solved as easily as the artificial problem that uses the multiplier, one might as well remain with the original model.

*The Multistage Regulated Firm*

As a final example of a model requiring its own analysis, we can think of the variables in Model (4.1) as applying to inputs or outputs from more than one stage in a firm's production process. For example, one of the variables can be capital which is manufactured at one stage of production; the capital can then be combined with a labor input to supply service to final customers. Or, the regulated firm can be viewed as both producing, transmitting, and distributing its service.

A characteristic of the multistage model is that the firm usually has some control over the price that one of its production stages sets for the next stage. A prototype of the objective function is

$$\text{Maximize } \pi = [R(z,y) - C(k,z,y)] + [R^*(k,y) - C^*(y)], \quad (4.26)$$
$$z,y,k$$

where profits to the parent company are seen to be the sum of profits from its two stages. $R$ and $C$ indicate the revenues and costs in the final stage of production, and $R^*$ and $C^*$ are the revenues and costs of the earlier stage. The price $k$ is seen to influence revenues in the earlier stage and costs at the later stage of production. Thus, even in the absence of regulatory constraint, the variable $k$ provides a way of transferring profit from one stage to another.[m] Not surprisingly, this variable also influences the analysis substantially when a regulatory constraint is imposed.

Dayan has done some rather intensive theoretical work in this area.[4] He uses an objective function similar to (4.26) and looks at a variety of regulatory constraints, such as one which regulates only one stage of the productive process, one which imposes a single overall constraint on profit, and one in which each stage is separately constrained. By using analytic procedures that are closely related to those employed here, he derives a set of theorems that provide a very illuminating contrast and supplement to our own.

Dayan also traces out a history of natural gas industry regulation, and uses his theoretical results to suggest how the methods of regulation prevailing in the past offered incentives to either integrate forward or backward into other stages, and at other times gave incentives toward divestiture. He thus uses the theory to provide insight into the means by which regulatory policies can influence market structure.

---

[m]See, for example, Irwin (1971), Williamson (1971), Garfield and Lovejoy (1964), Kahn (1971), Phillips (1969), and Needham (1969).

**Part II:
Rate of Return Regulation**

# 5 Averch-Johnson Model

**Introduction and Summary**

In Part I, a general theory of optimal response to regulation has been described. Much of the richness of interpretation that this theory makes possible lies hidden until one studies in detail some particular versions of the model. Certainly the most important and relevant specialization is the regulatory model of Averch and Johnson. This model not only triggered the initial interest in the analytic approach to regulation but also has served as the focal point of most of the subsequent literature on regulatory models. It asserted some of the first theorems about behavior under constraint, theorems which have since been modified and elaborated upon both by economists and by others concerned with the regulatory process. The model has been extended in a number of ways, each of which offers interesting insights. For these reasons, and because of the practical importance of rate-of-return regulation, the major portion of Part II of this book will be devoted to the Averch-Johnson model.

Our version of the AJ model differs from the original by permitting operation off the production frontier and by explicitly including the acquisition cost of capital as a parameter. In other respects, our model is the same as that of Averch and Johnson: it portrays a profit-maximizing firm in which two factors of production, labor and capital, are combined to produce a single output. A regulatory constraint limits the firm's earnings to a fair return (assumed to be larger than the cost of capital) on each unit of investment.

The first question that Averch and Johnson asked was whether a firm in such circumstances would allocate resources between labor and capital in an efficient manner. They found that the answer was no: because additional use of capital adds to the rate base while that of labor does not, the firm can earn additional profits by substituting capital for labor in production. As a result, the firm ends up using more capital and less labor than are consistent with minimizing costs at the level of output selected.

The second question that Averch and Johnson asked was whether there is any distortion in pricing between products because there is a single overall constraint on rate of return rather than separate constraints limiting return in each market. Their assertion here is that

the firm may have an incentive (that it would not have in the absence of regulation) to enter these markets, even if the cost of doing so exceeds the additional revenues.[1]

In contrast, we show that, in a labor-capital model in which two products share the same capital facilities, the expansion path between products is based on the same ratio rule that is followed by the classical revenue-maximizing firm: there is no unusual distortion between products, although there is still the misallocation between labor and capital inputs.

Other theorems are also arrived at in this chapter. One of the most important of these is that the firm regulated by a rate-of-return constraint will not find it optimal to operate in the inelastic region of the revenue curve. Thus, if empirical evidence reveals that a firm is operating in an inelastic region, we can assert that the firm is not behaving in accordance with the AJ model. Another theorem asserts that the point of largest output on an isorate-of-return contour is not associated with minimum-cost production, but rather is one at which the firm uses an overly labor intensive technology. A rate-of-return constraint can, therefore, cause a misallocation favoring the labor input if the firm's objective is revenue or output maximization rather than profit maximization.

## Components of Model

The Averch-Johnson model portrays the firm as maximizing profit subject to a regulatory constraint that limits the firm's earnings to, at most, a fair return on its capital investment:

$$\text{Maximize } \pi(L,K) = R(L,K) - wL - rcK \qquad (5.1)$$
$$L, K$$

$$\text{Subject to } \frac{R(L,K) - wL}{cK} \lesseqgtr s, \; s > r,$$

where
$L$ = physical units of labor
$K$ = physical units of capital
$w$ = wage rate per physical unit of labor (constant)
$c$ = acquisition cost per physical unit of capital (constant)
$r$ = market cost of borrowing funds (constant)
$s$ = fair return on investment set by regulator (constant)
$C(L,K) = wL + rcK$ = total costs
$R(L,K) = p(q)q(L,K)$ = revenues as determined by the firm's demand and production functions
$q(L,K)$ = a continuous and twice differentiable production function which transforms physical units of labor and capital into output of the firm; production requires both inputs, $q(L,0) = q(0,K) = 0$
$p(q)$ = inverse demand function which uniquely determines the price of the product given the output level, $p' < 0$

$$\pi(L,K) = R(L,K) - C(L,K) = \text{profit} = \text{revenues minus costs}$$

$$i = \frac{R(L,K) - wL}{cK} = \text{actual rate of return earned by the firm.}$$

*Description of Components*

In Model (5.1) the decision variables chosen by the firm are the labor and capital inputs to production. These are transformed by the production function into the output of the firm. Price is a residual having precisely that value which just clears the market in the constrained system. The process of price adjustment is thus implicit rather than explicit in the model. The regulator determines the largest acceptable rate of return, and the firm responds through its decision variables with a price that will be in accord with that rate of return.[a]

Labor input is total manhours worked and presumably is calculated by assigning appropriate weights to each such hour to account for differences in skill and wages. The assumption that the average cost per manhour is constant means both that the optimal mix of types of labor does not change when the level of operation changes, and that the firm does not have monopsonistic power in the labor market.

Capital input is the cost of tying up the assets required for production. The aggregate capital stock presumably includes both tangible assets, such as plant, and financial assets, such as working capital. By multiplying each unit of plant by its cost, the capital stock is expressed in dollars as $cK$. Since the acquisition cost is depicted as a constant, the mix of capital equipment is the same over different levels of output, and the firm does not influence the price it pays for capital goods.

The cost of capital, $r$, is the minimum return which the firm must have in order to be able to continue to raise capital funds over the long run. This cost is assumed to be known.[b] Furthermore, the cost is assumed to be independent of the mix of financial instruments employed.

Westfield[2] explains the lack of symmetry between the capital part and the labor part of the total cost term. Output, labor usage, and revenues are flows that take place over each unit of time, but capital is a stock which is available throughout the period of operation. Expressed mathematically, the total present value, $V$, of the firm is

$$V = \int_{t=0}^{\infty} [R(L,K) - wL] e^{-rt} dt - cK \qquad (5.2)$$

---

[a]If we admit that in actuality there are price structures rather than a single price, this description says that regulation is on rate of return rather than on price structure. This does seem a reasonable approximation to how most commissions have worked. For other methods of modelling the price adjustment process, see Davis (1973), Joskow (1972, 1973), Klevorick (1973) and Perrakis and Sahin (1972).

[b]This is, of course, a questionable assumption since many regulatory hearings are devoted entirely to the attempt to determine a value for cost of capital. See Myers (1973).

where $e^{-rt}$ discounts the stream of net operating revenues at the firm's market cost of capital. Equation (5.2) assumes that the time stream of returns commences immediately and is the same throughout the period. Upon integrating, we have $V = \dfrac{R(L,K) - wL}{r} - cK$ or

$$\pi = rV = R(L,K) - wL - rcK . \tag{5.3}$$

Thus, while profit is expressed in dollars per unit time, the present value of the firm is expressed in dollars. The cost of capital effectively converts the present value to an annuity yielding $rV$ each time period. Profit is this annuity.[c]

The AJ version of the profit function is $\pi = R(L,K) - wL - rK$ with the acquisition cost $c$ implicitly set equal to one. We have been explicit about introducing $c$ in our version of the model because $c$ appears in places where $r$ does not [such as in the constraint in Model (5.1)], and because $c$ turns out to have comparative statics properties that are quite different from those of $r$.

The regulatory fair return, $s$, is assumed to exceed the cost of capital, $s > r$. This notion that the regulator will permit the firm to earn a return that is larger than the minimum required to acquire capital is open to some dispute. However, the assumption $s > r$ is crucial in a theoretical sense, since it permits a unique solution to regulatory Model (5.1), as we shall see.

Sometimes the rate of return actually earned by the firm exceeds the "fair rate" explicitly permitted by the regulator; yet the regulator does not insist upon a price adjustment to reduce the return. In such cases, $s$ should probably be thought of as the ceiling return implicitly permitted by the regulator.

In Model (5.1), the $cK$ in the denominator of the constraint is the same as the $cK$ in the objective function of the firm. Thus, the model ignores the possibility that the rate base used by a particular commission may be different from the firm's invested capital. Disparities can occur in reality, of course. Regulators can exclude investments deemed improper and may (or may not) make "fair value" adjustments when higher replacement costs cause the net plant in service to be underestimated or overestimated on the firm's book.

The rate-of-return constraint can be translated into a profit constraint by multiplying both sides by $cK$, thereby obtaining $R(L,K) - wL \leqq scK$, and then subtracting $rcK$ from each side to obtain

$$\pi \leqq (s - r)cK . \tag{5.4}$$

Rate-of-return regulation is therefore a type of profit ceiling regulation, under which the profit ceiling rises with increases in capital use, but is completely

---

[c]The construction of (5.2) and (5.3) has assumed that all capital is bought today, that it never deteriorates and that no change is expected in the wage rate or revenue function over time. Dansby (1972) has relaxed some of these assumptions by including in the AJ model depreciation and the yearly replacement of a portion of the equipment. His method results in a capital stock that remains constant over time. This then permits him to examine the effects of various depreciation policies within the AJ framework.

unaffected by increases in labor use. Equation (5.4) makes it clear that if $s = r$, the constraint reduces to a zero-profit constraint, and the profit-maximizing firm is then presumably indifferent among the combinations of variables that permit it to break even in its operation.

Equation (5.4) also indicates that a fixed rate of return is not the same as a fixed total profit. When the fair rate is set at a level such as $s$, the profits of the firm depend on the amount of capital used. Therefore, the constraint (5.4) is not of the form usually used in a welfare-maximizing model or in a revenue-maximizing model.[d] In those models, the constraint is of a break-even or minimum dollar profit variety in which the right-hand side of the constraint is generally a constant; it does not vary with the size of the firm's decision variables.

If unconstrained profit is larger than that which is permitted under regulation, then equality holds in the constraint. The firm operates most profitably by earning exactly the maximum return permitted by the regulator. Model (5.1) can then be rewritten as

$$\text{Maximize}_{L,K} \quad (s - r)cK \qquad (5.5)$$

$$\text{Subject to} \quad \frac{R(L,K) - wL}{cK} = s, \; s > r.$$

This version of the model shows that the effect of the constraint upon the firm's behavior is to encourage the firm to maximize its use of capital because the objective in (5.5) is equivalent to maximization of $K$. The constraint in Model (5.5) ensures the firm does not choose so much $K$ that it fails to attain the ceiling profit permitted at $K$.

*Graphical Approach*

Zajac[3] has provided a geometric interpretation of the AJ model. Labor and capital can be combined productively in any of the ways indicated by the profit hill depicted in Figure 5-1. As in Chapter 4, the contour lines on the hill are the firm's isoprofit lines. There is exactly one combination of labor and capital that yields maximum profits to the firm, which is that combination corresponding to the topmost point of the profit hill $M$. The firm is not able to operate at this point, however, because of the rate-of-return constraint. This constraint is a plane hinged on the $L$-axis, with the surface being given in terms of profits by the equation $\pi = (s - r)cK$. If the fair rate and cost of capital are equal ($s = r$), the constraint lies on the floor of the $KL$-plane. As the fair rate is increased, the slope of the plane increases.

The points of intersection between the plane and the profit hill are equal

---

[d]See, for instance, Baumol and Bradford (1970), Baumol (1967), Peacock and Rowley (1972), and Azariadis, Cohen, and Porcar (1972).

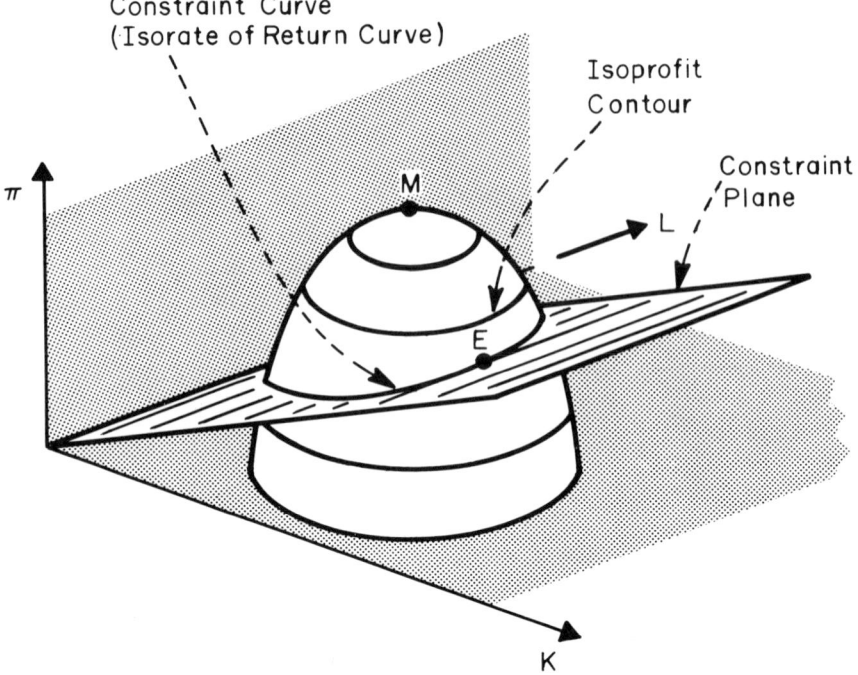

**Figure 5-1.** Rate-of-Return Regulation.

rate-of-return points, but they are not equal-profit points since they intersect many isoprofit lines (as is evident in Figure 5-1). These points form a constraint curve and the firm's objective is to operate at the point on this constraint curve yielding the highest profits. Since the constraint plane rises as $K$ increases, the highest value of $\pi$ on the intersection curve coincides with the largest $K$-value on this curve, that is, equilibrium point $E$ lies on the largest $K = K^*$ line that touches the profit hill in Figure 5-1.

It is convenient to look at a two-dimensional representation of Figure 5-1 and a very attractive means of doing this is given in Figure 5-2.[e] The figure has two components: the bottom depicts a projection of the profit hill into the $K\pi$-plane while the top shows the projection into the $KL$-plane. To understand how the projection into the $K\pi$-plane is obtained, imagine shining a light on the profit hill of Figure 5-1 and looking at the shadow cast by the hill on the $K\pi$-plane. This shadow is the hill in Figure 5-2. For each value of $K$, that $L$ has been selected which renders the highest possible profit, and the locus of these points traces out the silhouette. In the lower figure, the constraint $\pi = (s - r)K$ appears as a ray emanating from the origin with slope $(s - r)c$; the intersection at the point $E$ gives the solution to the constrained maximization problem.

---

[e] I am indebted to Gibb Oram for devising this figure.

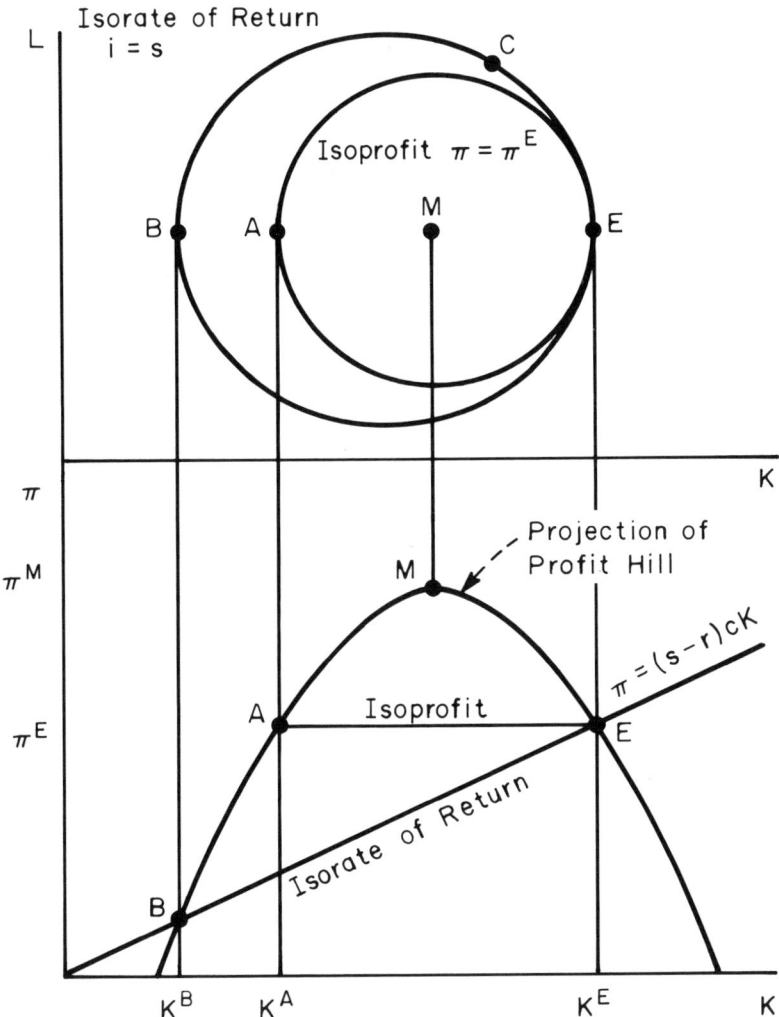

**Figure 5-2.** Isorate of Return and Isoprofit Contours.

An isoprofit line in the bottom part of Figure 5-2 is a line parallel to the $K$-axis such as $AE$; in the $KL$-plane, the isoprofit line becomes an isoprofit contour as the various combinations of $L$ as well as $K$ are considered as possibilities. The lowest and highest $K$ points on the isoprofit contour $\pi = \pi^E$ correspond precisely to the $K^A$ and $K^E$ values of the lower figure.

The isorate-of-return line in the bottom part of Figure 5-2 is the ray $BE$. This can be drawn as a contour in the $KL$-plane with end points $K^B$ and $K^{\bar{E}}$. Since all points on the line segment $BE$ have lower profit than all points on the isoprofit segment $AE$, it is apparent that the isorate-of-return contour $i = s$ in the $KL$-plane lies everywhere outside the isoprofit contour $\pi = \pi^E$, except at the point $E$ where the two curves touch. The top part of Figure 5-2 thus illustrates nicely the principle that the solution to the constrained system occurs at the intersection of the isoprofit contour and the isoconstraint contour.

Another way to get at the relationship between the isoprofit and isorate-of-return contours can be obtained by contrasting what happens to profit as we move along the isorate-of-return contour from point $C$ to point $E$ in the top part of Figure 5-2. The actual rate of return, $i = \dfrac{R(L,K) - wL}{cK}$, can be rewritten (by adding and subtracting $\dfrac{rcK}{cK}$) as

$$i = \frac{\pi}{cK} + r. \qquad (5.6)$$

As we move along the contour, $i$, $r$, and $c$ stay the same, but $K$ increases. To maintain the equality in (5.6), then, profit must increase also. As we move downward along the isorate-of-return contour away from $E$, by the same reasoning, profit decreases. Hence $E$ (the largest $K$ value) is the point of highest profit on the isorate-of-return curve.

## Major Theoretical Results

*Analytic Formulation of Model*

In order to derive systematically the theoretical propositions which arise in an Averch-Johnson model, we use an analytic formulation of the model which is compatible with the presentation in Part I:

Maximize $\pi(L,K,L^*,K^*) = R(L,K) - w(L + L^*) - rc(K + K^*)$ (5.7)
$L, K, L^*, K^*$

Subject to $\pi(L,K,L^*,K^*) \leqq (s - r)c(K + K^*)$, $s > r$,

where $\quad L^* = $ number of units of labor wasted with cost per unit of $w$
$\quad\quad\ \ K^* = $ number of units of capital wasted with cost per unit of $rc$.

In Model (5.7), the firm can, if it chooses, operate off the production frontier by wasteful expenditures either on staff or on capital which can go into the rate base. The index of x-inefficiency is $x = wL^* + rcK^*$. As in Part I, operation off the production frontier increases cost but does not alter revenue, which depends only on the amounts of $L$ and $K$ that are used productively.[f] The Lagrangian is

$$\phi(L, K, L^*, K^*, \lambda) = (1 - \lambda)[R(L, K) - w(L + L^*) - rc(K + K^*)] \quad (5.8)$$
$$+ \lambda[(s - r)c(K + K^*)] .$$

The Kuhn-Tucker conditions are

$\phi_L:$ $\quad (1 - \lambda)(R_L - w) = 0$ $\hfill (5.9)$

$\phi_K:$ $\quad (1 - \lambda)R_K = (1 - \lambda)rc - \lambda(s - r)c$ $\hfill (5.10)$

$\phi_{L^*}:$ $\quad \lambda \leqq 1, L^*(1 - \lambda)(-w) = 0$ $\hfill (5.11)$

$\phi_{K^*}:$ $\quad \lambda \leqq \dfrac{r}{s}, K^*c(-r + \lambda s) = 0$ $\hfill (5.12)$

$\phi_\lambda:$ $\quad R(L, K) - wL - scK = 0$ $\hfill (5.13)$

$\quad L > 0, K > 0, \lambda \geqq 0, L^* \geqq 0, K^* \geqq 0.$ $\hfill (5.14)$

*Lagrange Multiplier Theorem*

Proposition 3.1, limiting the range of the Lagrange multiplier, is readily established for the AJ model. In fact, the theorem can be stated in even tighter form.

---

[f]Model (5.7) offers us one way of taking into account the possibility of operation off the production frontier in an AJ model. Another method, suggested in a letter from Perry Shapiro is

$$\text{Maximize } \pi = pq - wL - rcK$$
$$L, K, q$$
$$\text{Subject to } \pi \leqq (s - r)cK, \; s > r$$
$$q \leqq q(L, K)$$

where $q(L, K)$ = potential production
$\qquad q$ = actual production.

The similarity of Shapiro's method to ours is clear, since in his objective function revenues are determined by actual rather than potential production. It is not surprising then to find that Shapiro was able to use his formulation to derive essentially the same set of propositions that we do here.

*Proposition 5.1: The Lagrange multiplier in a rate-of-return model is less than one; more precisely, it is less than or equal to the ratio of the market cost of capital to the fair rate of return on capital.*

*Proof::* By (5.14) and (5.12), $0 \leq \lambda \leq \frac{r}{s}$. Since the fair rate $s$ exceeds the cost of capital by assumption, the multiplier is always strictly less than unity.

*End of Proof*

Thus, by including rate base padding as an alternative open to the firm, the proof that the multiplier is bounded below one follows immediately from the necessary conditions.[g]

To bound $\lambda$ away from zero, all that is needed, as in Chapter 3, is that the constraint cut the profit hill below its maximum and that the profit hill be concave. Because both demand and production function relationships are included in the revenue term in the AJ model, concavity of the revenue function is equivalent to concavity of the profit function.

Since $\lambda < 1$ from Proposition 5.1, Equation (5.9) reduces to

$$R_L = w, \qquad (5.15)$$

which along with Equation (5.13) gives two equations in two unknowns, labor and capital. The levels of use of the productive inputs can thus be determined without knowing the optimal value of $\lambda$.[h]

*Marginal Revenue Theorem*

Equation (5.15) can be used to prove a second proposition about rate-of-return regulation, one which has virtually been ignored in the literature.[i]

*Proposition 5.2: The profit-maximizing firm constrained to earn no more than a fair return on its capital investment always finds it optimal to operate in an elastic region of the revenue curve.*

---

[g]This proof effectively counters the assertion made in Pressman and Carol (1971, 1973) that $\lambda$ may not be bounded between zero and one. For other proofs limiting the range of $\lambda$ in the AJ model, see Chapter 3, footnote a.

[h]Indeed, many of the AJ theorems can be proved without reference to $\lambda$. See, for example, Zajac's (1972b) method using vector analysis. See also the comparative statics analysis in Chapters 6 and 8.

[i]For example, there is no reference to it in Averch and Johnson (1962), Westfield (1965), Takayama (1969), Baumol and Klevorick (1970), Bailey and Malone (1970), or Zajac (1970).

*Proof:* Decomposing $R_L$ we obtain

$$R_L = R'q_L \tag{5.16}$$

for
$R_L$ = marginal revenue product of labor
$R' = p + qp'$ = marginal revenue, $p' < 0$
$q_L$ = marginal physical product of labor, $q_L > 0$.

Substituting (5.16) into (5.15) we obtain

$$R'q_L = w.$$

Since $w > 0$, and $q_L > 0$, $R'$ must also be positive.

*End of Proof* [j]

Proposition 5.2 may prove useful in testing the appropriateness of the AJ model. If empirical results indicate that a firm is operating in the inelastic region of the revenue curve,[k] then we can assert that the AJ model does not offer a valid explanation of the firm's behavior.

*Operation off the Production Frontier*

Proposition 5.2 strongly suggests that operation off the production frontier will not be an optimal alternative in an AJ model, for from Chapter 4, waste can never be a preferred action when marginal revenue is positive. Hence, the next AJ proposition should come as no surprise.

*Proposition 5.3:* The firm whose profits are limited to a fair return on capital investment will, if marginal physical product of capital is positive, have no incentive to operate off the production frontier.

*Proof:* From (5.11) and Proposition 5.1, $L^* = 0$. To show that $K^* = 0$, suppose the contrary, namely that $K^* > 0$. Then, the latter part of condition (5.12) yields $\lambda = \frac{r}{s}$. When this is substituted into (5.10) the result is $(1 - \frac{r}{s})R'q_K = 0$, which is

---

[j] We have assumed rather than proved that $q_L > 0$. It is possible to give a continuity argument to convince ourselves that $q_L$ is indeed positive at the solution to a rate-of-return model. The essence of the argument is that (5.15) is only true if $R'$ and $q_L$ are both positive or both negative. In order for both to be negative, there must have been an intermediate value of fair return at which $q_L = 0$ since $q_L$ starts out positive for the monopolist. But at such a value, (5.15) would not hold. Hence, $q_L > 0$. See Dayan (1972).

[k] See, for example, Fisher and Kaysen's (1962) study of the electric industry. Other studies, such as those by Wilson (1970) and by Erickson, Spann, and Ciliano (1973) indicate a demand elasticity of about unity or slightly higher.

impossible if $q_K > 0$, since $\frac{r}{s} < 1$ and $R' > 0$ (by Proposition 5.2). Hence, when the marginal physical product of capital is positive, $K^* = 0$, and the firm's optimal policy is to engage in no nonproductive use of capital.

End of Proof[1]

Proposition 5.3 asserts that padding of the rate base is not profitable so long as the marginal physical product of capital is positive at the solution to a rate-of-return model. Since for telecommunications and electric utilities, the product is essentially a time-shared rental of productive capacity, the assumption of positive marginal physical product of capital does not seem troublesome. By a straightforward expansion of capacity, the firm can handle a larger volume of demand; the additional capital installation increases total possible carried load.[m]

There are many instances in the literature in which the AJ model is thought of as implying that padding the rate base is an optimal alternative under the regulatory constraint. For example, Hughes, in commenting on Wein, quotes the more important forms of behavior arising in an AJ model as including

excess capacity (more generally, any redundant capital) [as well as] substitution of capital for other inputs.[4]

Even as late as 1971 Westfield described the AJ effect as entailing nonproductive cost inflations.[5] Yet, the preceding proof has shown that such an interpretation is not strictly correct. Wasteful use of capital is a possible response of the firm, and it can at times add to constrained profit, but it is not the firm's most profitable response to rate-of-return regulation. Instead, for the firm whose marginal physical product of capital is positive, an entirely productive use of capital has been found preferable to one entailing waste.

*Choice of Overly Capital Intensive Technology*

Other types of capital-intensive response may, however, be attractive to the firm. Although Proposition 5.3 has excluded physical padding of the rate base, it has not excluded other possibilities such as substitution of capital for labor in production. Indeed, the major theoretical result about rate-of-return regulation concerns the existence of an incentive for precisely such a misallocation.

*Proposition 5.4: The profit-maximizing firm constrained to earn at most a fair return on investment selects a production technique that uses more capital and less labor than are consistent with minimum-cost operation.*

---

[1]This proposition was demonstrated using a somewhat different argument in Bailey and Coleman (1971) and in Edelson (1971). A more thorough treatment which includes a rather interesting graphical interpretation appears in Zajac (1972). The first author to emphasize the dependence of the proposition on the $q_K > 0$ assumption was Dayan (1972).

[m]An analysis of the responses that will be most profitable for a regulated firm which encounters the $q_K = 0$ condition is given in Dayan (1972). See also Emery (1973) and Chapter 8.

*Proof:* See proof of Proposition 4.3.

*End of Proof*

The usual equation which displays the Averch-Johnson misallocation result is obtained by first using Proposition 5.1 to divide by $(1-\lambda)$ in (5.10):

$$R_K = rc - \frac{\lambda}{1-\lambda}(s-r)c. \tag{5.17}$$

We then use the result from Proposition 5.2 that $R'$ is positive, to divide (5.17) by (5.15), and find that

$$\frac{R_K}{R_L} = \frac{R'q_K}{R'q_L} = \frac{q_K}{q_L} = \frac{rc}{w} - \frac{\lambda}{1-\lambda}\frac{(s-r)c}{w}. \tag{5.18}$$

To see that (5.18) entails a misallocation of resources, note that efficient operation requires tangency between an isoquant and an isocost line,[n] that is,

$$-\frac{dL}{dK} = \frac{q_K}{q_L} = \frac{rc}{w}, \tag{5.19}$$

Comparing Equations (5.19) and (5.18), we see that for the firm regulated by a rate-of-return constraint

$$-\frac{dL}{dK} = \frac{q_K}{q_L} < \frac{rc}{w}, \tag{5.20}$$

so that the regulated firm is using relatively too much capital and too little labor in its production process.

The preceding discussion has relied upon the property that at an efficient point, the isoprofit contour must be tangent both to an isocost line and to an

---

[n]Equation (5.19) is derived from a model in which the firm is assumed to minimize the cost of production for any given level of output $q^*$ it chooses to produce, i.e., it

$$\text{Minimizes } C(L,K) = wL + rcK$$
$$L, K$$
$$\text{Subject to } q(L,K) \geqq q^*.$$

The Lagrangian of this model is

$$\phi(L,K,\mu) = wL + rcK + \mu[q(L,K) - q^*].$$

The necessary conditions corresponding to $L$ and $K$ are $w = \mu q_L$ and $rc = \mu \cdot q_K$. Since $q_L$, $q_K$, $w$, and $rc$ are all positive, the Lagrange multiplier is also positive. Equating the two solutions for $\mu$ then yields (5.19).

isoquant (the efficient point has the minimum cost and maximum profit of any point on an isoquant).º To demonstrate graphically that the solution point of a rate-of-return model is not efficient, we need only point out that in an AJ model, the solution point on the isoprofit contour is given by

$$\frac{\pi_K}{\pi_L} = \frac{R_K - rc}{R_L - w} = \frac{-\frac{\lambda}{1-\lambda}(s-r)c}{0} \quad (5.21)$$

that is, by a point with infinite slope. In the top portion of Figure 5-2, the tangent to the isoprofit curve at $E$ is a vertical line, and hence does not have the slope of an isocost line.

Figure 5-3 illustrates that the efficient point $D$ is simultaneously on the isocost line $ADB$, the isoquant $q = q^E$ and the isoprofit contour $\pi = \pi^D$. A point such as $E$ at which the tangent to the isoprofit contour is vertical occurs on a contour $\pi = \pi^E$ which offers a profit lower than the amount that could be attained at the given output. The lower profit occurs because the isocost curve which passes through point $E$ is associated with a larger dollar amount than that reflected by $ADB$. The firm is engaged in excessively capital intensive operation; it uses more capital ($\Delta K$ units) and less labor ($\Delta L$ units) than are consistent with minimum-cost production at the selected output. The excessive capital intensity can be interpreted as a distortion in the firm's internal valuation of factor costs since the slope of the tangent to the isoquant at the solution point $E$ in Figure 5-3 is more shallow than that of a true isocost line.[p]

Because of the central place of Proposition 5.4 in the Averch-Johnson literature, it is natural to ask whether the effect "is merely an intellectual curiosity" or whether it describes "serious distortions in the behavior of regulated firms."[6] Unfortunately, no definitive empirical treatment of the issue seems to have been published. There have been a number of studies which suggest that regulation of the electrics has not caused very much in the way

---

ºTo see this, note that an isoprofit contour ($\pi_K dK$ and $\pi_L dL = 0$) is tangent to an isoquant when

$$-\frac{dL}{dK} = \frac{\pi_K}{\pi_L} = \frac{q_K}{q_L}.$$

Expanding $\pi_K$ and $\pi_K$, we have $\pi_K = R_K - rc$, $\pi_L = R_L - w$, so that

$$(R'q_K - rc)q_L = (R'q_L - w)q_K$$

which reduces to (5.19).

[p]See Lie (1973) for a more thorough discussion of this point.

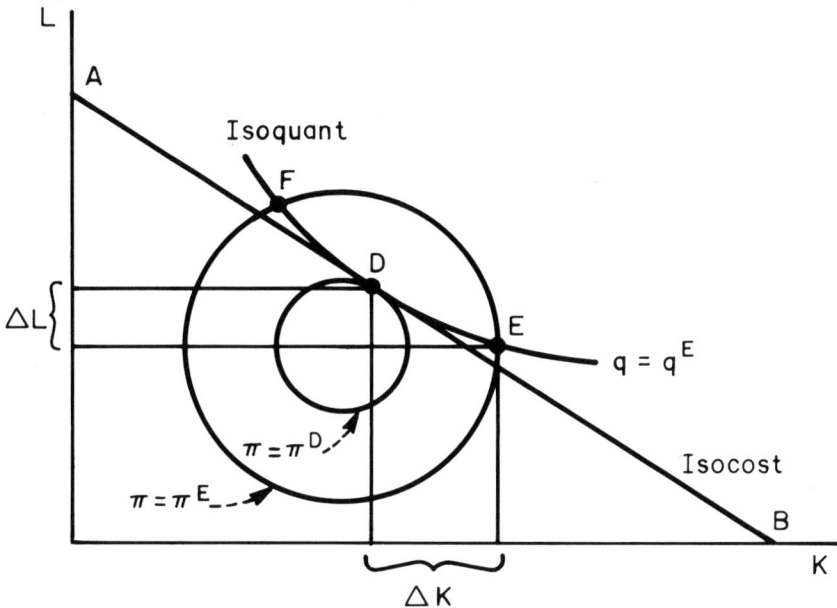

**Figure 5-3.** Theorem on Use of Overly Capital-Intensive Technology.

interpreted to mean that the AJ effect serves largely to increase inefficiency rather than to increase output. Alternatively, the results could mean that regulation is not effective, or that the effect of regulation is to alter price structure, rather than average price. Spann[r] has recently suggested that for steam electrics there is some evidence of an AJ effect at the plant level. On the other hand, Corey cites

warnings of possible curtailments of electric service due to capacity inadequacies, and expressions of public demand for an improved environment coupled with occasional allegations that management may be unwilling to spend the money necessary to protect our environment,[8]

---

[q]See, especially, Moore (1970) for electrics and MacAvoy and Noll (1973) for gas; see also Stigler and Friedland (1962), Greene (1971), and Jordan (1972).

[r]Spann (1974) uses a three-input (labor, capital, and fuel) model and the transcendental-logarithmic (trans-log) production function derived by Christensen, Jorgenson and Lau (1970). The use of a fuel variable in no way distorts the analytics, since fuel enters in the same fashion as labor.

Note that it is not possible to directly measure excess capacity and dub this an AJ effect. In the case of a point-to-point transmission facility in telecommunications, for example, Faulhaber (1972) shows that the combination of growing demand and economies of scale can result in optimal excess capacity of approximately 50 percent of total capacity. See also Courville (1974).

and in telecommunications. Vinod[7] has suggested the possibility of overly labor intensive operations. These tendencies do not seem compatible with Proposition 5.4. They may have arisen because the Averch-Johnson assumption that $s > r$ has not held true in recent years.[s] Or perhaps the static AJ effect may have been neutralized by dynamic influences.[t]

*Sufficiency Conditions*

Since we have proven that operation off the production frontier is not optimal in an Averch-Johnson model, (5.1) can be analyzed by using the Lagrangian rather than the Kuhn-Tucker conditions. Second-order conditions then require that the bordered Hessian, $D$, have a positive value

$$D = \begin{vmatrix} (1-\lambda)R_{LL} & (1-\lambda)R_{LK} & w - R_L \\ (1-\lambda)R_{KL} & (1-\lambda)R_{KK} & s - R_K \\ w - R_L & s - R_K & 0 \end{vmatrix} > 0$$

Expanding this, and using the first-order condition (5.15), we have

$$D = -(s - R_K)^2 (1-\lambda) R_{LL} > 0. \tag{5.22}$$

Diminishing revenue returns to labor (concavity of the revenue function) means that $R_{LL} < 0$. We have already established that $\lambda < 1$. Thus, (5.22) does hold in the Averch-Johnson model.[u]

The satisfaction of (5.22) is particularly interesting in view of the fact that there is no convexity of the feasible region in the AJ model. Any particular isorate-of-return contour, $i = s$, divides the $KL$-plane into the two regions shown in Figure 5-4. All points in the unshaded region correspond to a rate of return in excess of the rate $s$, and do not satisfy the regulatory constraint in Model (5.1). All points outside this region offer a return less than $s$. These points are thus feasible, as are all points lying on the $i = s$ contour itself. The feasible region is not convex since the line joining the two points $A$ and $B$ does not lie everywhere within the feasible region.

What we have thus established is that even though the feasible region is not convex, we can nevertheless find a global maximum to the AJ model. The geometry portrayed in Figure 5-1 is correct in its indication that there is a unique optimal level of capital and labor that can be chosen by the regulated firm.

---

[s]See Baumol and Klevorick (1970), Rosoff (1969, 1971).

[t]See Nelson (1972).

[u]This proof was first given in Baumol and Klevorick (1970). They used (5.22) to establish the bound on $\lambda$.

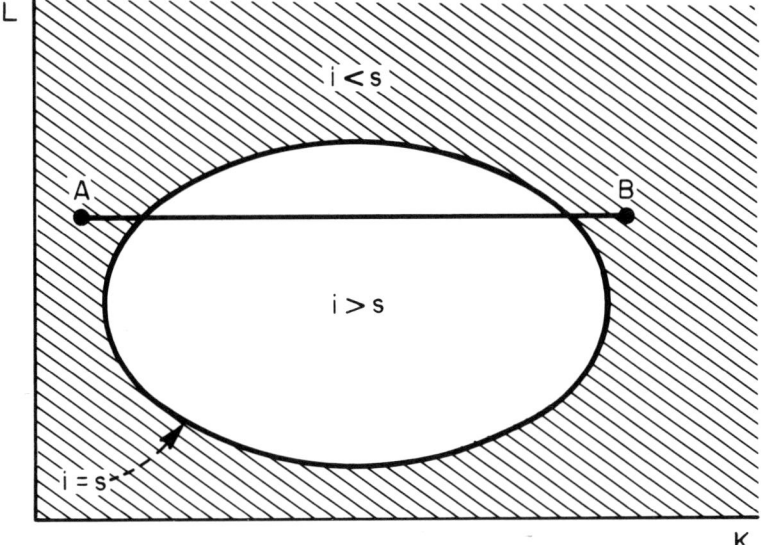

Figure 5-4. Nonconvexity of Feasible Region.

*Choice of Overly Labor-Intensive Technology*

Another interesting result follows from the properties of an isorate-of-return contour.

*Proposition 5.5:* The point at which output is maximized on a given rate-of-return curve is not characterized by either overly capital intensive operation or by minimum-cost production, but rather is one at which the firm misallocates by using too little capital relative to labor.

*Proof:* The geometry is displayed in Figure 5-5 where it is seen that the point of highest output (point $E$) on the $i = s$ curve occurs at the intersection of the isorate-of-return curve with an isocost curve having slope $\frac{sc}{w} > \frac{rc}{w}$. To prove the proposition, differentiate totally the isorate-of-return curve $\frac{R - wL}{cK} = s =$ constant, $s > r$, thereby obtaining

$$\left[ \frac{1}{cK}(R_K) - \frac{R - wL}{cK^2} \right] dK + \frac{1}{cK}(R_L - w) dL = 0, \text{ or } -\frac{dL}{dK} = \frac{R_K - sc}{R_L - w}.$$

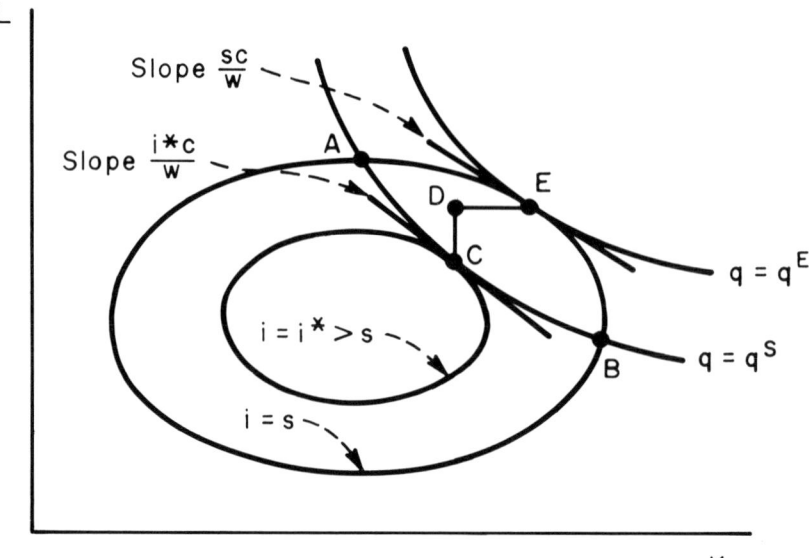

**Figure 5-5.** Theorem on Use of Overly Labor-Intensive Technology.

At the point of highest output, this is tangent to an isoquant,

$$-\frac{dL}{dK} = \frac{q_K}{q_L}, \text{ so that } \frac{R_K - sc}{R_L - w} = \frac{q_K}{q_L}, \text{ or } R'q_K q_L - scq_L = R'q_K q_L - q_K w.$$

This simplifies to $\frac{q_K}{q_L} = \frac{sc}{w} > \frac{rc}{w}$, so that overly labor intensive operation occurs whenever the isorate-of-return contour is at a level higher than the market cost of capital, $r$.

*End of Proof*

Proposition 5.5 says that if a firm's objective is to maximize output, given that rate of return is held at the level $s$, $s > r$, then, the firm adopts an overly labor intensive operation.[v] Proposition 5.5 can be also interpreted as asserting that a revenue-maximizing firm, whose rate of return is fixed at $s$, $s > r$, uses too little capital in its resource allocation. In particular, the statement is true whenever the solution point occurs in the elastic region of the revenue curve.

---

[v]These results can easily be contrasted with those arising for isoprofit contours as shown in Figure 5-3; the point of highest output on a given isoprofit contour must involve an efficient allocation of resources, but the point of highest rate of return on the contour does not.

Since the existence of advertising and quality-improving alternatives ordinarily ensures a positive marginal revenue, Proposition 5.5 thus holds for cases that may be likely to arise in reality.

Notice also that when the firm's objective is revenue or output maximization, the regulatory constraint serves, with the inequality reversed, as the minimum-return requirement for the firm. This assumption is what guarantees a binding constraint, for it says that the internal target return the firm would set, if not regulated, is at least as large as the regulatory fair rate.[w]

In a two-input single-output model of the type presented here, it is possible that demand and technology conditions will be such that the revenue-maximizing output yields a return on capital larger than the regulatory rate. Under such circumstances, the revenue objective requires that the firm produce the $q^S$ level of output. Since the efficient output $q^E$ in Figure 5-5 is larger than this amount, the firm must absorb some inefficiency to remain at $q^S$. Obvious possibilities are that it operate either at point $A$ or point $B$ in Figure 5-5 by substituting either labor for capital or capital for labor, or that it operate at $E$ but offer managerial emoluments in an amount $CD$ and pad the rate base by an amount $ED$. Thus, there is some indeterminacy in the status of resource allocation and some possibility of operation off the production frontier.[x]

The analysis can be turned around to yield some insight into revenue-maximizing models. The economist has always been pleased that in such models resources are not misallocated and the firm operates on the efficient expansion path.[y] This result is now shown to be quite dependent on the assumption that the internal constraint is one involving profit rather than rate of return.

*Proposition 5.6: The revenue-maximizing firm subject to the constraint that its rate of return at least equal some specified level misallocates resources by using too little capital relative to labor if the constraint is active.*

*Proof:* The model is

$$\text{Maximize } R(L,K)$$
$$L, K, x$$

$$\text{Subject to } R(L,K) - wL - x \geqq scK.$$

---

[w]Baumol and Klevorick (1970) were the first to argue that the firm's internal return requirement is likely to be at least as large as the regulatory fair rate. The fact that the firm would earn more than the regulatory rate, if it could, ensures that it will settle for at least the regulatory rate, and not below it. The constraint thus binds from above.

[x]The full flavor of these results was not perceived in Bailey and Malone (1970), where it was asserted that for the revenue- or output-maximizing firm, a binding rate-of-return constraint must lead to the undercapitalization result. For further discussion of this point, see Edelson (1971), Atkinson and Waverman (1973), Bailey (1973), and McNicol (1973).

[y]See Baumol (1967).

The Lagrangian is

$$\phi(L, K, x, \mu) = R(L, K) + \mu[R(L, K) - wL - x - sck]$$

The relevant Kuhn-Tucker conditions are $R_L = \dfrac{\mu}{1+\mu} w$, $R_K = \dfrac{\mu}{1+\mu} rc$, $x\mu = 0$.
If $R' > 0$ at the optimal solution, $\mu > 0$, $x = 0$, and resource allocation is given by $\dfrac{q_K}{q_L} = \dfrac{sc}{w} > \dfrac{rc}{w}$. If $R' = 0$, then $\mu = 0$, so that $x$ can be positive (operation off the production frontier can occur). A negative marginal revenue ($R' < 0$) is not possible at an optimal solution since the Kuhn-Tucker conditions would be violated.

*End of Proof*

Intuitively, the revenue-maximizing firm is now insisting that profit exceed some fraction of its capital investment. If the constraint is binding the firm below the revenue-maximizing output, the firm can come closest to its revenue objective by minimizing the effect of the constraint, that is, by minimizing investment. Therefore, a rate-of-return constraint causes a misallocation of resources in the classical revenue-maximizing model as well as in the regulatory model presented in Bailey-Malone.

**Two-Output Version of Model**

Averch and Johnson were interested not only in the allocation of resources between the labor and capital inputs to production but also wished to investigate possible distortions in the mix of outputs in the regulated multi-product firm. Their hypothesis was that the existence of a single constraint applied to all markets, rather than separate constraints applied to each market separately, would lead to such distortions. The model that they used, unfortunately, did not combine labor and capital inputs with more than one output, nor was it analyzed in the same detail as the single output model described earlier. Rather, examples were given of behavior patterns that could appear: there was not any explicit determination of the conditions under which these hypothesized patterns constitute the firm's optimal response to the regulatory constraint.

We now analyze a two-output model in which both labor and capital are used as inputs. To avoid issues arising because the two products utilize technologies of differing capital intensity, we shall limit ourselves to the case where production of the two products involves a sharing of capacity.

It is convenient for the purposes of the analysis to construct an alternative version of the Averch-Johnson model, which is

Maximize $\pi = R(q_1, q_2) - wH(q_1, q_2 K) - rcK$ (5.23)
$q_1, q_2, K$

Subject to $\pi \leq (s - r)cK$,

where $H(q_1, q_2, K)$ is a labor requirement function that determines the minimum amount of labor required to produce outputs $q_1$ and $q_2$, with the quantity of capital capacity at level $K$.[z]

When we use a labor requirements function in the specification of the model, the revenue function reflects only demand conditions, thus avoiding a confounding of demand and production conditions as in Model (5.1). The main advantage of (5.23), however, is that it permits us to see quite easily how a single rate-of-return constraint acts when applied in an overall fashion to two products which share the same facilities.

The Lagrangian for Model (5.23) is

$$\phi(q_1, q_2, K, \lambda) = (1 - \lambda)[R(q_1, q_2) - wH(q_1, q_2 K) - rcK] + \lambda(s - r)cK.$$

The first-order conditions for $q_1$, $q_2$, and $K$ are

$$(1 - \lambda)\left[R_{q_1} - wH_{q_1}\right] = 0 \qquad (5.24)$$

$$(1 - \lambda)\left[R_{q_2} - wH_{q_2}\right] = 0 \qquad (5.25)$$

$$-H_K = \frac{rc}{w} - \frac{\lambda}{1-\lambda} \frac{(s-r)c}{w}. \qquad (5.26)$$

The interpretation is clear. The AJ condition giving the relative use of capital and labor shows up in precisely the same form as it did before [compare (5.26) to (5.18)], but the familiar ratio rule holds between products since the ratio of (5.24) and (5.25) is

$$\frac{R_{q_1}}{R_{q_2}} = \frac{H_{q_1}}{H_{q_2}}.$$

Hence, the existence of the single constraint extending over both markets need not introduce inefficiency in output proportions: the rule used equates the

---
[z]Klevorick (1971) was the first to use a labor requirement function in connection with the AJ model; he considered the single output case. McNicol (1973) offers a graphical description of the labor requirement function model.

additional revenue per dollar spent in market 1 with that of market 2. Notice, however, that distortion between labor and capital still appears in (5.26). Thus, we are not able to say, as we could in the symmetric constraint case dealt with in Chapter 4, that the regulatory constraint offers the profit-maximizing firm an incentive to behave as if it were a revenue-maximizing firm subject to its own internal profit requirement. In the current case, the revenue-maximizing rule for the relative outputs of products does appear, but the asymmetry in the constraint prevents any further equivalence from being established.

# 6 Fair Rate of Return

## Introduction and Summary

Since the fair rate of return is a policy parameter under the direct control of a regulatory agency, we are naturally interested in inquiring into the nature of the firm's response to changes in the level of this parameter. Using the comparative statics technique, we find that while there is always a misallocation between capital and labor at the output selected and while this distortion, as measured by the ratio of the marginal products, does get more severe as the constraint is tightened, the distortion ordinarily does not become so extreme that the regulator's ability to effect an output increase is hampered.

Instead, the increase in capital usage is sufficiently large that output increases monotonically as the firm's return is reduced from the monopoly rate toward the cost of capital. More precisely, output increases unless capital is an inferior factor of production, that is, unless the economically most efficient method of expanding output requires a contraction of physical plant.

The important policy issue is, of course, whether there exists an optimal value for the fair return parameter, one for which the net gain to society from the increased output is just equal at the margin to the increased cost from the AJ inefficiency. It is possible to show that, in a partial equilibrium framework, welfare is always increased if the fair return is set below the monopoly return. Thus, some amount of regulation is worthwhile. We also show that whether the fair return should be set larger than the cost of capital or just equal to the cost of capital depends not only on demand and production conditions, but also on one's assumption about the firm's operating point when $s = r$.

The simplest supposition is that the firm operates at the end point of the AJ path when $s = r$. In a partial equilibrium model we prove, contrary to Sheshinski,[a] that an interior solution ($s > r$) may not exist and that an end point solution ($s = r$) may instead be optimal. A general equilibrium approach preserves the result that both $s > r$ and $s = r$ are candidate solutions to the optimal rate-of-return problem. However, the true nature of the tradeoff is shown to entail the valuation by society of the regulated good or service relative to the valuation of the other goods and services that are available. The opportunity cost is therefore measured in terms of the amount of other goods and services foregone (exchange efficiency) as well as in terms of the regulated firm's productive efficiency.

---
[a]Sheshinski (1971) does not use risk or uncertainty arguments in establishing this result, and these questions are also ignored in our analysis.

In the situation considered by Klevorick[1] where the firm chooses to operate efficiently at the $s = r$ point, the partial equilibrium approach indicates that $s = r$ is optimal only in the case of constant or decreasing average costs. The general equilibrium approach shows that when exchange efficiency is taken into account, $s = r$ is always optimal.

Another important property of the expansion path generated by lowering the fair rate of return is that the path does not change if the constraint ceiling $(s - r) cK$ is replaced by the more general formulation $G(K)$, $G' > 0$. This invariance explains why the "graduated fair return" method of regulation does not work; altering the form of the ceiling does not make the firm's expansion path more efficient; instead it serves only to vary the precise operating point on the path. The property also leads to the result that the AJ expansion path is independent of changes in depreciation policy and tax policy, although the precise operating point on the path will change with changes in these parameters.

## Regulatory Expansion Path

Since in an Averch-Johnson model the firm operates on the production frontier, we can dispense with the waste variables $L^*$ and $K^*$. The model then becomes

$$\text{Maximize } \pi = R(L,K) - wL - rcK \qquad (6.1)$$
$$L, K$$

Subject to $\pi = (s - r)cK$, $s > r$.

Using the propositions from the last chapter, the first-order conditions are

$$R_L = w \qquad (6.2)$$

$$R_K - rc = -\frac{\lambda}{1 - \lambda}(s - r)c, \quad 0 < \lambda < 1 \qquad (6.3)$$

$$R(L,K) - wL - scK = 0. \qquad (6.4)$$

*Optimal Levels of Capital, Profit, Labor, and Output*

The comparative statics results of an increase in $s$, the regulatory ceiling on rate of return, are summarized in Table 6-1.

*Proposition 6.1: In an AJ model, the firm increases its capital usage as the fair return is lowered from the monopoly rate toward the firm's cost of capital.*

## Table 6-1
## Comparative Statics Results of a Change in Fair Rate of Return

|  | Capital, $K$ | Labor, $L$ | Output, $q$ | Profit, $\pi$ |
|---|---|---|---|---|
| Rate of return $s$ | − | ?† | −* | + |

*The sign holds if capital is not an inferior input (or, more simply, if $q_{LK} > 0$).
†The corresponding sign is negative if $R_{LK} > 0$.

*Proof:* Differentiating totally Equation (6.4), we obtain

$$(R_L - w)dL + (R_K - sc)dK = cKds.$$

Using Equation (6.2), and rearranging gives

$$\frac{dK}{ds} = \frac{cK}{R_K - sc}. \tag{6.5}$$

It is easily established, by manipulating Equation (6.3), that

$$R_K - sc = -\frac{c(s-r)}{1-\lambda} < 0, \tag{6.6}$$

where the negative sign follows because $\lambda < 1$ and $s > r$. Thus,

$$\frac{dK}{ds} < 0, \tag{6.7}$$

with the appropriate negative sign being entered in Table 6.1.

*End of Proof*[2]

Equation (6.6) indicates that the marginal revenue product of capital at a constrained optimum will be lower than it would be if the true cost of capital were equal to the regulatory fair return $s$. This is not surprising since it has already been established that the marginal revenue product is set below the true cost of capital [Equation (6.3)], which is itself below the fair return. The right-hand side of Equation (6.6) appears frequently in the comparative statics analysis of the AJ model, and hence the sign information given by (6.6) will be used extensively both in this chapter, and in Chapter 8.

Equation (6.7) says that a rise in the rate-of-return ceiling actually decreases the firm's demand for capital. Stated in this way, we are aware of a strongly counterintuitive aspect of the proposition. Somehow if the fair return goes up we would expect the firm to take advantage of the added increment in profit for each additional quantity of capital it employs, and therefore to increase not decrease its demand for capital. Instead, the AJ model says that a higher rate of return means that the firm chooses a more monopolistic output (along with the associated smaller capital).

Proposition 6.1 is easily verified graphically. We use the lower part of Figure 5-2 which is redrawn here as Figure 6-1. The projection of the profit hill is not altered by a change in the fair rate of return since profit is defined entirely by the demand curve, the production function, and the factor costs, $r$, $c$, and $w$. The constraint ray does change position, however, as the fair return is lowered from $s_1$ to $s_2$ to $s_3$, $s_1 > s_2 > s_3$, with each new ray having a smaller slope. The intersection points forming the equilibrium solutions are denoted $A$, $B$, and $C$, and it is obvious that larger quantities of capital are used at the lower intersections. It is also obvious from Figure 6-1 that the level of profit goes down as the constraint is tightened.

Thus, the second comparative statics result about the AJ expansion path should come as no surprise.

*Proposition 6.2:* As the fair rate of return is set closer to the cost of capital in an AJ model, the level of constrained profit declines.

*Proof:* Differentiate $\pi = (s - r)cK$ with respect to $K$, $L$, and $s$, substitute (6.5) for $\dfrac{dK}{ds}$, and use (6.3) and (6.6) to obtain

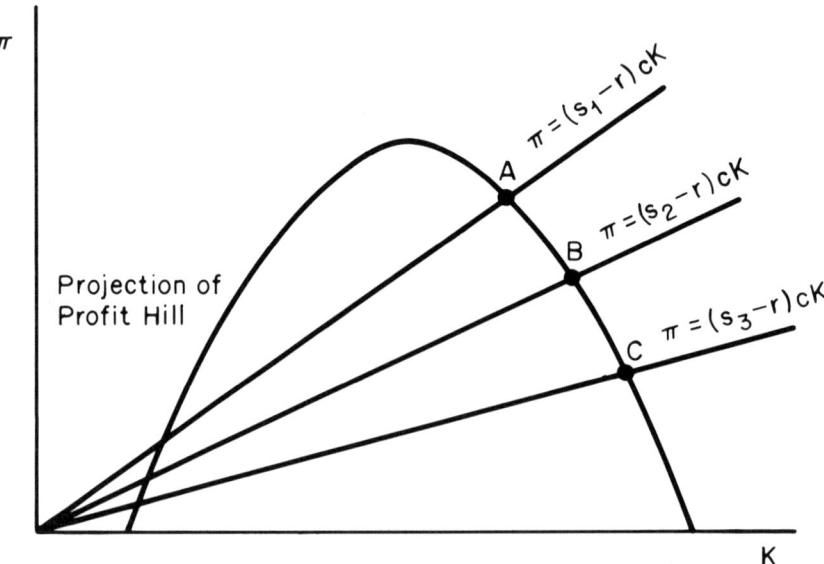

**Figure 6-1.** Capital and Profit Response to Changes in Fair Return.

$$\frac{d\pi}{ds} = (s-r)c\frac{dK}{ds} + cK = \frac{[(s-r)c + (R_K - sc)]cK}{R_K - sc} = \frac{(R_K - rc)cK}{R_K - sc} > 0.$$

The positive sign is precisely what is reported for $\frac{d\pi}{ds}$ in Table 6.1.

*End of Proof*

A third theorem can be derived about the labor input.

*Proposition 6.3: Labor usage will increase as the rate of return decreases if labor and capital are complements in the production of revenue, and labor usage will decrease as the rate of return is lowered if labor and capital are substitutes in the production of revenue.*

*Proof:* Differentiate (6.2) totally to obtain

$$\frac{dL}{ds} = -\frac{R_{LK}}{R_{LL}} \frac{dK}{ds}. \tag{6.8}$$

Proposition 6.1 established that $dK/ds < 0$. Expanding $R_{LL}$ gives

$$R_{LL} = R'q_{LL} + R''q_L^2. \tag{6.9}$$

By (6.2), $R' > 0$, by concavity of the revenue curve, $R'' < 0$, and by diminishing returns to labor, $q_{LL} < 0$. Hence, $R_{LL} < 0$, so that there are diminishing revenue returns to labor.

Expanding $R_{LK}$ gives

$$R_{LK} = R'q_{LK} + R''q_L q_K. \tag{6.10}$$

If the marginal physical products of labor and capital are positive, that is, if $q_L > 0$, $q_K > 0$, and if we make the reasonable assumption that capital and labor complement each other in the production of a variable output so that $q_{LK} > 0$, then it is clear the sign of $R_{LK}$ can be either positive or negative. Consequently, $\frac{dL}{ds}$ can be either positive or negative. More specifically, if $R_{LK} > 0$, so that labor and capital complement each other in the production of revenue, then $\frac{dL}{ds} < 0$; if $R_{LK} < 0$ so that labor and capital are substitutes in the production of revenue, then $\frac{dL}{ds} > 0$; if $R_{LK} = 0$, then $\frac{dL}{ds} = 0$. *End of Proof*[3][b]

---

[b]Lindenberg (1973) has shown that $\frac{dL}{ds} < 0$ for a constant elasticity of demand function and homogeneous production function.

In spite of the indeterminacy in the sign of $\frac{dL}{ds}$, it can be established that output will generally increase as regulation is tightened.

*Proposition 6.4: Except in the anomalous case in which capital is an inferior input, output increases as the fair rate of return is set closer to the cost of capital.*

*Proof:* By differentiating the production function

$$\frac{dq}{ds} = q_L \frac{dL}{ds} + q_K \frac{dK}{ds} . \qquad (6.11)$$

Using (6.5) and (6.8) in (6.11)

$$\frac{dq}{ds} = \left[ \frac{-q_L R_{LK} + q_K R_{LL}}{R_{LL}} \right] \left[ \frac{cK}{R_K - sc} \right] \qquad (6.12)$$

The key expression is obviously $(-q_L R_{LK} + q_K q_{LL})$. Expanding, using (6.9) and (6.10), and taking note of cancellations, we have

$$-q_L R_{LK} + q_K R_{LL} = R'(-q_L q_{LK} + q_K q_{LL}). \qquad (6.13)$$

As before, we suppose that there are eventually diminishing returns to labor, $q_{LL} < 0$ and that $q_K > 0$ and $q_L > 0$. Since $R' > 0$ by (6.2), the reasonable assumption that labor and capital are complements in the production of a variable output, $q_{LK} > 0$, is seen to guarantee that the sign of (6.13) is negative. Alternatively, the assumption that capital is not an inferior input will give the same result. To see this, note that the mathematical definition of an inferior input is[c]

$$\text{labor not inferior implies } q_L q_{KK} - q_K q_{LK} < 0 \qquad (6.14)$$

and

$$\text{capital not inferior implies } q_K q_{LL} - q_L q_{LK} < 0. \qquad (6.15)$$

Substituting (6.9) and (6.13) into (6.12) we get

$$\frac{dq}{ds} = \left( \frac{R'(q_K q_{LL} - q_L q_{LK})}{R' q_{LL} + R'' q_L^2} \right) \left( \frac{cK}{R_K - sc} \right) < 0 ,$$

---

[c]See Ferguson (1971), Bear (1965), Bilas and Massey (1972) and Bear (1972).

where the negative sign follows by $R' > 0$, $R'' < 0$, $q_{LL} < 0$, (6.6), and the noninferiority assumption (6.15).

*End of Proof*[4]

*The Factor Noninferiority Assumption*

An intuitive definition of factor inferiority is that a factor is inferior if its usage declines when output is expanded at constant factor prices. In terms of Figure 6-2, capital becomes inferior at point $D$ since all points above $D$ use progressively smaller amounts of total capital as output is increased. Thus, when a factor is inferior, the efficient expansion path (the path traced out by intersections of isoquants and isocost lines) is negatively sloped.

Using this definition of factor inferiority, we then ask ourselves whether it seems reasonable that capital could be an inferior factor in the regulated industries. Since output in these industries is essentially a time-shared rental of productive capacity (the telecommunications or electricity networks), it seems obvious that expanding output entails expanding capacity. Capacity should then be a normal rather than an inferior input.[d]

Baumol and Klevorick[5] describe (6.15) partly in terms of noncomplementarity of capital and labor. Unfortunately their description seems to make violation of (6.15) more plausible than it really is.[e] The reason is that the concepts of substitution and complementarity in production are not as straightforward as they may at first appear. We are used to thinking in terms of isoquants on which capital and labor are necessarily substitutes, that is, if more capital is used, then less labor must be used if output is to remain on the same isoquant. Yet, in the proof of Proposition 6.4, the factors are considered complementary. The paradox is explained by the fact that output is not held fixed in the analysis. As Hicks puts it

> in the case of constant costs and two factors, the two factors are necessarily complements in the production of a variable output, and necessarily substitutes in the production of a constant output.[6]

---

[d]To emphasize how standard the assumption of factor noninferiority is, consider the case of the unregulated profit-maximizing monopoly. It is standard practice to state that if one of the input factors increases in price, then there will be substitution of the relatively cheaper for the now more expensive factor, but that equilibrium output will decline. Yet, this result depends on the assumption of factor noninferiority just as does Proposition 6.4, as is shown in Dayan (1972).

Note also that factor inferiority is impossible in any homogeneous production function, that is, in any production function characterized by

$$m^a q(L,K) = q(mL, mK),$$

where $a$ is the degree of homogeneity. For homogeneous production functions, the efficient expansion path is a straight line with positive slope.

[e]See, for example, Johnson (1973).

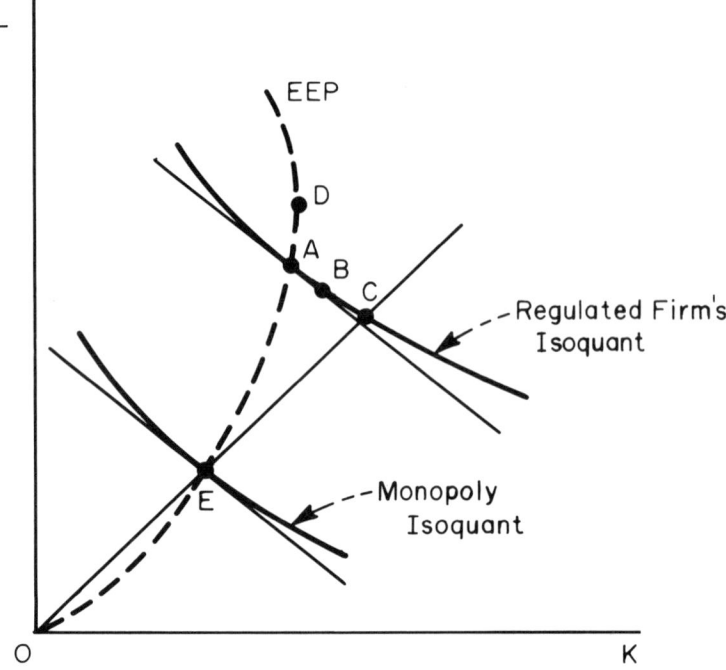

**Figure 6-2.** Factor Inferiority and the Capital-Labor Ratio.

*Relative Distortion in Resource Allocation*

The misallocation result has sometimes been stated in the form: the profit-maximizing firm constrained to earn no more than a fair return on investment adopts a capital-labor ratio that is larger than that which is efficient at the given output. This form is correct. An alternative statement, used by Stein and Borts,

> the capital-labor ratio of the regulated firm will be larger than that which prevailed when the firm was unregulated.[f]

does not always hold. Nor can the capital-labor ratio always be used to measure the degree of distortion in resource allocation, as Scherer suggests when he attempts to measure the distortion as[7]

---

[f]Stein and Borts (1972), p. 962. These authors state this result without qualifying it, but actually prove their statement only for homogeneous production functions. Baumol and Klevorick (1970) were the first to point out that the proposition does not hold in general. They did so by solving the AJ model for an explicit revenue function in which the capital-labor ratio actually decreases as the regulatory constraint is tightened.

$$\frac{d(K/L)}{ds}.$$

To see this, note that the capital-labor ratio is the slope of the line connecting the origin to any point in Figure 6-2. The efficient expansion path is a ray if the production function is homogeneous. In this case, we can indeed compare directly the capital-labor ratio of the regulated firm and that of the monopoly. If the expansion path bends (variable proportions are best at different output levels, as when different technologies are used at high outputs than at low outputs), then there is no reason to believe that the capital-labor ratio which is appropriate for the profit-maximizing firm is the one which is best when output is greater than the monopoly level. In terms of Figure 6-2, it is apparent that even if the firm misallocates by producing at $B$ rather than at $A$, the capital-labor ratio that results can be smaller than that of the unregulated monopolist.

An alternative measure of the relative distortion is

$$\frac{d(q_K/q_L)}{ds}, \tag{6.16}$$

for this gives the amount by which the ratio of marginal products deviates from the ratio of factor prices. By differentiating (6.16) directly, and using the expressions for $\frac{dK}{ds}$ and $\frac{dL}{ds}$, Lie[8] has been able to establish that the sign of (6.16) is positive. This result coincides with our intuitive expectation that there is a sense in which resource allocation is getting worse as the constraint is tightened. What happens is that the marginal product of capital monotonically decreases relative to that of labor as the fair return is lowered.

*Geometry of EEP and AJP*

To summarize our results about the Averch-Johnson expansion path, we turn to Figure 6-3. The efficient expansion path (*EEP*) consists of all tangencies between isoprofit contours and the isoquant which just touches them. Since the isocost line is also tangent at such a point, and has a negative slope ($\frac{dK}{dK} = -\frac{rc}{w}$), the path must proceed along a negatively sloped portion of the isoprofit contour such as is indicated in Figure 6-3.

The regulatory expansion path (*AJP*) is, by definition, that path of capital, labor, output, and profit traced out as the fair rate of return is reduced from the monopoly level to the firm's cost of capital. It consists of all points lying at the

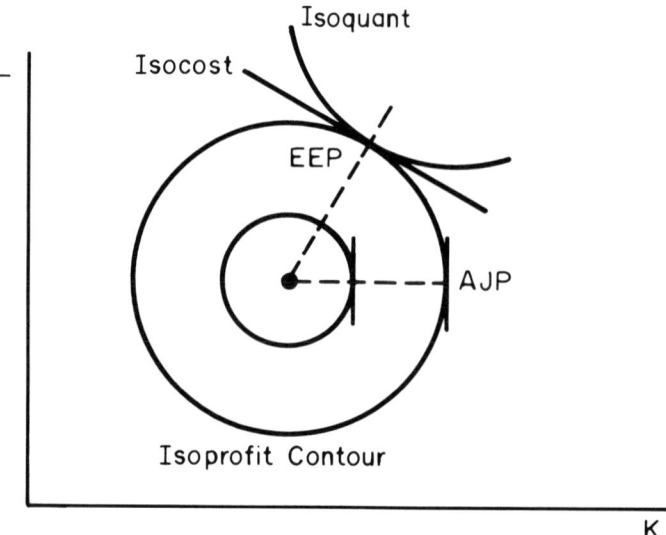

**Figure 6-3.** AJ and Efficient Expansion Path.

intersection of an isoprofit contour with the vertical tangents shown in Figure 6-3. Intuitively, since the total profit permitted the firm increases to some extent with $K$, it will pay the firm to move to the right-most point on any isototal profit curve, since this $K$ gives the highest profit ceiling.

Mathematically, the slope of the isoprofit contour is obtained by differentiating totally $R(L,K) - wL - rcK = \pi^*$ and by rearranging

$$-\frac{dL}{dK} = \frac{R_K - rc}{R_L - w} \qquad (6.17)$$

At the optimal point in an AJ model, this slope is infinity since the denominator is zero from (6.2), whereas the numerator is finite and nonzero from (6.3). Visually, it is apparent that the AJ path lies everywhere below the efficient path, so that for any fixed level of output the AJ point involves more capital and less labor than the efficient point. It is also clear to the eye that the firm never finds pure substitution of capital for labor along the monopoly isoquant as attractive an alternative as simultaneous use of overly capital intensive technology and increase in output. The firm prefers a path along which revenues as well as capital increase to any alternative which entails increases only in capital base.

Figure 6-4 indicates that the AJ path always ends before its intersection with the revenue-maximizing isoquant, $q^S$.[g] Graphically, if the $\pi = 0$ contour and the

---
[g]Some portions of this proof were suggested by Craig Bender.

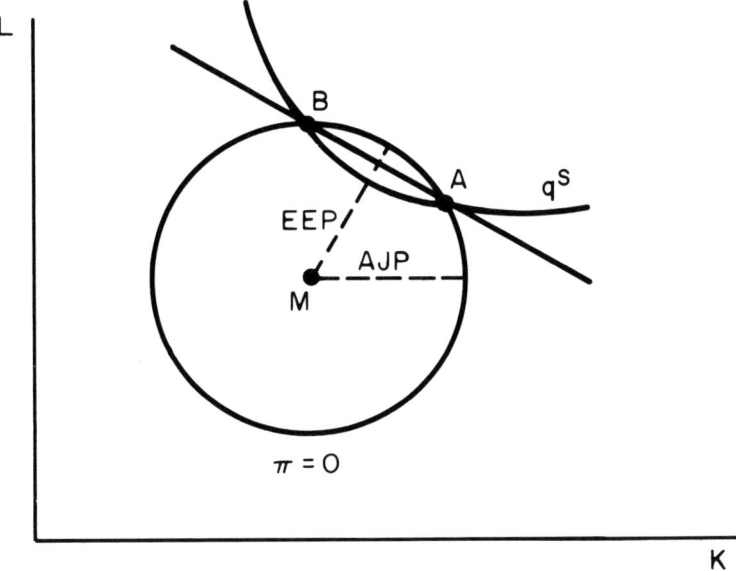

**Figure 6-4.** End Points of *AJP* and *EEP*.

$q^S$ isoquant intersect, they do so in a region where $\frac{dL}{dK}$ is finite and negative. To demonstrate, note that Equation (6.17) reduces to the familiar ratio of the factor prices when $R' = 0$; the isocost line thus passes through the intersection points $A$ and $B$ of the $q^S$ curve with the $\pi = 0$ curve as illustrated in Figure 6-4. The slope $\frac{dL}{dK}$ is indeed negative at this intersection point. Thus, no matter how close to $r$ the regulator sets the fair rate $s$, he will never be able to get the firm to increase output to the extent that maximizes revenue.

## Invariance Property of Path

### Graduated Fair Return

If the functional form of the AJ constraint ceiling is changed from $(s - r) cK$ to some other function such as $G(K) = [\sigma(K) - r] cK$, it seems possible that the new expansion path might differ from both the efficient and the AJ path. Yet, from Proposition 4.4 this cannot be so.

*Proposition 6.5: The expansion path under rate-of-return regulation is independent of the functional form of the investment-related constraint.*[h]

---

[h]This proposition first appeared in a letter written by William J. Baumol to Alvin K. Klevorick in 1970.

*Proof:* As long as the constraint has form $G(K)$, $G_K > 0$, $\lambda \neq 1$, so that (6.2) holds. But whenever $G_L = 0$, the denominator in (6.17) is zero at the optimal operating point, and hence the slope of the tangent to the isoprofit contour is infinite.

*End of Proof*

It is a simple matter to check that Propositions 6.1-6.4 hold for any capital related constraint $G(K)$ with $G_K > 0$. The analysis thus offers illumination on the controversy about the graduated fair return method of regulation. In proposing this method, Klevorick envisioned a function $\sigma(K)$ which might be equal to the current fair rate $s$, up to some threshold value of $K$, and would be graduated downward as $K$ increased.[9] It was hoped that the downward graduation would create a penalty as the amount of capital used by the firm increased, thereby discouraging the inefficient substitution of capital for labor. Unfortunately, these hopes were not realized as can be seen in Figure 6-5.

The silhouette of the profit hill in Figure 6-5 is constructed in precisely the same fashion as that in Figure 5-2, so that for any level $\bar{K}$ of capital, the labor used is that which gives the maximum possible profit. It is apparent geometrically that the firm constrained to earn $\sigma(K)$ has the same operating point and the same efficiency as a firm constrained to earn $s_2 = \sigma(\bar{K})$. The graduated fair rate is equivalent to a reduction in the constant fair rate from the level $s_1$ to the level $s_2$. Thus, while it is true that for different levels of the graduated fair return $\sigma(K)$, the equilibrium point can be shifted from one part of the expansion path

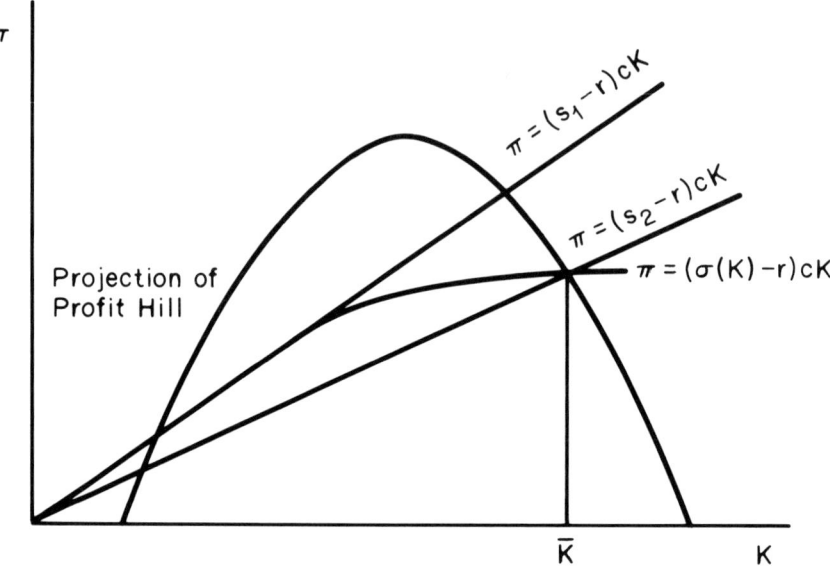

**Figure 6-5.** Graduated Fair Return.

to another, exactly the same change can always be accomplished by an appropriate change in the level of a constant fair rate of return. Further, the tightening of the constraint which is implicit in the graduated fair return serves to increase rather than decrease the actual amount of capital employed, hence running counter to the original intent of the method.[i]

*Other Cases of Invariance Property*

A second circumstance to which Proposition 6.5 applies arises when the regulator detects and disallows at least some of the capital it considers to have arisen from the tendency to misallocate. Just as happens with the graduated fair return, the firm's position along the AJ path will change but, as long as $G_K > 0$, the path itself will not be altered by the greater vigilance of the regulatory agency.

Proposition 6.5 is also relevant in an AJ model in which capital equipment and plant deteriorates in its economic usefulness over time. Dansby has studied such a model in which the firm's investment and equipment replacement policies are such that $K$ is kept constant.[10] The firm may use any depreciation policy (straight line, double declining balance, and so on) acceptable to regulators. It is shown that although the AJ path is independent of the depreciation policy chosen, the operating point on the path will be influenced both by $s$ and by the depreciation policy. It is also shown that acceleration of depreciation acts in the same fashion as does a decrease in the fair return $s$; in both cases, the regulated firm is given an incentive to increase the level of capital investment and output. The regulator has, in essence, the choice between two adjustments, either of which can produce the same changes in behavior.

Still a third situation in which the AJ path is invariant to policy changes arises if corporate income and/or property taxes are incorporated into an AJ model.[j] For the income tax, the model becomes

$$\text{Maximize } \pi = (1-t)[R(L,K) - wL - rcK]$$
$$L, K$$

$$\text{Subject to } \pi \leqq (s-r)cK,$$

where $t$ = corporate profit tax rate. To convince oneself that there is a change of

---

[i]The proof as described here is presented somewhat more elaborately in Bailey and Coleman (1970). The first conjecture suggests that the tightening of the graduated fair return might put into motion forces that increase rather than decrease capitalization appeared in Kahn (1968). The first mathematical disproof of the proposition was given by Wichers (1971) [see also the confirmation by Klevorick (1971a)]. All the proofs are subsumed, however, by Proposition 4.4 which establishes the result over a much broader class of circumstances.

[j]See also Aten (1973) and Dayan (1973).

operating point, it is helpful to look at Figure 6-6a which shows two profit hill projections; the larger one corresponds to a zero income tax and the smaller one to a 50 percent income tax. At any level of capital, the smaller hill has a profit precisely one half that of the larger hill. The regulatory constraint ray is a function only of the values of $s$, $r$, $c$, and $K$ and does not shift position when the income tax rate is changed. In a partial equilibrium setting, then, the solution

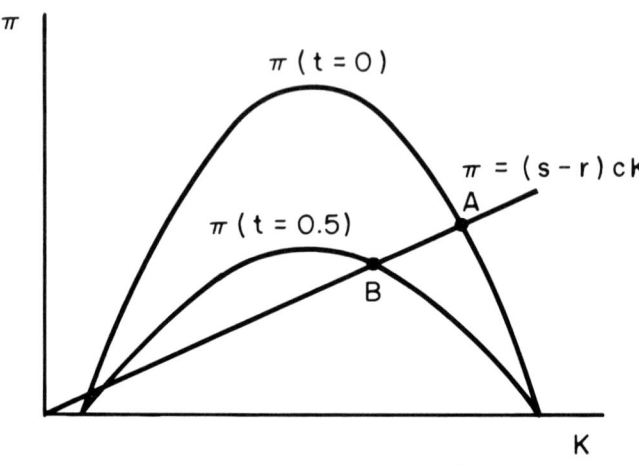

(a) Change in Operating Point

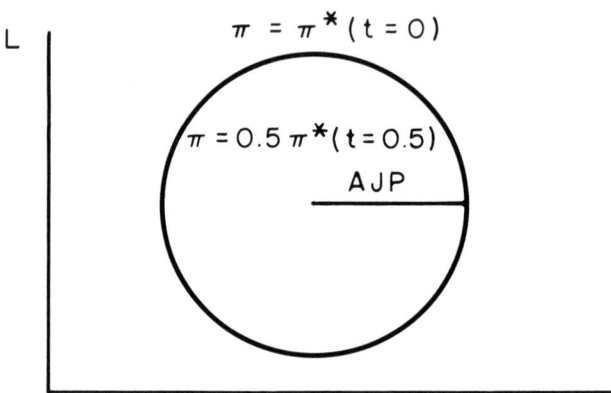

(b) Invariance of AJP

**Figure 6-6.** Corporate Income Tax.

point for the regulated firm shifts from $A$ to $B$ when the income tax is imposed. There has been a reduction in capital usage and in profit, but the AJP does not shift position. This is illustrated in Figure 6-6b in which it is seen that the effect of the tax is just to renumber each isoprofit contour, that is, the isoprofit contour $\pi = \pi^*$ becomes, after a 50 percent tax, $\pi = .5\,\pi^*$.

For the corporate property tax, the appropriate model is

$$\text{Maximize } \pi = R(L,K) - wL - rcK - kcK$$
$$L, K$$

$$\text{Subject to } \pi \leqq (s-r)cK$$

where the tax, $k$ is viewed as a tax on the total dollar value of capital equipment and property owned by the firm. As was the case with the income tax, an increase in property taxes does alter the equilibrium operating point. The graphical depiction in the $K\pi$-plane is shown in Figure 6-7a. The effect of the tax is to shrink the profit hill by an amount $kcK$; hence the hill shifts by a larger amount for large values of $K$ than for small values. The consequence of the shift is, as before, a movement from point $A$ to point $B$ in which both profit and capital decrease.

The invariance of the expansion path can be seen by rewriting the constraint in terms of rate of return. We have

$$R - wL - (r+k)cK = (s-r)cK$$

or

$$i = \frac{R - wL}{cK} = s + k. \tag{6.18}$$

It is clear from (6.18) that a change in $k$ just renumbers the isorate-of-return contour. In terms of Figure 6-7b, the isorate-of-return contour $i = .10$ is the relevant contour for either a model with fair rate set at .10 and a tax of zero, or for a model having a fair rate of .09 and a tax of $k = .01$.

To establish that the renumbering feature is all that is needed to prove the invariance of the path, we can draw upon our previous results. We have proved that the AJP can be viewed as being generated either by the right-most points on isoprofit contours or by the right-most points on isorate-of-return contours (see Figure 5-2). In the property tax case, it is the latter method of generating the path that establishes the invariance; in the case of the income tax, it is the former.

*Expansion Path in True Investment Model*

In reality, the firm borrows money not only for its investments in capital equipment but also to cover a part of its wage bill. The amount borrowed over

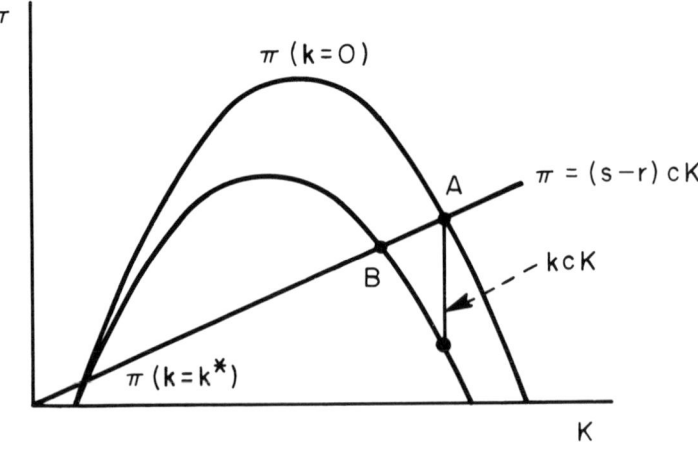

(a) Change in Operating Point

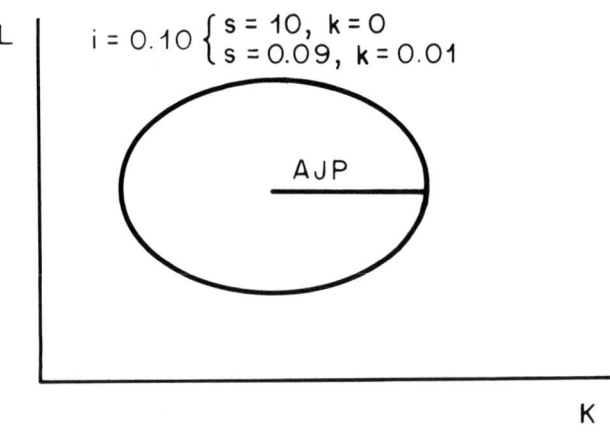

(b) Invariance of AJP

**Figure 6-7.** Corporate Property Tax.

the course of a year depends on the turnover periods of the two types of expenses. In classical economic terms, we can view the firm as having both fixed and circulating capital, each of which has its own turnover period, with the turnover period of the fixed capital being the larger.[k] For example, the turnover period for fixed capital might be twenty years, while that for circulating capital could be on the order of a month or two.

---

[k] See, e.g., Smith (1937 edition) and Ricardo (1971 edition). William Baumol suggested the link between this work, and that in regulatory modeling.

The aspect of this that is important in regulatory modeling is that the true investment cost the firm incurs in any year is

$$r(bwL + mcK)$$

for
$wL$ = yearly wage bill
$cK$ = yearly capital bill
$b$ = turnover period for circulating capital
$m$ = turnover period for fixed capital, $m > b$.

The true investment cost thus includes both labor-related and investment-related components. Hence, the rate-of-return constraint will now appear as

$$\pi \leqq (s - r)(bwL + mcK),$$

where the constraint ceiling rises not only when capital increases but also when labor increases. The asymmetry condition $G_L = 0$ no longer applies. Because of this, the expansion path of the firm will differ from the AJ path.

Figure 6-8 illustrates the situation for a model of the form

Maximize $\pi = R(L,K) - (1 + br)wL - (1 + mr)cK$
$L, K$

Subject to $\pi \leqq (s-r)(bwL + mcK),$

where the relevant first-order conditions reduce to

$$\frac{R_K}{R_L} = \frac{(1+mr)c}{(1+br)w} \frac{\left[1 - \frac{\lambda}{1-\lambda}\frac{(s-r)m}{(1+mr)}\right]}{\left[1 - \frac{\lambda}{1-\lambda}\frac{(s-r)b}{(1+br)}\right]}.$$

If the turnover period for circulating capital is zero ($b = 0$), then we have the asymmetric expansion path of the AJ model. If the turnover period is the same for the one factor as for the other ($m = b$), then the regulated firm would expand along the efficient expansion path, just as it does under symmetric regulation. In the more realistic case ($m > b$), the expansion path lies somewhere in between the other paths. Thus, for the situation most likely to correspond to the true borrowing requirements of a regulated firm, the expansion path entails misallocation, but to a smaller extent than that in the usual AJ model.

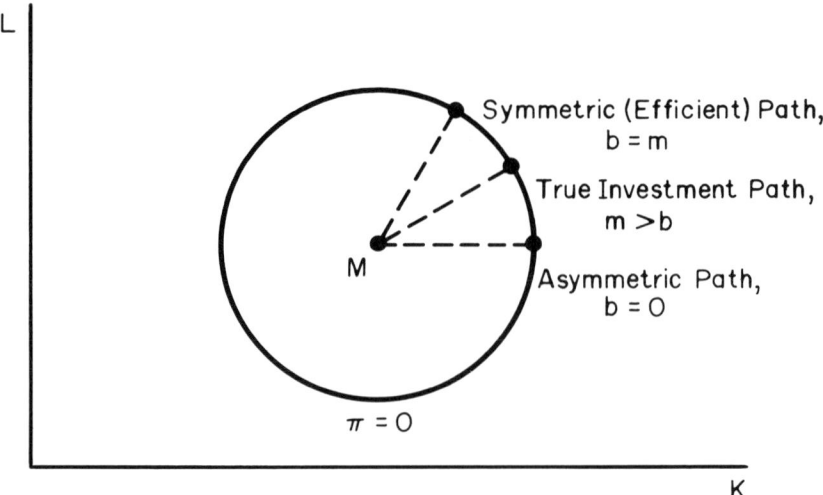

**Figure 6-8.** True Investment Model.

**Optimal Fair Return**

*Partial Equilibrium Models*

In partial equilibrium terms, the selection of an optimal fair return involves a tradeoff between increased output versus increased production inefficiency. A relatively high value of the fair return is beneficial in reducing the amount of inefficiency introduced by the AJ effect, but it also serves to keep down the output of the regulated firm. The obvious question then is whether there is an optimal value of the fair return parameter, one for which the gain in output just compensates at the margin for the loss in efficiency.

Candidate values for the optimal fair return obviously include the monopoly return, the cost of capital, and all returns that lie between these two values. Using basic theory and simple notation, we first show that $s > r$ and $s = r$ can both be solutions to the optimal fair return problem if it is supposed that the firm operates at the end point of the AJ path when $s = r$.[1] However, the monopoly return will never be a candidate solution; instead, some amount of regulation will always prove to be worthwhile.

*Proposition 6.6: In a partial equilibrium framework, the optimal fair return is always lower than the return of the unregulated monopolist. If the regulated*

---

[1] Strictly speaking, the AJ path is defined only for $s > r$. By the end point on the path, we mean that point for $s = r$ which would cause no discontinuous jump in the path.

firm is assumed to operate on the AJ path for all s ≧ r, then s > r is optimal if average cost lies below marginal cost at the end point of the AJ path, and s = r is optimal if average cost equals or exceeds marginal cost at the end point of the AJ path.

*Proof*: The optimal return is that for which the price obtained from increasing output by a marginal amount just equals the additional cost of supplying this output. For the regulated firm, the relevant marginal cost is, of course, that associated with the AJ path ($MC_{AJ}$) rather than that on the efficient expansion path ($MC$). Thus,

$$\frac{dW}{dq} \gtreqless 0 \text{ as } p \gtreqless MC_{AJ}. \tag{6.19}$$

At the monopoly output there is no inefficiency so that $MC_{AJ} = MC$. The monopolist sets $MR = MC$, and since $MR < p$, we have

$$\left.\frac{dW}{dq}\right|_{\text{Monopoly Return}} > 0.$$

Therefore, welfare is increased by lowering the fair return from the monopoly level.

At the end point of the AJ path, $\pi = 0$. Thus, price must equal $AC_{AJ}$ at this point, so that (6.19) becomes

$$\left.\frac{dW}{dq}\right|_{\text{End Point } AJ \text{ Path}} \gtreqless 0 \text{ as } AC_{AJ} \gtreqless MC_{AJ}$$

Welfare is still increasing (there is an end point solution $s = r$) if increasing returns are strong enough so that marginal costs are below average costs at the end point of the AJ path. If, on the other hand, $p = MC_{AJ}$ for some value of $s$ entailing positive profit, then this interior value of $s$ is optimal.

*End of Proof*[m]

Proposition 6.6 is illustrated graphically in Figure 6-9. Figure 6-9a portrays a case where the interior solution, $s > r$, is optimal. Here efficient production is assumed to have constant marginal costs (curve $MC = AC$), while the AJ expansion path yields marginal costs that are rising (curve $MC_{AJ}$) because of the inefficiency in input proportions introduced by the AJ phenomenon. Average costs on the AJ path then lie below marginal costs. The unconstrained

---
[m] I am grateful to Eric Lindenberg for suggesting many aspects of this proof.

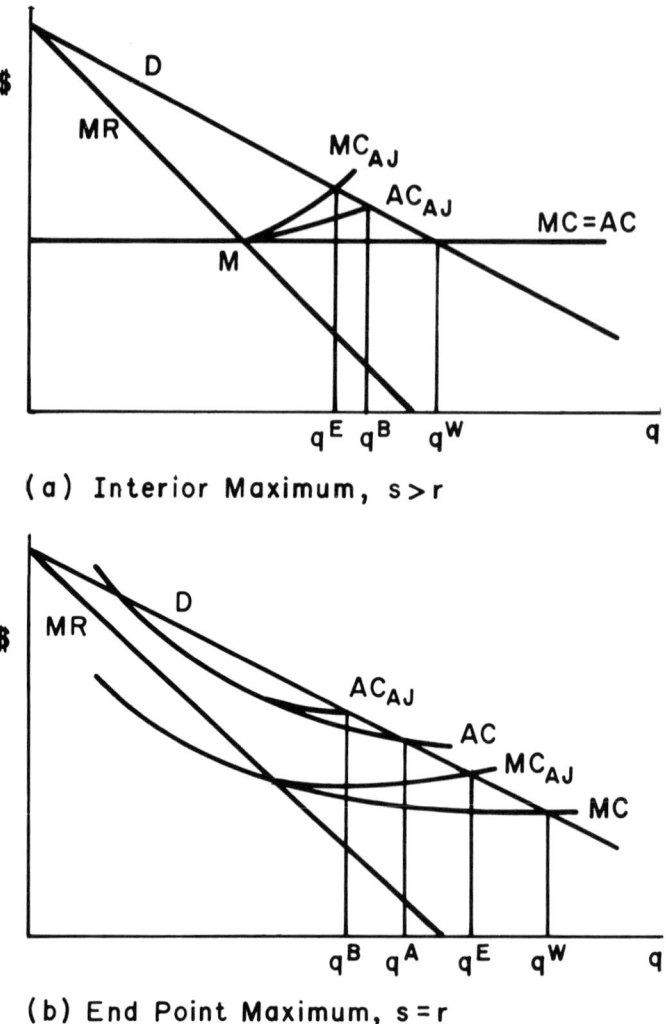

**Figure 6-9.** Optimal Fair Return in Partial Equilibrium Model.

welfare optimum occurs where $p = MC$, with $q^W$ the associated output. The break even point for a firm that is regulated occurs at $q^B$ where $p = AC_{AJ}$. At $q^B$, the fair return $s$ equals $r$. The second-best welfare optimum for the regulated firm occurs at $q^E < q^B < q^W$, where $p = MC_{AJ}$. It is clear that $s > r$ at this output since profit is positive.

Figure 6-9b illustrates a case where the end point solution for the fair return parameter is optimal ($s = r$). Here, the firm is portrayed as having decreasing average costs, so that the marginal cost curve lies below the average cost curve.

The usual welfare optimum is defined to occur at output $q^W$, which entails a loss for the firm. The analogous optimum under regulation occurs at the $p = MC_{AJ}$ point, but this also entails a loss for the firm. The break even point on the AJ path occurs at output $q^B$, where $\frac{dW}{dq} > 0$. Thus, the end point solution $s = r$ is the best that can be obtained.

Proposition 6.6 can be related to the work of Sheshinski.[11] He was the first author to explore the issue of an optimal fair return, and constructed a model which led, in essence, to Figure 6-9a. What he neglected to do was to point out the possibility that the solution $s = r$ may be optimal; instead, he left the reader with the impression that an interior $s$ ($s > r$) will always maximize social welfare.

Klevorick[12] recognized that either an interior or an end point solution was possible. However, he focused attention on the case where there was a discontinuity of behavior at $s = r$. In his work, the firm remains on the AJ path for $s = r + \epsilon$, $\epsilon > 0$, but when $\epsilon = 0$, the firm operates at the efficient point on the $\pi = 0$ contour. Under this assumption, he showed essentially the following:

*Proposition 6.7: Suppose the regulated firm operates efficiently when* s = r. *Then, in a partial equilibrium model where the costs, as measured by the firm, are constant or decreasing on the average,* s = r *is the optimal fair return. Otherwise,* s > r *is optimal.*

*Proof:* When there are constant average costs, $p = MC = AC$ so that the welfare optimum can be attained on the efficient point of the $\pi = 0$ contour ($q = q^W$ in Figure 6-9a). Since the firm is assumed to operate efficiently when $s = r$, the optimal fair return equals the market cost of capital.

If there are decreasing average costs, the $p = MC$ condition entails negative profits. The break even point on the efficient expansion path ($q^A$ in Figure 6-9b) is associated with an output closer to the welfare optimum, $q^W$, than is any inefficient point such as the AJ point $q^B$ on the $\pi = 0$ contour. Therefore, $s = r$ offers the highest welfare given that the firm is constrained to break even in its operations.

By similar reasoning, when marginal cost exceeds average cost, the optimal $s > r$.

*End of Proof*

This proposition is, however, quite misleading as the general equilibrium model we now present makes abundantly clear.

*General Equilibrium Model*

By casting the model into a general equilibrium framework, we immediately encounter a tradeoff that has not been taken into explicit account by any of the discussants to date. The cost that needs to be looked at is not simply the marginal cost associated with the AJ expansion path. Rather, what must be considered as well is the opportunity cost connected with the substitution of the good or service produced by the regulated firm for other goods and services provided by society. The tradeoff involved in the general equilibrium setting thus involves not only the productive efficiency within the regulated firm, but also the exchange efficiency between the regulated good and other of the goods offered by society.

Figure 6-10 illustrates the important features of the general equilibrium model.[n] Figure 6-10a depicts the social production possibility locus. The monopoly output appears on the vertical axis, and the other goods and services of society are aggregated into an output marked "competitive output" on the horizontal axis. The social optimum occurs at point $W$ where the social indifference curve, $I$, is just tangent to the production frontier. The unregulated monopoly firm produces at point $M$ at which there is exchange inefficiency—relatively too much of the competitive output and too little of the monopoly output is offered. This is the standard result that the monopoly, by setting $MR = MC$ rather than $p = MC$, ends up producing too small a quantity. Point $M$ is on the efficient frontier since there is minimum-cost production in both sectors.

The AJ path is depicted by the dashed line. It is clear that as the constraint is tightened, the output of the regulated firm is increased and the competitive output is thereby reduced. However, because of the AJ production inefficiency, the expansion path lies in the interior of the efficient production frontier for society.

Figures 6-10b and 6-10c depict the two types of solutions under the assumption that the firm operates on the AJ path when $s = r$. The critical feature is seen to be the relative slopes of the social indifference curve, $I'$, and the AJ expansion path, denoted $EM$. In Figure 6-10b the tangency occurs at the point where $s = r$. In this case, society rates the monopoly output very highly relative to the competitive output, as shown by the small absolute slope of the indifference curve (a small marginal rate of substitution of the competitive for the monopoly output). Thus, society is willing to trade the monopoly good for the competitive good even when the inefficiency imposed is very great. In Figure 6-10c the social indifference curve is such that an $s > r$ is chosen. In this case, the competitive output is sufficiently attractive relative to the regulated firm's output that less productive inefficiency is tolerated by society.

Under the alternative assumption of efficient operation when $s = r$, the firm suddenly moves from the AJ path (point $E$ in Figure 6-10a) and goes to the efficient point $W$ on the social production frontier. In this case, $s = r$ is precisely the optimal fair return, and it is optimal quite independently of whether there are increasing, decreasing, or constant marginal costs in the regulated industry. Thus, when the exchange efficiency in terms of the other goods and services

---
[n] I am indebted to William Baumol for devising the figure, and for suggesting much of the interpretation that goes along with it.

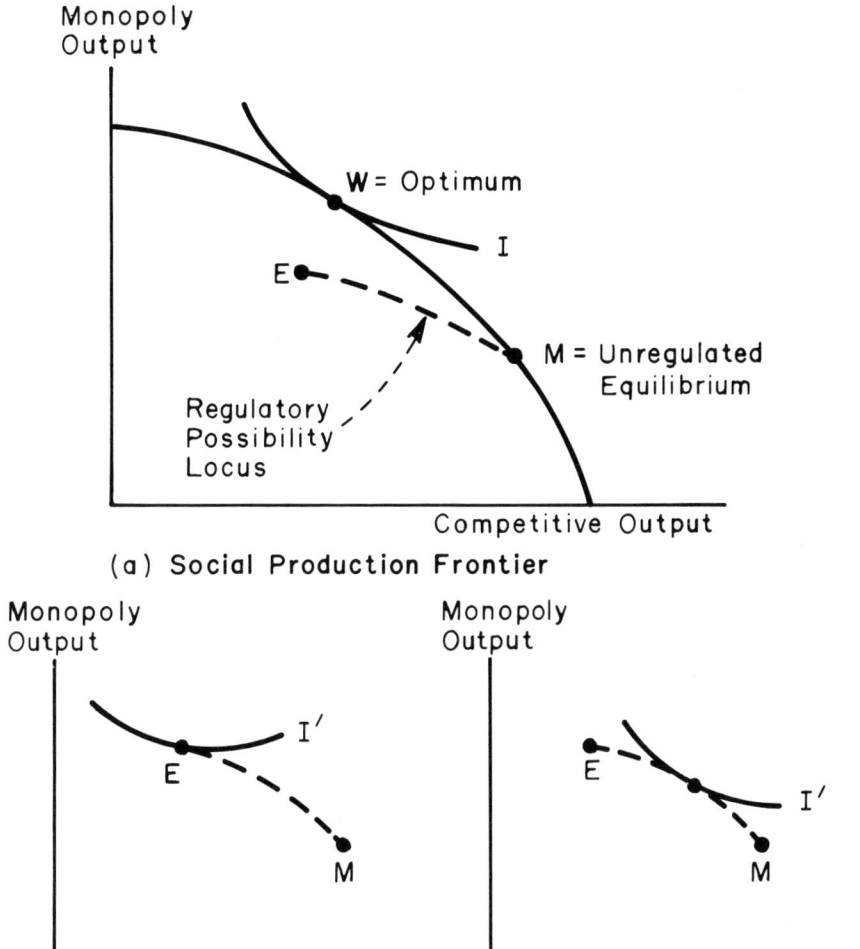

**Figure 6-10.** Optimal Fair Return in General Equilibrium Model.

provided by society is accounted for properly, the dependence of the results on the slopes of the cost curves within the regulated firm are seen to be less illuminating than they seemed at first. Both Propositions 6.6 and 6.7 served to obscure somewhat the true nature of the tradeoff, for they focused only on the productive efficiency of the firm, and ignored the exchange efficiency with the other goods available in the society.

# 7

# Effect of Lagged Regulation[a]

## Introduction and Summary

Although the Averch-Johnson model depicts the regulatory constraint as imposed continuously, in practice there are delays before prices are adjusted in the regulatory process. This chapter includes lagged regulation in the analysis by supposing that a change in the firm's level of capitalization (and hence in its rate of return) is followed by a time interval—the regulatory lag—after which price is adjusted to bring the rate of return back to the fair level.

It is found that regulatory lag can mitigate the incentive to adopt an overly capital intensive technology. In particular, although it may not always pay for the firm to alter its resource allocation from the overly capital intensive level indicated by Averch and Johnson, there is some length of the lag interval above which the firm will misallocate by successively smaller amounts, with attendant increases in output from the AJ level. Thus, the analysis shows that regulatory lag can be effective in encouraging the adoption of a more optimal use of resources.[b]

A second finding is that if the regulator sets the fair return precisely equal to the cost of capital, the usual indeterminacy of output that arises under the zero-profit constraint no longer occurs. The delays between price adjustments give the firm an incentive to move to the efficient production point.

## Effect of Lag When $s > r$

### Initial Operating Point

If the regulator permits a fair return somewhat above the firm's cost of capital, and if regulation is continuous, then a firm finding itself at any point other than $D$ in Figure 7-1 would improve its profit outlook by moving immediately to $D$. To accomplish this shift, the firm could increase its capital $K$ to the level required at $D$; the change in the rate of return thus effected would generate an

---

[a]This chapter is taken from Bailey and Coleman (1971).

[b]The model highlights the potential advantages of regulatory lag, and thus is in the tradition of Bonbright (1961, p. 147), Baumol (1970a, p. 195), and Wein (1968, p. 230). Other authors feel that the suggestion that one institute delays for theoretical reasons "offends one's sense of orderliness and efficiency" [Lewis (1966), p. 230]. See also Phillips (1969, pp. 709-12).

111

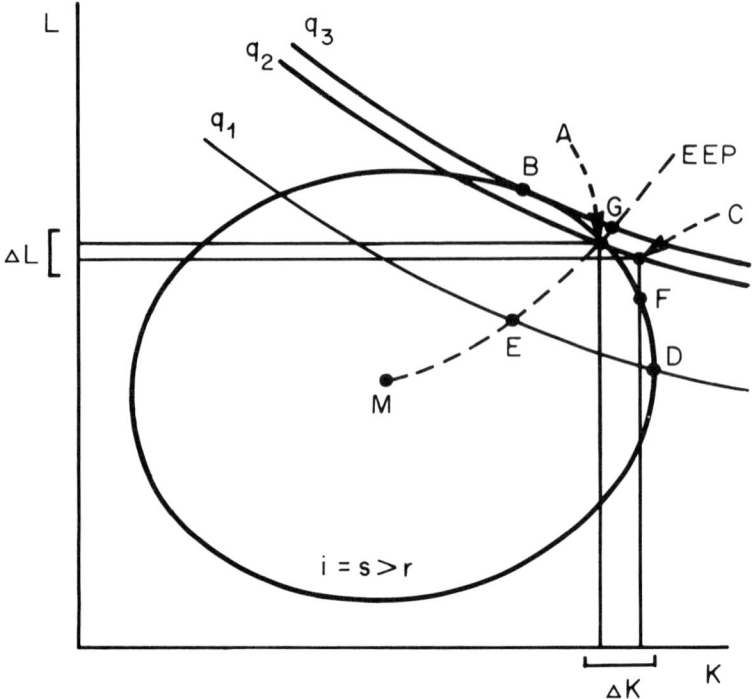

**Figure 7-1.** Lagged Regulation and the Incentive to Misallocate.

instantaneous price adjustment, after which the firm would change its labor $L$ to bring operation to the point $D$. We wish to determine how the firm's actions are modified if a lag is encountered in the regulatory process. The lag that is envisioned is a response time which elapses before the regulator reacts to a change in rate of return by changing price.[c]

The conclusions may be expected to depend on the initial operating point of the firm. Without loss of generality, it may be assumed that the firm is initially operating on the constraint curve between points $A$ and $D$. It is easy to show that if the firm is operating at a point on any other part of the constraint curve, then there is a point between $A$ and $D$ such that operation at this point improves the profit outlook of the firm regardless of the length of the lag. No matter which point between $A$ and $D$ the firm starts at, the equations obtained are identical in appearance. Therefore, for ease of presentation, we shall assume that the firm is initially operating at point $A$, and later mention the conclusions corresponding to other starting points.

---

[c]In our model, price adjustments are treated in a symmetric fashion. The regulator increases price if the firm operates below the fair return, and decreases price if the firm earns more than the fair return. An asymmetric treatment which permits price decreases, but not price increases, is given in Peles and Stein (1973).

## Nature of the Tradeoff

In order to enjoy the higher profits at point $D$, the firm must increase its capitalization. Such an increase causes costs to rise while price remains the same, so that the firm earns lower profits during the lag interval $T$. Thus, the actions taken by the firm depend on a tradeoff between the loss in profits until time $T$, and the gain in profits after time $T$. The idea that lag creates a tradeoff is helpful in giving us some insight into the results that might be expected. We observe first that when the lag is zero (the AJ model), it is always advantageous for the profit-maximizing firm to adopt an overly capital intensive technology since there is no initial loss to be made up. At the other extreme, when $T$ is infinity (no further price adjustment), the firm maximizes profits by producing at minimum cost. With lags of intermediate lengths, it seems reasonable to expect that the firm might not be able to recover the loss incurred by employing capital of the full AJ amount, but that some reduced level of misallocation might instead be worthwhile. We show that such an intermediate level will often be optimal, but that when the lag interval is short, operation at the AJ point is still the firm's most profitable course of action.

If the firm operates at point $A$, using labor $L$ and capital $K$ and earning annual profits $\pi = (s-r)cK$, then the constraint is being satisfied and there is no need for further regulatory action. Since costs, demand, and so on are assumed to remain constant, the present value of the firm's total future profits is given by

$$\pi_0 = \pi \sum_{j=0}^{\infty} d^j = \frac{\pi}{1-d} \qquad (7.1)$$

where $d$ is the value of next year's dollar, and equals $\frac{1}{(1+r)}$ if the discount rate of money is taken to be equal to the firm's market cost of capital.

The firm, seeking to maximize the discounted stream of future profits, wishes to compare the profit stream given by (7.1) with one it would obtain if it operated closer to point $D$. To effect such a change, the firm moves down its isoquant to a point such as $C$ in Figure 7-1. By doing so, the capital costs are increased by an amount $rc \Delta K$. Since production is kept constant, labor costs decrease by $w \Delta L$, and we have

$$q(L,K) = q(L - \Delta L, K + \Delta K) = q_2. \qquad (7.2)$$

However, $w \Delta L$ is less than $rc \Delta K$ since costs are being increased when we move away from $A$; thus profits decrease by $(rc \Delta K - w \Delta L)$ each year until the price adjustment is made. After time $T$, the regulator resets price so that the firm operates at a point such as $F$ on the constraint curve. Profits are then increased to $\pi + (s-r)c\Delta K$ since the rate base has been increased. Of course, this expression is valid only for values of $\Delta K$ that are not greater than that required to increase capital to the AJ amount; if $K + \Delta K$ exceeded the AJ level of capital, the firm would be unable to earn sufficient profits to meet the constraint. The significance of having the firm end up at a point such as $F$ is, of course, that the expansion path of the firm will be shifted somewhere between the AJ path and the efficient path. Thus, regulatory lag will be found to improve efficiency in a way that could not be accomplished by changing the functional form of the profit ceiling.

Figure 7-2 shows the effect of discounting on the profit stream. The area under the solid lines gives the discounted present value of the profits earned by continuous operation at $A$, while the area under the dashed lines gives the present value of profits if the firm adopts an overly capital intensive technology. Mathematically, the profit stream is given by

$$\pi_1 = (\pi - (rc\Delta K - w\Delta L))\sum_{j=0}^{T-1} d^j + (\pi + (s-r)c\Delta K)\sum_{j=T}^{\infty} d^j,$$

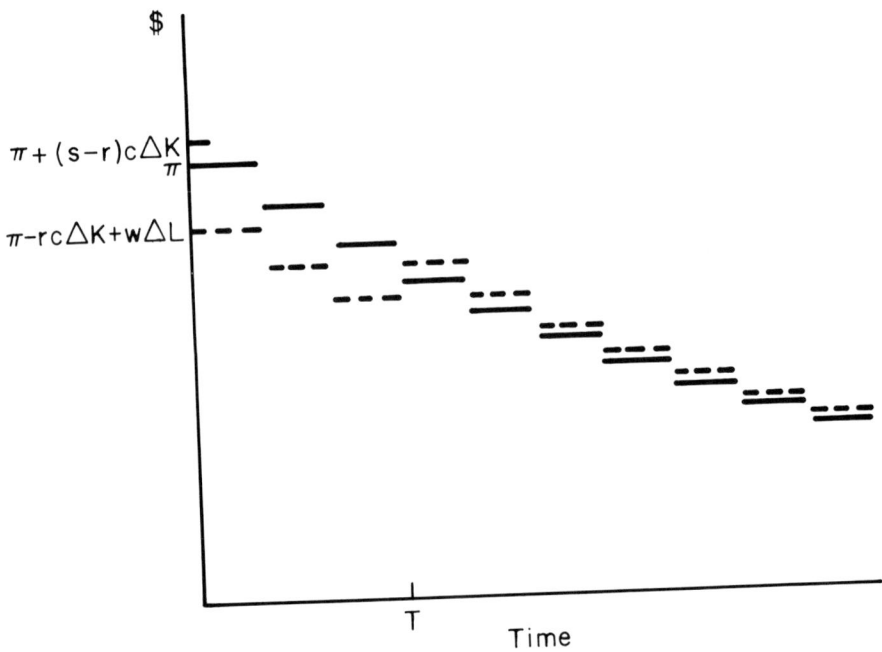

**Figure 7-2.** Effect of Lag on Discounted Profit Stream.

or, upon summing and rearranging,

$$\pi_1 = \frac{\pi}{1-d} - \frac{(rc\Delta K - w\Delta L)(1-d^T)}{1-d} + \frac{(s-r)c\Delta K d^T}{1-d}. \quad (7.3)$$

An overly capital intensive technology is worthwhile if and only if the present value given by (7.3) exceeds that of (7.1), that is,

$$\pi_1 - \pi_0 = \left[ (s-r)c\Delta K \frac{d^T}{1-d} \right] - \left[ (rc\Delta K - w\Delta L) \frac{1-d^T}{1-d} \right] > 0. \quad (7.4)$$

This inequality shows that the level of profits, $\pi$, earned at the initial point $A$ is irrelevant to the decision to overcapitalize. Instead, it is the incremental profits and losses accruing from the increase in capital $\Delta K$ which are important. Equation (7.4) expresses mathematically the tradoff that is required; it states that the firm finds it advantageous to increase capital by the amount $\Delta K$ so long as the additional profits it obtains by so doing (first bracketed term) exceed the initial losses (second bracketed term). A visual interpretation is available from Figure 7-2. The areas between the solid and dashed lines to the left of $T$ are the incremental losses and those on the right are the incremental gains.

It should be pointed out that the analysis does not depend on the "annual" nature of the variables involved: lag, profit, interest, and so on, could refer to any other convenient period of time, such as a month, for example. In fact, whenever two alternative courses of action are compared, exactly the same decisions are made if $T$ is defined in a continuous rather than a discrete environment; that is, if we replace

$$\sum_{j=0}^{T-1} d^j \text{ by } \int_0^T d^x dx.$$

*Change in the AJ Path*

We would expect there to be an "optimal" value of $\Delta K$ lying between zero and the AJ amount, that is, a value which maximizes the gain in profits.

*Proposition 7.1: When the fair return exceeds the cost of capital, then the final operating point for a firm encountering regulatory lag will, for large enough* values of the lag interval, involve a lower level of capital and a higher level of output than that of a firm which is regulated continuously.

*Proof:* Differentiate the gain in profits (7.4) with respect to $\Delta K$, regarding $\Delta L$ as a function of $\Delta K$, and obtain

$$\frac{d}{d\Delta K}(\pi_1 - \pi_0) = (s-r)c \frac{d^T}{1-d}\left[rc - w\frac{d\Delta L}{d\Delta K}\right]\frac{1-d^T}{1-d}. \qquad (7.5)$$

Observe that $-\dfrac{d\Delta L}{d\Delta K}$ is the slope of the production curve at point $C$ in Figure 7-1, for upon differentiating (7.2), we have

$$\frac{d\Delta L}{d\Delta K} = \frac{q_K(L-\Delta L, K+\Delta K)}{q_L(L-\Delta L, K+\Delta K)}.$$

Two features of (7.5) are immediately apparent. First, no matter what the value of $T$ is, if $\Delta K$ is small enough (that is, point $C$ is close to point $A$), then $\dfrac{d\Delta L}{d\Delta K}$ is so close to $\dfrac{rc}{w}$ that (7.5) is positive. This means that the firm's optimal policy always entails misallocation by at least some small amount.[d]

The second feature of (7.5) to notice is that if $T$ is small enough, (7.5) is positive no matter how large the value of $\Delta K$. Hence, for small $T$, the firm maximizes gain by choosing $\Delta K$ as large as possible; that is, the firm uses the AJ amount of capital. For larger values of $T$, say $T > T'$, the derivative (7.5) can be made zero. We then have

$$\frac{d\Delta L}{d\Delta K} = \frac{rc}{w} - \frac{d^T}{1-d^T}\frac{(s-r)c}{w}. \qquad (7.6)$$

Equation (7.6) determines the optimal level of capital for each $T > T'$; namely, the firm will choose whatever $\Delta K$ makes the slope of the production function at point $C$ in Figure 7-1 equal to the right-hand side of (7.6). If (7.6) yields a $\Delta K$ larger than the AJ amount, then the firm's optimal decision is to use exactly the AJ level.

*End of Proof*

---

[d]Note, however, that this conclusion will not necessarily hold if price adjustments have a cost associated with them. Suppose that the firm incurs expenses of $N$ dollars in order to justify its request for a price adjustment. Equation (7.4) then becomes

$$(s-r)c\Delta Kd^T - (rc\Delta K - w\Delta L)(1-d^T) - N(1-d) > 0.$$

Since the term involving $N$ has a negative sign, the inequality may be false for all values of $\Delta K$, no matter how small, so that no amount of misallocation would be worthwhile.

It is interesting to note that the optimizing equation (7.6) is strikingly similar to the one obtained in the AJ model [Equation (5.18) of Chapter 5]. In each case, the left-hand side is the magnitude of the slope of an isoquant at the point where the firm would operate after making an optimal decision (point $D$ on the isoquant $q_1$ in the AJ model and some point the right of $A$ on the isoquant $q_2$ in our model). The difference in sign on the left-hand sides is accounted for by the fact that we have defined $\Delta L$ in such a way that it must be positive when $\Delta K$ is, so that $\Delta L$ increases when labor decreases. On the right-hand sides, it is clear that $d^T$ plays the same role in this equation as $\lambda$ does in the AJ analysis.

In computing (7.6) the firm is assumed to be interested in all future profits to be earned. It may be more realistic to assume that the firm's planning horizon is finite rather than infinite. A planning horizon of $n$ years is incorporated by summing only the first $n$ terms in our equations. Equation (7.6) then becomes

$$\frac{d\Delta L}{d\Delta K} = \frac{rc}{w} - \frac{d^T - d^n}{d^T} \frac{(s-r)c}{w} .$$

Thus there would be a somewhat lower use of capital in this case, a reasonable result since the introduction of the finite horizon in no way alters the initial losses, but it does cut off some of the eventual gains.

*Other Starting Points*

We have obtained equations based upon the assumption that the constrained firm is initially employing minimum-cost technology. The same equations are obtained no matter where between points $A$ and $D$ in Figure 7-1 the firm starts out. However, the quantity $\Delta K$ now refers to the change in capital required to move from the new starting point toward $D$, rather than the change required to move from $A$ toward $D$. The quantity of $\Delta L$ still refers to the change in labor which occurs when the firm increases capital by $\Delta K$ while holding production constant.

When the starting point is arbitrary, it may not be worthwhile for the firm to adopt a higher level of capital. To see this, divide Equation (7.4) by $\Delta K$ and let $m$ be the slope of the production curve at the starting point ($m < \frac{rc}{w}$). Then, as $\Delta K$ approaches zero, we obtain

$$scd^T - rc + wm(1 - d^T) \geq 0 ,$$

which is not always true. Indeed, for an arbitrary starting point, it can be asked whether it is worthwhile for the firm to move back to a less overcapitalized production alternative. This question is nearly symmetric to the one that has been analyzed and if a similar two-period approach is used, it might be found that the firm would earn enough extra profits in the lag period to offset the loss to be incurred in the future. Unfortunately, when the firm can move into the interior of the constraint curve, it is less clear that the two-period approach gives an "optimal" policy for the firm to follow. The more complex approach has been avoided here since it would not only have complicated the description of the model, but would also have obscured the tradeoffs we wished to consider.

**Two Graphical Examples**

*Enlargement versus Minimum Cost*

A special case that is of some interest can be examined by setting $\Delta L$ equal to zero in (7.4). This corresponds to the firm's enlarging its capital investment by adding $\Delta K$ to its rate base $K$; but, rather than making productive use of it immediately, the firm leaves the extra capital idle until a price adjustment has been made. This situation has been given considerable attention in the literature as one way the firm might "pad its rate base."[e] When $\Delta L = 0$, Equation (7.4) reduces to

$$\pi_1 - \pi_0 = \frac{cs\Delta K}{1-d} (d^T - \frac{r}{s}) > 0. \tag{7.7}$$

Thus, the firm would find it worthwhile to enlarge its rate base with some idle capital if, and only if $d^T > \frac{r}{s}$; furthermore, since the left-hand side of (7.7) is the gain, the firm's optimal decision is to choose $\Delta K$ as large as possible if $d^T > \frac{r}{s}$. Hence the firm would make an all-or-nothing decision between remaining at $A$ and enlarging its capital base to the AJ level.

A graphical representation is easy to obtain and is given in Figure 7-3. For each value of $T$, the corresponding line divides the unit square into two parts, one being the region in which minimum-cost production is better than enlargement, and the other being the region in which enlargement is worthwhile. Thus, for example, when the reaction time is one year ($T = 1$), the firm would use minimum-cost production on the left of the 45° line and would enlarge its capital investment by the AJ amount on the right. The area in which the minimum-cost production is used increases with increasing values of $T$. When no regulation is anticipated ($T = \infty$), the firm operates at minimum cost independently of the values of $d$ and $\frac{r}{s}$. The desirability of enlargement can be measured by the distance below the appropriate $T$-curve: on the curve, it takes

---

[e]See Wein (1968) and Zajac (1972).

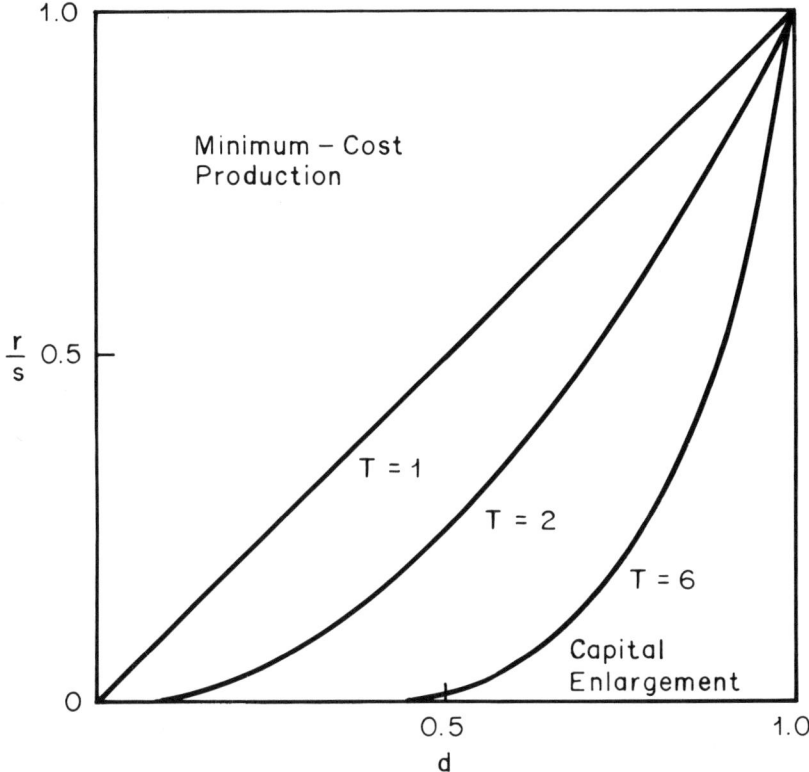

**Figure 7-3.** Minimum Cost Versus Enlargement.

the firm an infinite length of time to recover the loss; as we move down below the curve, recovery occurs in a finite, progressively smaller number of years.

In spite of the graphical appeal of this enlargement case, the result is of limited theoretical interest, since a profit-maximizing firm would always prefer misallocation to enlargement. In terms of this version of the AJ model, we can readily demonstrate this by noting that the initial loss in profits under enlargement ($rc \Delta K$) is greater than the initial loss under misallocation ($rc \Delta K - w \Delta L$), while the eventual gain, ($s - r$) $c \Delta K$, is the same in either case. It should be mentioned, however, that in practice excess capacity has advantages which are not reflected in our model; for instance, it can serve as a buffer against uncertain demands, and it is presumably easier to implement than factor substitution is.

*Overly Capital Intensive Technology*

Since a graphical representation was obtained in the enlargement case, it is natural to seek one for the more important misallocation alternative. To illustrate the details of the misallocation, it is convenient to examine a special case of the Cobb-Douglas production function, namely

$$Q(L,K) = \beta L^{1/2} K^{1/2} . \tag{7.8}$$

This particular form is selected because it has the attractive feature of permitting us to eliminate the variables $w$ and $\Delta L$ from (7.6), which now becomes[f]

$$\frac{r}{s}\left[1 - \left(1 + \frac{\Delta K}{K}\right)^{-2}\right] = \frac{d^T}{1-d^T}\left(1 - \frac{r}{s}\right) . \tag{7.9}$$

In Figure 7-4, the percentage change in capital usage $\frac{\Delta K}{K}$, is plotted as a function of $d$ for $T = 1$, $T = 3$, and $T = \infty$ when $\frac{r}{s} = 0.95$. Any particular $T$-curve partitions the area into two sections: if the AJ level of capital usage lies in the right-hand section, then that is the optimal level to adopt; if the AJ level falls within the left-hand section, then the firm's optimal decision is to choose a reduced level of

---

[f]The derivation is fairly straightforward. From Equation (7.2) we have

$$\beta L^{1/2} K^{1/2} = \beta (L - \Delta L)^{1/2} (K + \Delta K)^{1/2}$$

which is easily manipulated into the form

$$\Delta L = \frac{L \Delta K}{(K + \Delta K)} .$$

By using (7.3) and the fact that minimum-cost technology is employed at the point $A$, we have

$$-\frac{dL}{dK} = \frac{\partial Q/\partial K}{\partial Q/\partial L} = \frac{L}{K} = \frac{rc}{w} .$$

This is used to eliminate $L$, so that

$$\Delta L = \frac{rc}{w} \frac{K \Delta K}{K + \Delta K} .$$

Differentiating with respect to $\Delta K$, we obtain

$$\frac{d \Delta K}{d \Delta L} = \frac{rc}{w} \left(\frac{K}{K + \Delta K}\right)^2$$

which is substituted into (7.6) and manipulated to get (7.9).

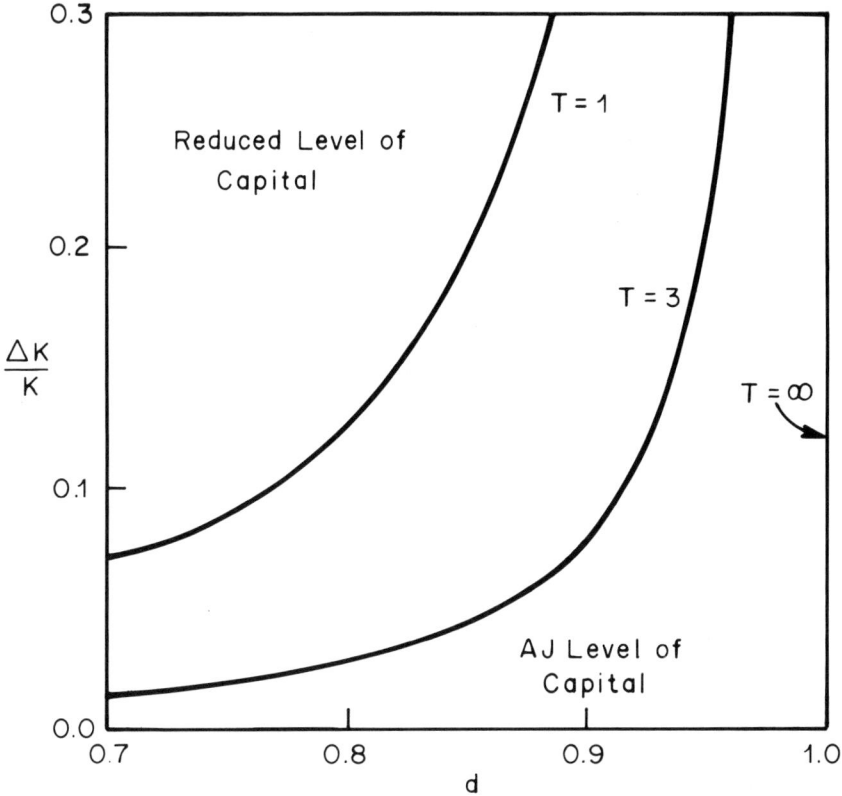

**Figure 7-4.** Optimal Level of Capital Usage for Particular Example.

$\frac{\Delta K}{K}$, that level vertically below the AJ level on the $T$-curve. We note that for smaller values of the ratio $\frac{r}{s}$, the right-hand section gets larger, that is, the $T$-curves shift upward and to the left. We also note that the $T$-curves are asymptotic to the line $d = (\frac{r}{s})^{1/T}$; therefore, for that portion of the area lying to the right of this asymptote, the firm's decision will be independent of $\frac{\Delta K}{K}$.

Thus, using the AJ amount of capital, like capacity enlargement, is always worthwhile when $d^T > \frac{r}{s}$; but when $d^T < \frac{r}{s}$, the level of capital may have to be reduced. For example, if the regulatory lag is three years and $d = 0.9$, then we find from Figure 7-4 that in order to maximize profits, the firm must limit its capital to $0.07932K$, even though the firm might like to increase its capital by $\Delta K = 0.1 K$, say, in order to move to the AJ point $D$. In this case, the firm has found it must misallocate by a smaller amount than it would have done in the no-lag case; the firm would therefore ultimately produce at some point on the constraint curve between $A$ and $D$ rather than at $D$.

**Zero-Profit Constraint**

If the regulatory agency has set the fair rate as close to the cost of capital as it can (given the various uncertainties about how the cost of capital might actually be determined), then the constraint curve, as shown in Figure 7-5, is the outline of the base of the profit hill—those points at which the firm earns zero profit.

Figures 7-1 and 7-5 appear similar, but there is one important difference between them. In Figure 7-1, the point $B$ of maximum output occurs at a point on the constraint curve at which production costs are not minimized (see Chapter 5). The isoquant $q_3$ of Figure 7-1 intersects the efficient locus at a point

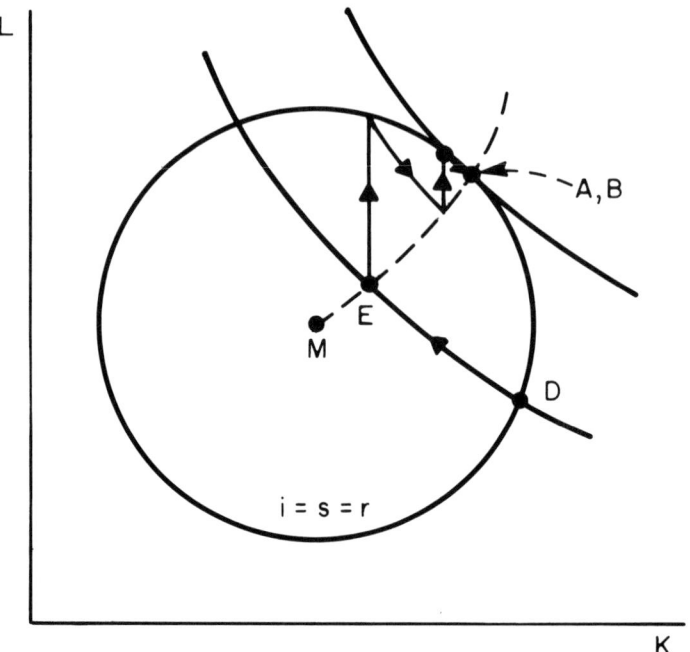

**Figure 7-5.** Efficient Operation under Zero-Profit Regulation.

such as $G$ where profits are larger than at point $B$, even though rate of return is smaller. However, when $s = r$, the point of maximum output and the point on the efficient locus coincide and are denoted by the point $A, B$ in Figure 7-5. To show this, we observe that if they did not coincide, then $q_3$ would intersect the efficient locus at a point such as $G$ in Figure 7-1, different from $B$, and lying outside the base of the profit hill. Profits at $B$ are zero, and since $G$ is on the efficient locus, profits there are greater than at $B$. But any point outside the base of the profit hill must have negative profits, a contradiction. Hence, $G = B = A$.

If regulation is continuous, the firm will have no preference among these points. Hence no conclusion can be drawn about the firm's allocation of resources between labor and capital.[g] When regulatory lag is introduced, the firm compares the profit stream obtainable at the current price with the profit streams obtainable by changing the level of capital. Such a change in capital and therefore in rate of return, is followed by a lag of duration $T$, after which a price change brings the firm's rate of return back to the fair level $s$ and profits back to zero. Since the only opportunity for positive profits is before the price adjustment, the firm will concentrate on maximizing its profits during the lag interval.

*Proposition 7.2: When the regulator sets the fair rate of return so that it exactly equals the firm's cost of capital, the combination of lagged regulation and the profit objective serve to drive the firm toward the minimum-cost maximum-output point on its zero-profit contour.*

*Proof:* Suppose the firm is originally at the AJ point, $D$ on the base of the profit hill (any other point could be used equally well). The firm can maximize profits by shifting its resource allocation to the minimum cost point $E$ on that isoquant (note the arrow in Figure 7-5). Since this point is in the interior of the constraint curve, the firm will then earn profits in excess of the constrained amount until the subsequent price adjustment forces the firm back onto the constraint curve. Eventually, by always moving to the minimum-cost point on its current isoquant, the firm will be driven to the minimum-cost, maximum-output point $A,B$, as is indicated in Figure 7-5. Moreover, this result holds no matter how small the length of the lag interval, so long as it is positive.

*End of Proof*

---

[g]For a treatment of the zero-profit case which combines lagged regulation and technological change, see Bailey (1972b).

# 8  Comparative Statics Analysis of AJ Model[a]

**Introduction and Summary**

In this chapter, the standard comparative statics method is used to examine the effects of changes in the values of some of the more significant parameters determining the behavior of the regulated firm: the cost of capital, the prices of capital inputs, the expenses of the firm, and various types of taxes.

Surprisingly, when the market cost of capital rises, while the fair rate of return remains unchanged, it does not pay the regulated firm to make any change in the quantities of capital or labor it uses or in the output it produces. This is paradoxical since we showed in Chapter 6 that as the fair rate is moved closer to the cost of capital (the other way of making regulation more effective), the firm moves out along the AJ expansion path using more capital and producing a larger output. There is thus a basic asymmetry in behavior when the cost of capital rather than the fair rate of return is the agent of tighter regulation.

Another implication of the cost of capital result is that the AJ effect may be more pronounced for firms whose market cost of capital is high relative to the fair return than it is for firms with lower market costs. In addition, $\frac{dK}{dr} = 0$ implies that increases in interest rates that are induced by governmental monetary policy may be ineffective in discouraging investment in the regulated sector. The response also provides a striking illustration that increased costs are not automatically passed on by a regulated firm to its consumers: in this case, the firm bears the entire effect of the cost increase through a decline in its profit.

A second result derived in this chapter asserts that an increase in the acquisition cost of capital goods causes a decline both in the regulated firm's use of capital and in its profits. This conclusion is consistent qualitatively with the expected behavior of the unregulated firm, but is in disagreement with the Westfield assertion that a conspiracy among the capital equipment suppliers can be advantageous to the regulated firm. In his words,

> even under the simplest assumptions—the conventional model of a profit-maximizing monopoly with an added restriction limiting its rate of return—a public utility may not only fail to suffer a decline but actually experience an increase in profit if suppliers of capital goods collude to raise their prices.[1]

---

[a]Much of the formal comparative statics analysis was derived jointly with Frank Gratzer. Kyu Lie and David Dayan also made contributions. We later discovered that many of the results had been derived earlier by Tasch (1968). A somewhat different approach is being published concurrently by McNicol (1973).

We show instead that as long as the marginal physical product of capital is positive (certainly the "simplest assumption"), an increase in the acquisition cost of capital is unambiguously disadvantagous to the firm. Thus, we demonstrate the invalidity of a proposition that has been cited extensively by numerous authors.[b]

*Changes in Costs of Production*

Table 8-1 summarizes the results of a comparative statics analysis for the AJ model, most of which will be derived explicitly later in the chapter. The first row of the table contains the sign information discussed in Chapter 6, that is, the assertion that a rise in the fair rate of return will decrease the use of capital and output and will increase total profit. The next three rows, which constitute the main topic of this chapter, report the qualitative behavior of the model in response to changes in the three cost-of-production parameters—the market cost of capital, the acquisition cost of capital, and the wage rate. The last two rows summarize the firm's response to changes in tax parameters. The columns labeled "M" contain the results pertaining to the unregulated monopoly firm; the columns labeled "AJ" give the corresponding results under rate-of-return regulation. Table 8-1 thus permits us to see at a glance when the qualitative behavior of the profit-maximizing firm under regulation differs from that of an unconstrained monopolist.

In deriving these results, it is assumed that neither factor is inferior. However,

**Table 8-1**
**Comparative Statics Properties of Monopoly versus Regulated Firm**

|  | Capital, $K$ | | Labor, $L$ | | Output, $q$ | | Profit, $\pi$ | |
| --- | --- | --- | --- | --- | --- | --- | --- | --- |
|  | M | AJ | M | AJ | M | AJ | M | AJ |
| Rate of return, $s$ |  | − |  | $?^{\ddagger}$ |  | −* |  | + |
| Market cost of capital, $r$ | − | 0 | $?^{\ddagger}$ | 0 | −* | 0 | − | − |
| Acquisition cost of capital, $c$ | − | − | $?^{\ddagger}$ | $?^{\ddagger}$ | −* | −* | − | − |
| Wage rate, $w$ | $?^{\ddagger}$ | − | − | $?^{\ddagger}$ | −* | −* | − | − |
| Income tax, $t$ | 0 | − | 0 | $?^{\ddagger}$ | 0 | −* | − | − |
| Property tax, $k$ | − | − | $?^{\ddagger}$ | $?^{\ddagger}$ | −* | −* | − | − |

*The sign holds if factors are not inferior (or, more simply, if $q_{LK} > 0$).
$^{\ddagger}$The corresponding sign is negative if $R_{LK} > 0$.

---

[b]Most such authors [e.g., Kahn (1970), Trebing (1968)], have cited the result without qualification; however, Corey (1971) questioned its validity earlier. By independent logic Emery (1973) and Dayan (1972) have derived alternative proofs of its invalidity.

the cases in which the result is affected by this assumption are indicated by an asterisk. Since there is no way to prejudge the sign of $R_{LK}$, we cannot determine the signs of several entries. This is indicated by a question mark in the table. The dagger indicates that each of these signs is negative if labor and capital are complements in the generation of revenue ($R_{LK} > 0$).

**Changes in the Market Cost of Capital**

*Lack of Responsiveness*

It seems natural to expect that a firm operating under rate-of-return regulation will respond to changes in the market cost of capital. If market forces cause the cost of capital to move closer to the fair return, we might also expect the firm to exhibit the same response pattern it displays when the fair return is moved closer to the cost of capital. In both cases, the regulatory constraint becomes more binding and it would seem from the symmetry between $s$ and $r$ in the right-hand side of the constraint

$$\pi = (s - r) cK, \tag{8.1}$$

that there should be a correspondence in behavior. Instead, under the assumption $s > r$, the theory reveals that the capital and output decisions of the regulated firm change only with changes in the fair rate-of-return figure, and are invariant to changes in the market cost of capital. The firm is not, however, indifferent to the magnitude of the cost of capital; quite the contrary, for the magnitude of that rate determines the amount of profit the firm will be able to achieve.

A graphical interpretation is given in Figure 8-1, which shows the projection of the profit hill and constraint on the $K\pi$-plane. Consider first the case where the fair return, $s$, is reduced by an amount $\epsilon$ to $(s - \epsilon)$. The profit possibility contour remains as it was at $\pi = R - wL - rcK$. However, the constraint ray shifts from $\pi = [s - r] cK$ down to $\pi = [(s - \epsilon) - r] cK$. The new intersection between the profit hill and constraint occurs at a point where the use of capital is increased from $K_1$ to $K_2$ and profit falls (see Figure 8-1a).

Now suppose instead that the cost of capital, $r$, increases by an amount $\epsilon$ to $(r + \epsilon)$, and hence moves closer to $s$. As before, the constraining ray shifts downward from $\pi = [s - r] cK$ to $\pi = [s - (r + \epsilon)] cK$. However, the profit possibility contour also shrinks to $\pi = R - wL - (r + \epsilon) cK$. For each particular value of $K$, the hill is now $\epsilon cK$ units lower than it was before. Hence, the hill shifts down more for larger values of $K$ than for smaller. Because the downward shift is precisely the same ($\epsilon cK$) for both the constraining ray and the profit hill, it follows that at the new intersection point profit is reduced precisely by

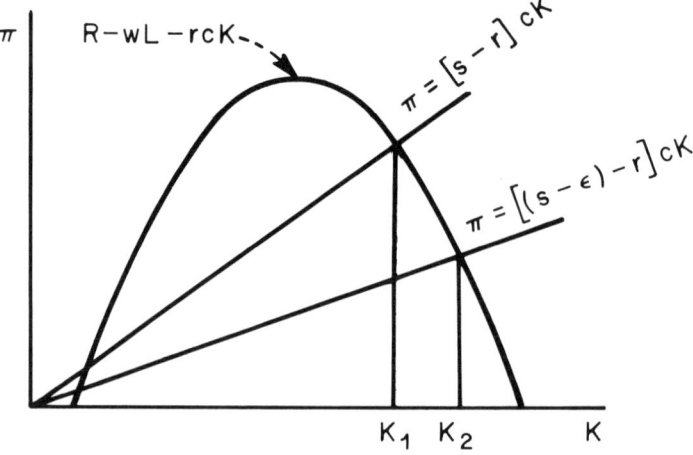

(a) Decrease in Fair Return

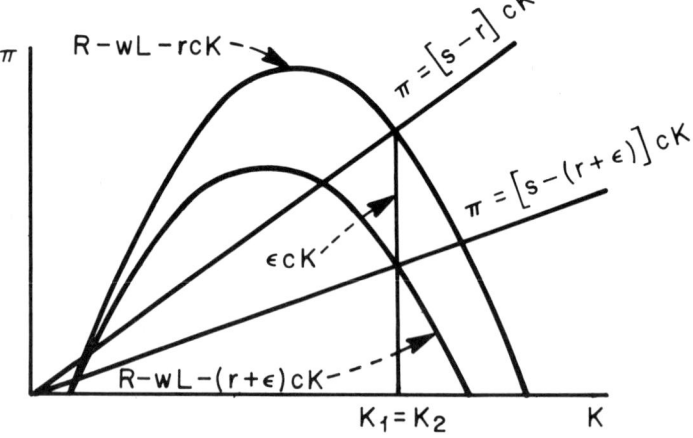

(b) Increase in Market Cost of Capital

**Figure 8-1.** Cost of Capital Versus Fair Return.

$\epsilon cK$. The value of $K$ at the new intersection is, however, exactly the same as it was before.

An intuitive explanation of the difference in behavior can be obtained by writing the equation of an isorate-of-return contour as

$$\frac{R(L,K) - wL}{cK} = i. \qquad (8.2)$$

It is apparent that the market cost of capital does not enter into this equation. Hence, a change in the cost of capital does not affect the isorate-of-return contour. Since, as was shown in Chapter 5, the AJ equilibrium occurs at the point of tangency between the isorate-of-return contour and a vertical line, it follows that the location of the AJ point is independent of $r$.

A word of caution is required here. The preceding result depends upon the assumption that equality holds throughout in the constraint. Thus, the analysis does not explicitly treat the case where there is a reduction in cost of capital that is so large as to render the constraint inactive. The result also depends on the assumption that positive profit is achievable. Thus, it assumes the change in cost of capital cannot be so large that the higher cost exceeds the fair return.

The formal mathematical derivation of the result is not difficult.

*Proposition 8.1: When the market cost of capital increases, everything else remaining unchanged, the optimal capital, labor, and output of the regulated firm remain unchanged, but profit falls.*

*Proof*: Utilizing the methods from Chapter 6, we differentiate totally the constraint $R(L,K) - wL - scK = 0$ to obtain $(R_L - w)\dfrac{dL}{dr} - (R_K - sc)\dfrac{dK}{dr} = 0$.

Since we established that $R_L = w$ and $R_K < sc$, it follows that $\dfrac{dK}{dr} = 0$. Putting this result into $R_{LK}\dfrac{dK}{dr} + R_{LL}\dfrac{dL}{dr} = 0$, we can infer that $\dfrac{dL}{dr} = 0$. Thus, $\dfrac{dq}{dr} = q_L\dfrac{dL}{dr} + q_K\dfrac{dK}{dr} = 0$ as well. To show the profit result, differentiate totally the constraint $\pi = (s - r)cK$, thereby obtaining $\dfrac{d\pi}{dr} = (s - r)c\dfrac{dK}{dr} - cK$, where the result $\dfrac{d\pi}{dr} < 0$ follows immediately from the fact that $\dfrac{dK}{dr} = 0$.

*End of Proof*

*Implications of the Result*

Perhaps the most important aspect of Proposition 8.1 is its potential usefulness in empirical studies. It is well known that for a model of unconstrained profit maximization, an increase in market cost of capital decreases the firm's demand for capital, and, if capital is a normal input, it also reduces the equilibrium output of the firm. Since we have shown that the AJ operating point is invariant to changes in cost of borrowing, there is thus a testable difference between the two models in terms of the nature of the firm's response. If an empirical study found that $\dfrac{dK}{dr} < 0$ and $\dfrac{dq}{dr} < 0$, for example, we could conclude that the firm was not behaving in accordance with the Averch-Johnson model. The test may have somewhat limited applicability, however, for the AJ model does not include the fact that interest charges are deductible as expenses. By including this possibility in the analysis, it would be found that the AJ model would yield the $\frac{dK}{dr} < 0$ result.

A second outcome from Proposition 8.1 is that we are now able to state conclusively whether the AJ misallocation becomes worse or better as the cost of capital is changed. If the cost of capital is $r_1$ rather than $r_2$, then the efficient expansion path is shifted from $EEP(r_1,w)$ to $EEP(r_2,w)$ as shown in Figure 8-2. Since the AJ operating point depends on $s$ and does not change with small changes in $r$, it does not shift position. Therefore, the new factor costs will necessarily mean a more overcapitalized production (a larger AJ effect); conversely, a lower interest rate to $r_0$ reduces the extent of the AJ misallocation.[c]

A third economic implication of our result relates to changes in cost of capital that are the result of deliberate governmental policy. Standard monetary policy calls for the government to increase the cost of borrowing during an inflationary period, as a means of discouraging investment, with the reverse policy prescribed for a period of recession. The simple analysis we have presented (which has ignored questions of debt-equity ratios, availability of funds, and so on) implies that such policy changes do not affect investment decisions in the regulated sector of the economy. Thus, for the government to achieve any given target modification in the level of investment, a disproportionate effect on the firms outside the regulated sector is required.

We have been careful not to imply that monetary policy always has very large and rapid effects on investment in the unregulated sector. Even in that sector, many studies[d] have found that changes in cost of capital affect investment only after long lags. These studies, which also investigate the regulated sector, all employ a user cost-of-capital measurement that includes both the market cost of borrowing and acquisition cost of capital. Thus, their conclusions reflect a response to changes in both costs rather than a response to changes in the cost of capital alone. Since the theoretical response of the regulated firm to changes in the two parameters differs, as we shall shortly show, the behavior reported in the cited works does not offer a clear test of our proposition.

An implication of the theory that seems rather perverse is that if the government wishes to affect investment in the public utility sector, then the appropriate policy involves changes in the fair return rather than reliance on manipulation of the cost of borrowing. Such a policy prescription calls for an increase of the fair return and hence the granting of even higher profits during an

---

[c]This conclusion can be misleading to the extent that a cost of capital increase reflects a nominal rather than a real increase in costs. The socially efficient path presumably reflects the true productivity of the two factors.

[d]See, for example, Kuh and Meyer (1963), Jorgenson (1965), and Nadiri (1972).

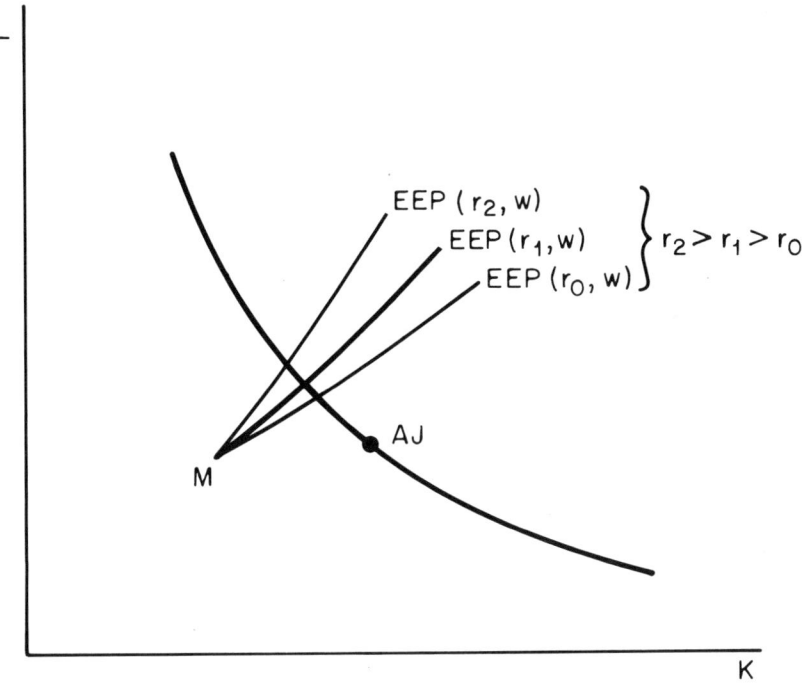

Figure 8-2. Inefficiency Worsens with Increase in Cost of Capital.

inflationary period and a lowering of the fair return with its associated reduction in profits during a recession.

Note, finally, that our analysis has shown that the optimal response to an increase in cost of capital entails no price increases. The incidence of the rise in interest rate is entirely upon the owners of the firm, with none of the cost shifted to the consumers. This conclusion contradicts the usual view in the folklore which holds that regulated firms are guaranteed a fair return, and hence can always shift the burden of any cost increase to the consumer.

The result also seems at odds with the price increase requests that have been made by virtually every public utility since the early 1970s. One explanation of these requests resides in our assumption that the fair return remains larger than the actual cost of capital even when the cost of capital increases. This assumption was almost undoubtedly violated in the late 1960s and early 1970s when nominal costs of borrowing reached unprecedented levels. In the short run, at least, firms were having to pay more for their new capital requirements than they were able to earn under the regulatory constraint. Under these circumstances, price increase requests clearly do not violate our proposition. Moreover, during this period there were inflationary cost increases in $w$ and $c$. Such increases, as we will see in the next section, do necessitate that the regulated firm raise its prices.

In the longer run, regulators may recognize that the real value of $s$ has in fact fallen; and, therefore, they may increase the fair return. In such a situation, the firm may be able eventually to pass some or all of the increased costs along to the consumer. The precise incidence will depend on the new $(s - r)$ differential as contrasted with the old.

### Increase in the Acquisition Cost of Capital

*Standard Qualitative Response*

We might be tempted to think that changes in the acquisition cost of capital have the same qualitative effects as changes in the market cost of borrowing, but as Table 8-1 shows, the results are not the same. Instead, the regulated firm responds to changes in the acquisition cost, $c$, in precisely the same qualitative fashion as does the unregulated firm; the increase in the one factor cost, while the other remains unchanged, causes a firm to substitute the relatively cheaper factor for the more expensive one. Thus, a rise in the acquisition cost causes the usage of capital to decrease. Moreover, overall costs of the firm are increased by a rise in acquisition cost so that profitability declines.

*Proposition 8.2: If there is an increase in the acquisition cost of capital, the regulated firm reduces its use of capital. Furthermore, at the new equilibrium, society gets less output, and the firm less profit.*

*Proof:* By the usual methods (see proofs of Propositions 6.3 and 6.4), it can be shown that

$$\frac{dK}{dc} = \frac{sK}{R_K - sc} < 0,$$

$$\frac{dL}{dc} = -\frac{R_{LK}}{R_{LL}}\frac{dK}{dc} = ?, \frac{dq}{dc} = R'(q_K q_{LL} - q_L q_{KL})\frac{sK}{R_{LL}(R_K - sc)} < 0, \text{ and}$$

$$\frac{d\pi}{dc} = (s-r)(c\frac{dK}{dc} + K) = \frac{(s-r)[csK + K(R_K - sc)]}{R_K - sc} = \frac{(s-r)KR_K}{R_K - sc} < 0.$$

*End of Proof*

A graphical interpretation is given in Figure 8.3. When the acquisition cost of capital increases from $c$ to $c + \epsilon$, the constraint ray shifts upward by an amount $(s - r)\epsilon K$. For any fixed level of $K$ the profit possibility contour shifts down by $r\epsilon K$. The new intersection takes place at a profit-capital combination $\pi_2 K_2$, which involves a lower profit and a smaller quantity of capital than those at the initial equilibrium, $\pi_1 K_1$.

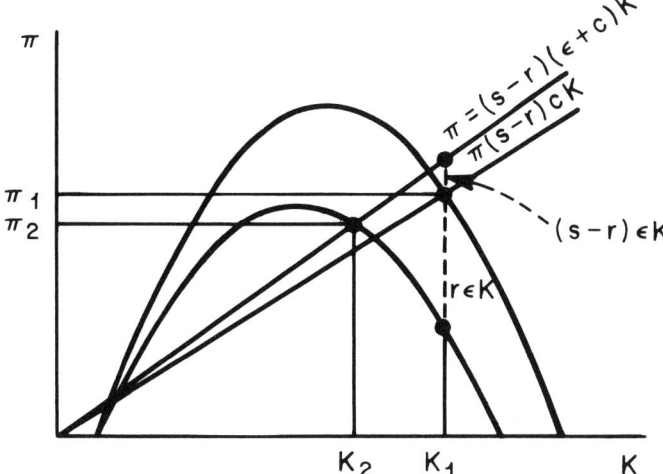

**Figure 8-3.** Profit Goes Down with Increase in Acquisition Cost of Capital.

*Contradiction of Conspiracy Conclusion*

Proposition 8.2 directly contradicts the oft-cited Westfield[2] result that a regulated firm can find it profitable to collude with the suppliers of its capital equipment. Instead, we have found that the regulated firm must lose from any conspiracy to increase price. It is naturally pertinent to investigate the source of such a discrepancy in conclusions.

Only two circumstances, neither of which are ordinarily assumed in a rate-of-return model, lead in Westfield's own analysis to the answers he reports. His first suggestion is that the firm is operating on a falling portion of the curve generated by $\max_L R(L,K) - wL$, that is, where

$$\frac{d}{dK}\left[\max_L R(L,K) - wL\right] = \frac{d}{dK}\left[R(\bar{L},K) - w\bar{L}\right] = R_K + (R_{\bar{L}} - w)\frac{d\bar{L}}{dK} < 0.$$

Since in a rate-of-return model $R_L = w$ at the optimal point, this reduces to the condition $R_K = R' q_K < 0$. However, by Proposition 5.2, $R' > 0$. Hence, Westfield's assumption reduces to $q_K < 0$, which means that capital is so redundant as to "cause physical output to decline."[3] This does not seem likely in an industry whose product is essentially a rental of capacity. Emery has recently put the matter in this way:

With the specified process function and acquisition price function for generating equipment, a utility has a virtually unlimited source of investment alternatives which offer a positive marginal physical product for dollar units of capital, and a Knightian Region III will not be reached in steam-electric generation.[4]

Westfield's second explanation relies on the existence in some states of reproductive or fair value methods of evaluating the rate base. Such methods attempt to reflect in the value of the rate base the costs required to duplicate the system today rather than the original cost. The incentive to pay inflated prices is easily explained: by paying a price premium now to acquire capital, some or all of the previous equipment can be evaluated at the new higher cost. The original AJ model ignores the reproduction cost methods; it implicitly assumes that original cost methods are being used; that is, in the AJ model, the current rate base appearing in the constraint is precisely the same as the current capital base in the firm's objective function. Emery has empirically tested to see if reproductive cost methods contribute to a Westfield effect, and has found that

empirical evidence, though mixed in nature, does not allow acceptance of a hypothesis that utilities subject to some form of reproduction cost valuation paid higher acquisition prices for similar plants than did utilities subject to some form of actual cost valuation.[5]

A third explanation of Westfield's assertion that the firm may want to pay a price premium for acquiring capital has been offered by Dayan.[6] Dayan points out that free capital would not be financially attractive to the regulated firm since the right-hand side of the constraint $\pi = (s - r)cK$ would then equal zero. Thus, as he goes on to show, if the firm could choose the value of $c$, it would pick some intermediate value, $c^*$, which is the value of $c$ such that operations are increased to the point where the marginal physical product of capital is just equal to zero, that is, at which $q_K = 0$. If the value of $c$ that is the current price in the marketplace exceeds $c^*$, then the results we have described hold: the firm's best policy is to keep $c$ as small as possible. However, should the actual cost, $c$, encountered in reality be smaller than $c^*$, then Westfield's results hold. The firm will find it more profitable to pay the price premium for capital rather than to substitute capital for labor or to adopt an actual physical padding of the rate base.

The outcome thus depends on the technology of the regulated firm, and the minimum cost at which capital can be supplied to it. If empirical studies show, as Emery[7] indicates is likely, that the marginal physical product of capital is positive in the industry, then the Westfield result cannot hold; otherwise, it may be valid. In sum, a careful study of the Westfield analysis reveals that his conspiracy conclusions are not valid under the standard interpretation of the AJ model, and only can arise in circumstances which do not seem particularly applicable or appropriate for the regulated public utilities.[e]

---

[e]There is, however, a case where it may be profitable to inflate acquisition cost. This occurs in a model of the regulated firm that is integrated vertically. Dayan (1972) has shown that, where the earlier stage of production is the supplier of the capital input, the firm may have an incentive to inflate the price of that input rather than to misallocate via the use of an overly capital intensive technology.

## Changes in the Wage Rate

*Formal Derivation*

By a reasoning analogous to that used to analyze the role of the acquisition cost of capital, we might expect that if the wage rate increases, the amount of labor used will decline, and that the optimal output and the level of profit will also decline. It is rather curious that under rate-of-return regulation, the result concerning the labor input cannot be derived, but both the output and profit conclusions do follow. Furthermore, when wages go up, capital usage can be shown unequivocally to go down, a result which would not always hold true in the absence of regulation.

*Proposition 8.3: If there is an increase in the wage rate, the capital usage and profit are reduced under rate-of-return regulation. If capital is not an inferior input, output is also reduced.*

*Proof:* By the usual manipulations, it can readily be shown that

$$\frac{dK}{dw} = \frac{L}{R_K - sc} < 0, \frac{dL}{dw} = -\frac{R_{LK}}{R_{LL}}\frac{dK}{dw} + \frac{1}{R_{LL}} = ?$$

$$\frac{dq}{dw} = \frac{[R'(q_K q_{LL} - q_L q_{LK})L + q_L(R_K - sc)]}{R_{LL}(R_K - sc)} < 0$$

and $\dfrac{d\pi}{dw} = (s-r)c\dfrac{dK}{dw} < 0.$

*End of Proof*

Figure 8-4a illustrates graphically what has happened. If the wage rate increases from $w$ to $w + \epsilon$, the increased costs cause profit to decrease by an amount $\epsilon L$ for any given level of capital usage. However, the constraining ray is not altered in the slightest. Therefore, capital and profit must both be lower.

*Economic Significance*

In the case of wage-rate changes, the derived differences in behavior between the AJ and monopoly firm do not in general seem sufficiently pronounced to be useful in empirical analysis. Indeed, if $R_{LK} > 0$, the signs become identical. However, McNicol[8] has recently argued that an analysis based on derived demands may be of some help in distinguishing effective from ineffective regulation. He uses the "labor-requirements" formulation, and obtains results for partial derivatives rather than for the total derivatives shown here.

The chief interest of the comparative statics analysis for the wage rate lies in its connection with fuel and other automatic escalator clauses that have been instituted in many electric and gas utilities.[f] These clauses, which apply to fuel

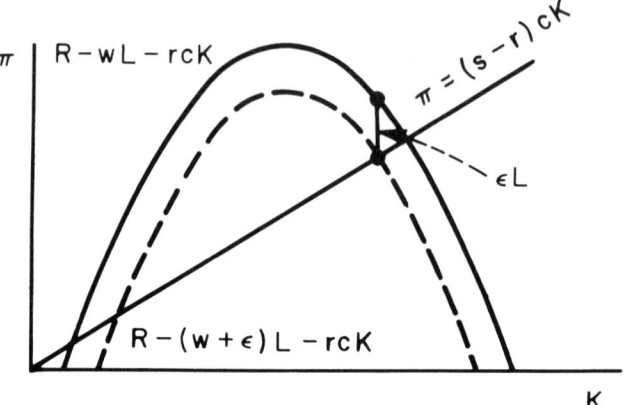

(a) Increase in Wage Rate

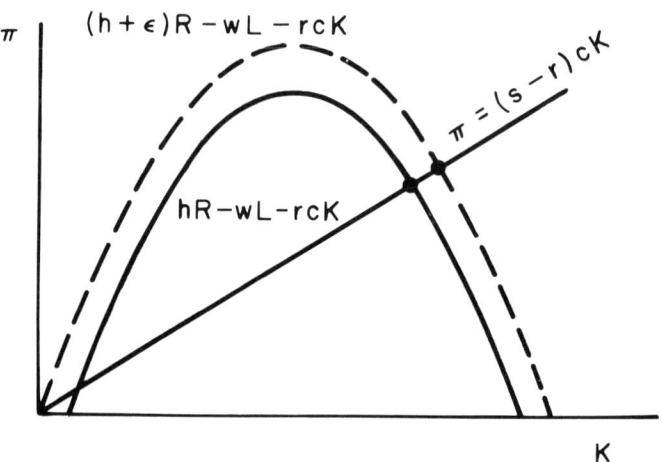

(b) Neutral Technical Change

**Figure 8-4.** Increases in Wage Rate and Technical Change.

---

[f]See Yoon (1973).

and other materials' costs that presumably are included in the expense term, serve to alleviate some of the hardships caused by regulatory lags during periods of rising costs. Without the automatic adjustment clauses, there are two sources of lower profits: (1) the reduction in profits that, as Table 8-1 indicates, will remain even if prices are adjusted optimally from the firm's point of view and (2) the delay in the institution of that price change. With the adjustment clause, there is still some erosion of profit; however, the erosion is alleviated by the increased speed with which a portion of the cost increases can be passed on to the consumer.

There are some measures which can help to offset the profit squeeze felt by the firm during periods of rising costs. The most obvious is technical change.[g] To illustrate the point, define output as $Q = hq(L,K)$, where $h$ is a measure of the degree of Hicks-Neutral technological change. The corresponding comparative statics results for capital and profit, derived by the usual methods, are

$$\frac{dK}{dh} = \frac{-R'q}{R_K - sc} > 0 \text{ and } \frac{d\pi}{dh} = (s-r)c\frac{dK}{dh} > 0 \text{ so that capital usage and profit}$$

both rise with an increase in $h$. Graphically, as a result of technological improvement, the profit possibility curve shifts upward while the constraining ray remains in place. The resulting capital increase and increase in profitability are apparent in Figure 8-4b.

Although we have not quantitatively compared the incentives to innovate of the regulated versus unregulated firm, we have at least established that the rate-of-return ceiling does not always stifle the incentive to innovate. The regulated firm finds that, in a period of rising costs, its profits decline. Since the decline occurs with increases in any of the cost parameters, the firm not only has an incentive to avoid payment of inflated costs, but also will seek out cost-reducing innovations. These innovations then offer the firm the possibility of restoring profits to their previous level. The constraint fixes the rate of return, but profit does not remain fixed; instead, it increases if technological change increases the efficiency of the productive factors.

## Changes in Tax Parameters

Table 8-1 summarizes the partial equilibrium response of the regulated firm to changes in corporate income tax and to changes in property tax rates. As was discussed in Chapter 6, tax increases always serve to decrease the capital usage and output of the firm as well as to reduce its profits. In fact, the tax increases play essentially the same qualitative role as would an increase in one of the factor costs. Table 8-1 also shows that changes in the income tax rate have implications for the effectively regulated firm that are different than those for its unregulated or ineffectively regulated counterpart.

---

[g]See Westfield (1971a). Westfield also treats a markup and a price ceiling method of constraint, and Harrod neutral (L-augmenting) and K-augmenting technological change. See Meyer and Straszheim (1971) and Haring and Humphrey (1971) for some other discussions of public utility regulation during inflationary periods.

# 9 Rising Cost of Capital

## Introduction and Summary

The inclusion of a rising cost of capital in an AJ model constitutes an important departure from the case in which the cost of capital is assumed to be constant as the firm's demand for capital increases. We find, for example, that the firm's optimal policy may be to purchase capital up to the point where its marginal cost just equals the fair return. This behavior differs from that in the AJ model, where fair return is always larger than cost of capital. The behavior does, however, agree with the regulatory folklore which argues that the fair return often equals rather than exceeds the cost of capital. Furthermore, since the marginal cost is above the average cost, the constraint does permit positive profit.

The rising cost of capital model provides an explanation for several other apparent discrepancies between the behavior usually predicted in the Averch-Johnson theory and that which is often proclaimed to be evident in the regulated sector of the economy. In particular, there will be a range of values of the fair return over which the firm will actually find it profitable to reduce (rather than increase as in the AJ model) its demand for capital as the fair return is lowered. The firm's decisions within this range can explain why production may end up in the inelastic region of the revenue curve (as opposed to the elastic region as in the other models of regulation). Operation off the production frontier is also a possibility, which contrasts with the usual AJ result that misallocation is always preferred to any padding of the rate base.

## Components of the Model

### Cost-of-Capital Schedule

The Averch-Johnson model assumes that the supply curve of capital is horizontal. However, we shall consider here the case where the marginal cost of capital schedule is upward sloping. The plausibility of such a slope is typically argued by Baumol as follows:

---

[a]The chapter is co-authored with T. Austin Finch; see Bailey and Finch (1973); see also Finch (1972).

The capital market that faces any one company is usually far from perfect. As the company's demand for funds increases, it is likely to find that the cost it must pay for them goes up. The amount of expansion that can be financed out of retained earnings is limited. Too large an issue of new stocks or bonds will drive down the price significantly, and financial institutions may place absolute limits on the amounts they are willing to lend or will increase their lending only if they are offered extremely attractive terms.[1,b]

Since the demand for public utility services is typically growing and since the firms must in each year raise a substantial portion of their new capital requirements from external sources, the rising cost of capital schedule would seem appropriate.[c]

Such a schedule has been considered in nontechnical analyses by both Bower and Shepherd.[2] Informalizing their work, we shall portray the cost of capital as rising with the size of the capital stock. This method at least approximates the preferred approach of portraying the cost of capital as rising with the amount invested in a given period. The model is

$$\text{Maximize } \pi = R(L,K) - wL - r(K)K \qquad (9.1)$$
$$L, K$$

where $r(K)$ = average cost of capital with $\dfrac{dr}{dK} > 0$. For simplicity, we assume that the acquisition cost of capital, $c$, equals unity.

The first-order conditions for (9.1) are

$$R_L = w$$

$$R_K = MC_K$$

where $MC_K$ = marginal cost of capital = $r(K) + r'(K)K > 0$, so that the quantity of funds which a profit-maximizing firm will seek is determined by the intersection of its marginal revenue product of capital curve with its marginal cost of capital curve.

By taking the ratio of the first-order conditions, it becomes clear that the

---

[b]See also Weston and Brigham (1972), p. 324 for a similar argument.

[c]We thus portray the cost of capital schedule as rising because of higher transactions costs of floatation as more borrowing is attempted at a particular moment of time. Not treated are increases arising from increasing costs of new issues over time, nor increases (if any) stemming from changes in the debt/equity structure of the firm. [See Modigliani and Miller (1958), Baumol and Malkiel (1967), and Miller and Modigliani (1966)]. Care must be exercised in order to avoid confusing the assumption of a rising cost of capital schedule for a particular firm with the idea that smaller firms might be riskier than larger firms, and hence have larger risk premiums on any source of external financing. [See Archer and Faerber (1966)].

efficient expansion path is not, as in the constant cost case, traced out by $\frac{q_K}{q_L} = \frac{r}{w}$, but rather is given by

$$\frac{q_K}{q_L} = \frac{r(K)}{w} + \frac{Kr'}{w} = \frac{MC_K}{w}. \qquad (9.2)$$

Thus, the expansion path is based on marginal rather than average factor costs whenever these two quantities diverge. Equation (9.2) says that a firm that faces a rising-cost-of-capital schedule has an expansion path which eventually becomes more labor intensive than that of a firm which faces the same initial factor costs but where $r$ remains constant. This follows immediately since the term $\frac{Kr'}{w} = 0$ in the constant cost of capital case. Thus, our intuition is correct: as capital becomes more expensive, the firm begins substituting labor for capital in its optimal production decision.[d]

Another change caused by the rising cost of capital assumption is that isocost lines (such as those in Figure 2-1) now become isocost curves which are concave to the origin. The usual sorts of interior tangencies with isoquants still however take place.

*Regulatory Constraint*

The top portion of Figure 9-1 shows that with rising capital costs a regulatory constraint can serve to limit the firm's willingness to raise capital funds. For a low fair-return value such as $s_1$, the added cost of a unit of capital is only less than the added return the regulator permits the firm to earn on this capital in the range, $0 < K < K_1$. For $K_1 < K < K_1^*$, the added cost exceeds the added return permitted by the regulator, but the average return $s_1$, is still larger than the average cost of capital. For quantity of capital $K > K_1^*$, the firm finds its fair return is below the average cost, and borrowing does not take place, at least in theory.

Because the $MC_K$ curve is rising and the fair return curves are horizontal lines, the intersection between the fair return and cost of capital corresponds to successively larger quantities of capital as the fair return is increased. This is depicted in the top portion of Figure 9-1. We might think, therefore, that as the constraint is loosened, the firm will increase its capital use, which is precisely the opposite of the corresponding conclusion for the usual AJ analysis.

---

[d]Notice that if the market cost of labor were rising with increased usage, we would obtain a condition similar to (9.2) only with $MC_L$ replacing $w$ in the denominator.

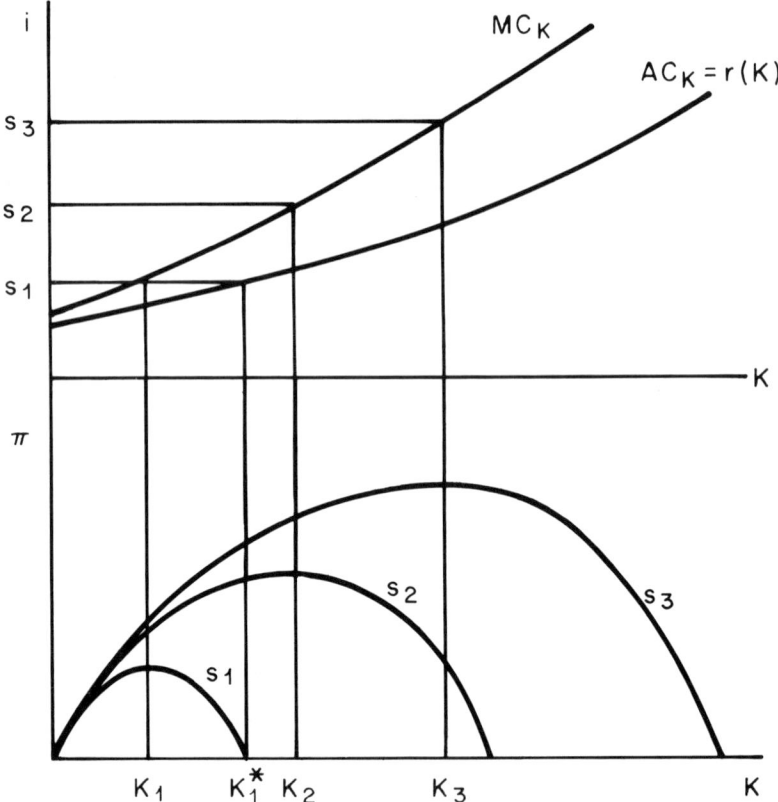

**Figure 9-1.** Rising Cost of Capital Leads to Hill-Shaped Constraint Curves.

In order to explore what happens, we construct the ceiling profit curve for the rising-cost-of-capital model. The rate-of-return constraint is

$$\pi = [s - r(K)]K. \tag{9.3}$$

Because the term $[s - r(K)]$ is not constant, the constraint locus in the $\pi K$-plane no longer takes the usual AJ form of a ray emanating from the origin. Instead if we

Maximize $[s - r(K)]K$
$K$

the first-order condition is

$$s = MC_K. \tag{9.4}$$

so that the constraint ceiling reaches a maximum at precisely that $K$ at which the fair return line intersects the marginal cost of capital curve. This is shown in Figure 9-1 by the light vertical lines connecting the top and bottom parts of the graph. Furthermore, the ceiling profit curve traced by (9.3) starts at the origin, and falls again to the origin at that $K$ at which $s = AC_K = r(K)$.[e] Figure 9-1 also shows that the ceiling profit curves always lie completely within one another as $s$ is lowered. The lack of intersection reflects the obvious property that the higher the fair rate of return the higher the total profit at any level of $K$.

Equation (9.4) indicates that the marginal cost of raising new capital may end up equaling the fair return. Yet, since the marginal cost of capital is higher than the average cost, it is possible that profit is positive.

It is tempting in looking at Figure 9-1 to think that the firm will always choose that quantity of capital at which Equation (9.4) holds. However, this is not always true; the reason is that the regulated firm's solution occurs at a point of intersection between the ceiling constraint and a curve representing the firm's profit possibilities. To find that equilibrium point, we must overlay on Figure 9-1 the information given by the firm's profit hill.

*Profit Hill*

The top part of Figure 9-2 includes the projection of the profit hill into the $\pi K$-plane. This hill will not be identical to the one for the case in which the cost of capital is constant, but it will have roughly the same shape and properties. The hill is constructed by choosing for each level of capital, that quantity of labor which yields the highest profit to the firm. Thus, labor usage is different at different points on this curve (see, for instance, Figure 5-2). Notice that the profit hill can be drawn without any information concerning the level of the fair return $s$, since the hill reflects only market and technological relationships. The other curves drawn in the top part of Figure 9-2 correspond to the regulatory constraints at various levels of the fair rate of return, $s_1$, $s_2$, and $s_3$.

**Graphical Analysis**

*Three Cases*

When the profit is effectively determined by the fair return $s_3$, the firm finds operation at the intersection of the profit hill and the $s_3$ curve to be its optimal alternative. As might be expected, the analysis in this case is no different qualitatively than that in the AJ model. When the ceiling reaches its maximum before its intersection with the profit hill, as happens when the fair rate of

---
[e]Note that if the cost of capital curve rises slowly, then the intersection given by (9.4) occurs at larger levels of $K$ than if the cost of capital curve has a steeper slope.

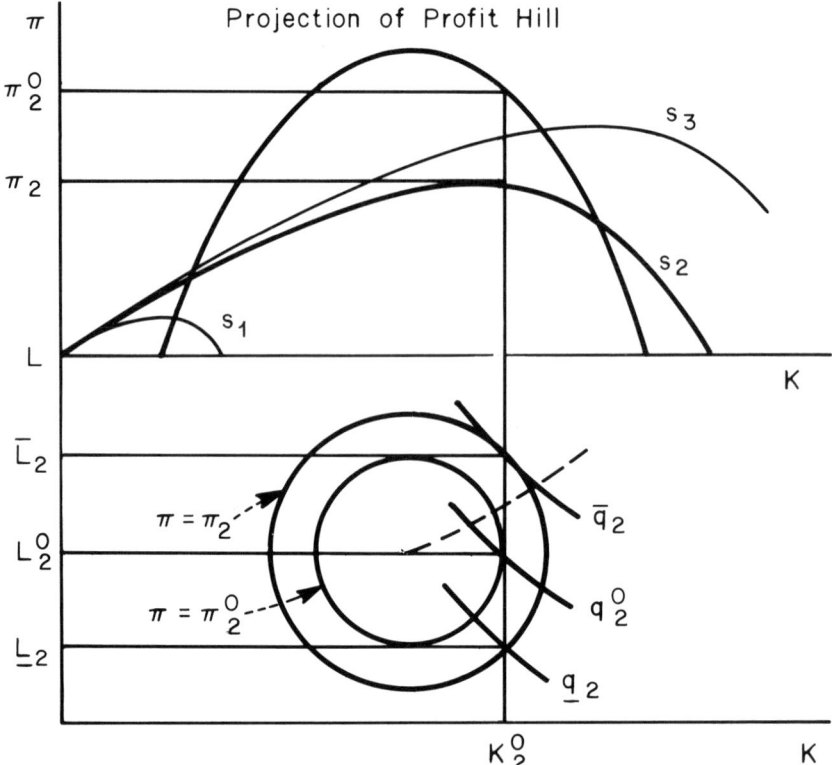

**Figure 9-2.** Indeterminacy in Labor Usage and Output Level.

return is at $s_1$, the best alternative open to the firm is again to produce at the intersection of the two curves. However, this now occurs in the falling part of the constraint curve determined by $s_1$. A third possibility is that the fair rate is set at a level such as $s_2$. Constrained profit is then maximized at $\pi_2$ which does not occur at an intersection of the constraint curve with the profit hill. Since $\pi_2$ lies below the maximum profit which is achievable at the level of capital $K_2^0$, there is some slack which must be absorbed if the system is to be in equilibrium.

*Indeterminacy in Operations*

The bottom portion of Figure 9-2 shows one way in which such absorption can take place. The $\pi = \pi_2$ contour in the $LK$-plane gives all combinations of capital and labor which can yield precisely the profit $\pi_2$. We know from the top portion of the figure that with the constraint $s = s_2$ the firm's optimal policy is to use $K_2^0$

worth of capital. Then, from the bottom part of Figure 9-2, there are two possible values of labor, $\overline{L}_2$ and $\underline{L}_2$ which yield profit $\pi_2$. Neither of these involves the use of labor $L_2^0$ which yields the maximum profit $\pi_2^0$ that is possible when $K = K_2^0$. One of these quantities of labor yields an output $q_2$ smaller than that if $L_2^0$ were used, and the other yields the larger output $\overline{q}_2$. The firm is indifferent between these two alternatives if its only objective is profits. If output maximization is a secondary objective, then the regulated firm produces the higher output $\overline{q}_2$. We know from the usual AJ analysis that $q_2^0$ is in the elastic portion of the demand curve, but there is no reason to suppose that $\overline{q}_2$ is always in the elastic region. The rising-cost-of-capital model can therefore explain the occurrence in the regulated sector of demands which are inelastic. This is an especially surprising result since all the other models, including those of symmetric as well as asymmetric regulation, limit demand to at most unit elasticity. It is an important result because it permits us to offer a theoretical explanation for behavior patterns which have been noted in the utility industries. In particular, we can explain how a regulatory model may be compatible with studies, such as that by Fisher and Kaysen,[3] which assert that demand for electricity may be price inelastic.

Along with the indeterminacy in the output selected, there is also an indeterminacy in resource allocation. This was first noticed by Bower who constructed a numerical example of a firm facing a rising-cost-of-capital schedule. He found that when

cost of capital rises with investment, overutilization of capital may not accompany rate-of-return regulation. In this case, paradoxically, a company, with prices regulated to permit some allowed return, may be inefficient because it uses less capital than it should.[4]

In terms of Figure 9-2, we know from the AJ analysis that $K_2^0 L_2^0$ is an overly capital intensive pair of inputs, and so $K_2^0 \underline{L}_2$ is also. However, the point $K_2^0 \overline{L}_2$ might represent either minimum-cost production, or an overly capital intensive technology, or (as is actually pictured) an overly labor intensive technology.

Figure 9-3 shows a three dimensional representation of the relationship between the $s_2$ constraint and the profit hill. It is seen that the constraint surface lies everywhere below the maximum of the profit surface. The lines parallel to the $L$-axis reflect the property that for any particular level of $K$ there is a maximum level of permitted profit which is the same over all $L$. The line on the constraint surface which has highest profit corresponds as in Figure 9-2 to capital usage $K_2^0$. The two levels of labor use lying on the outer surface of the profit hill are then $\underline{L}_2$ in the front, and $\overline{L}_2$ in the rear. The dashed line connecting these two points goes through the interior of the profit hill. This dashed line can be used, as Figure 9-4 indicates, to give another way of looking at the options open to the firm.

Figure 9-4 is constructed by passing a plane parallel to the $\pi K$-axis through

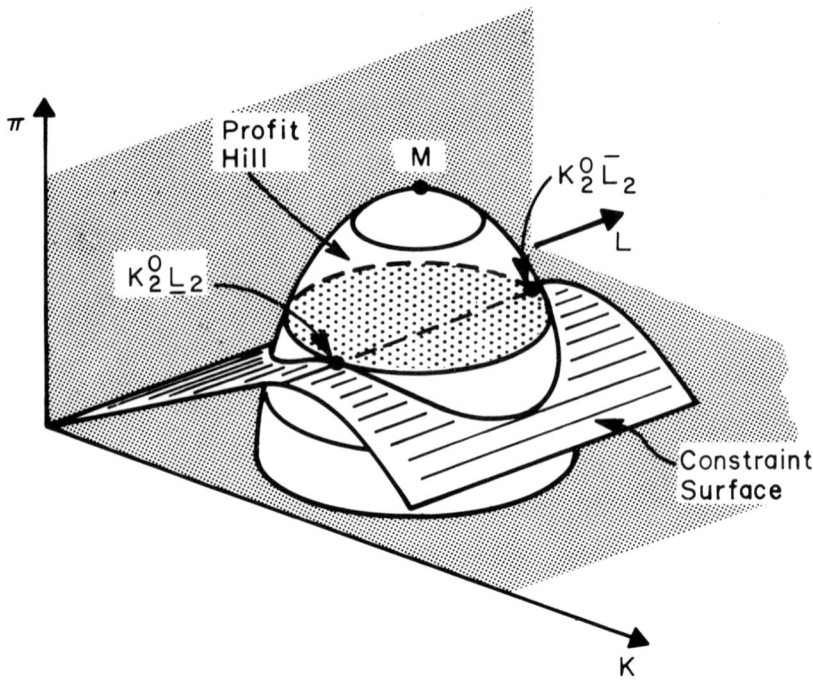

**Figure 9-3.** Profit Hill and Constraint Surface for Rising Cost of Capital Model.

the profit hill at $K = K_2^0$. The hill is thus a projection of the profit hill on the $\pi L$-axis at this quantity of capital. The isoprofit contour $\pi = \pi_2$ is a horizontal line parallel to the $L$ axis; as before, $\underline{L}_2$ and $\overline{L}_2$ are the amounts of productive labor that can be combined with a fully productive $K_2^0$, while permitting the firm to meet the constraint. If the firm chooses to employ some other quantity of labor, such as $L_2^0$, then it can absorb the excess profit $(\pi_2^0 - \pi_2)$ by some form of wasteful endeavor. This could include purely wasteful use of labor or of some of the capital in $K_2^0$, which would then constitute a degree of padding or "gold-plating." Thus, the usual theorem that waste is never optimal under rate-of-return regulation turns out to be untrue when the cost of capital is rising rather than constant.

The idea that the firm is willing to engage in waste even though these expenditures do not increase the maximum permitted profit seems to run counter to Proposition 3.6 in which if $G_x = 0$, the firm's optimal policy entailed no waste. However, the reason waste is a possibility in our present discussion is that the constraint is not rising in any productive or wasteful variable at the optimal solution to the regulated system. As a result, the firm can waste without suffering any loss in permitted profits.

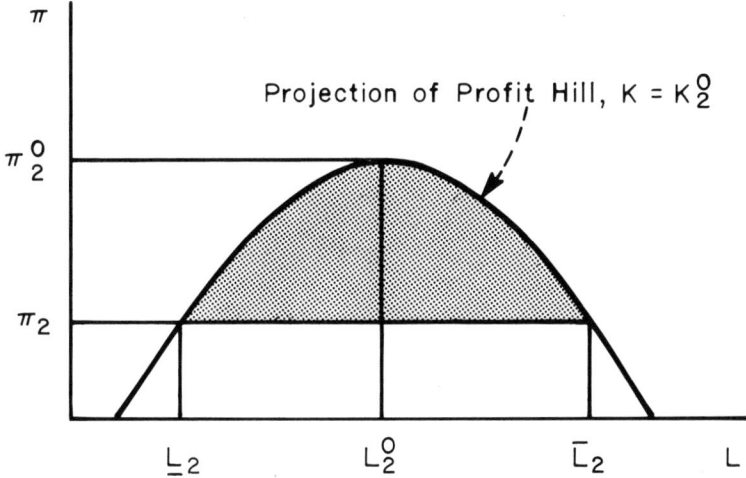

**Figure 9-4.** Possibility of Waste when Fair Return Equals Marginal Cost of Capital.

*Comparative Statics for the Fair Return Parameter*

By considering the whole range of levels of the fair return, we can get what amounts to a comparative statics result indicating the change in equilibrium behavior as $s$ is varied. Figure 9-5 summarizes the conclusions. The dotted lines indicate the capital rate-of-return pairs and the capital-profit pairs respectively, as the rate of return is lowered from the monopoly level $s^M$ to the break-even level $s^B$. There are two intermediate levels of fair return, denoted $\bar{s}$ and $\underline{s}$ which prove to be crucial for the analysis. By definition $\bar{s}$ is that fair return at which the top of the constraint curve occurs precisely at the rightmost intersection of the profit hill and constraint curve (see the lower part of Figure 9-5). There will always be such an $\bar{s}$ if the cost of capital increases over any portion of the profitable region of operation. By definition $\underline{s}$ is that fair return at which the top of the constraint curve occurs at the leftmost intersection of the profit hill and constraint curve. There need not always be an $\underline{s}$ as can happen, for example, if the profit hill intersects the $K$-axis at the origin.

If the fair return is started out at the monopoly level $s^M$ and lowered toward $\bar{s}$, the firm's profits are reduced from $\pi^M$ to $\bar{\pi}$ and capital use increases from $K^M$ to $\bar{K}$. Thereafter, as the fair return is lowered from $\bar{s}$ to $\underline{s}$ the firm's most profitable policy is to operate at the topmost point of the constraint curve. In this range, profit continues to be reduced from $\bar{\pi}$ to $\underline{\pi}$, but now capital use (and eventually output) will be reduced as well. The optimal policy with respect to capital use is thus reversed in this range of fair returns from what it was

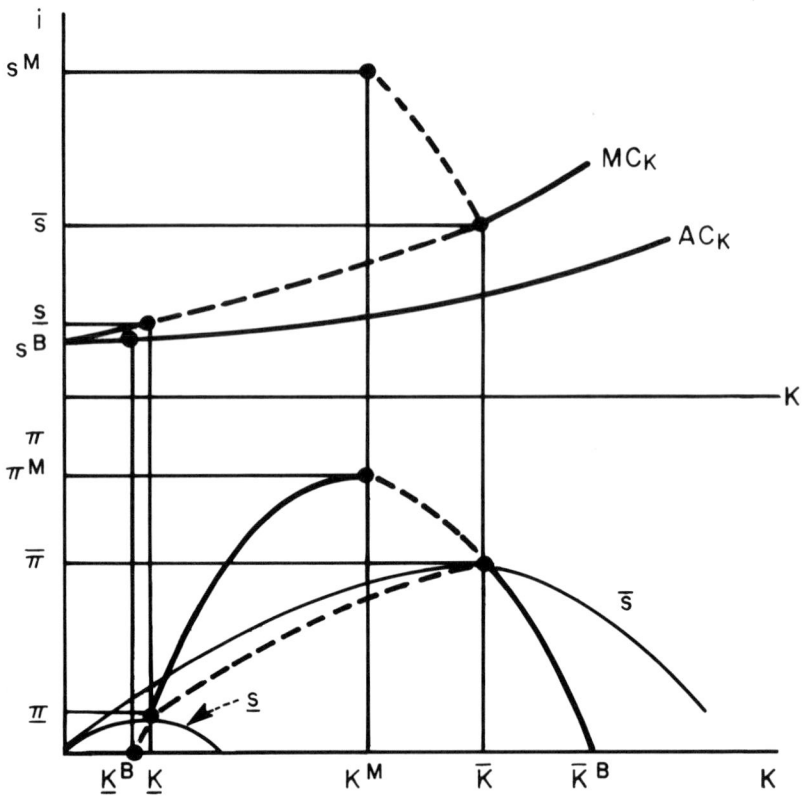

**Figure 9-5.** Comparative Statics for the Fair Return Parameter.

in the $s^M$ to $\bar{s}$ range.[f] Notice from the upper part of Figure 9-5 that the range $\underline{s} < s < \bar{s}$ is characterized by the firm's purchasing precisely that amount of capital at which the fair return is just equated to the marginal cost of capital, so that Equation (9.4) holds.

It is thus clear why regulated firms might not enthusiastically embrace overly capital intensive methods of operation.[g] Over the range $\underline{s} < s < \bar{s}$, the constraint is seen to limit the employment of capital to some prespecifiable amount. The capital is purchased up to the point where its marginal cost

---

[f]In his analysis of a rising cost of capital model for the regulated firm, Shepherd notes the changeover in behavior in which the firm's demand for capital decreases after some degree of tightness in the fair return constraint. However, he missed the precise conditions under which the changeover takes place, believing that the $\dfrac{dK}{ds} < 0$ result would hold so "long as permitted rate of return does not fall below the average cost of capital" [(1966), p. 350].

[g]See, for example, Corey (1971).

exceeds the allowed return. However, in this region the firm's demand for capital is always lower than the supply of capital it could actually draw upon. Hence, the apparent constraint on capital from the point of view of the firm's actions is not really an actual constraint on its supply of funds.

As the fair return is lowered below the level $\underline{s}$, the firm purchases capital at prices in excess of the obtainable return until it is gradually driven out of business with return $s^B$ and capital level $K^B$. The rising cost-of-capital model thus appears to provide quite a different description of a firm's behavior as it approaches bankruptcy than does the AJ model. In the AJ model, the firm keeps growing larger as the permitted return is lowered, and it is forced out of business at $\overline{K}^B$. In contrast, in the rising cost-of-capital model the firm is unable to attract that amount of new capital on profitable terms so that it is forced to cut back its operations before eventually being forced into bankruptcy. It is noteworthy that this second behavior pattern seems to agree far more closely than the first with observed behavior under regulation. Certainly the railroads and, more recently, the public utilities, seem to have lowered the quality of their service and, in some cases, have obviously tried to reduce its quantity when permitted earnings were exceptionally low.

## Mathematical Analysis

### Behavioral Properties

In a rate-of-return model in which the marginal cost of capital is rising, we have seen that the optimal response to regulation is different for different ranges of the fair return. The properties we have described are summaried in Table 9-1. For example, the top entry in the first column means that when the fair return exceeds the value $\overline{s}$, then the analysis concludes that $s > MC_K$. We now explain the various entries in this table somewhat more rigorously.

**Table 9-1**
**Rising Cost of Capital Theorems**

| Size of Fair Return | | | | | Conclusions of Analysis | | | |
|---|---|---|---|---|---|---|---|---|
| | $s$ | $\lambda$ | $x$ | $MR$ | $\dfrac{-dL}{dK}$ | $\dfrac{d\pi}{ds}$ | $\dfrac{dK}{ds}$ | $\dfrac{dq}{ds}$ |
| $s > \overline{s}$ | $> MC_K$ | $0 < \lambda < 1$ | 0 | $> 0$ | $< \dfrac{MC_K}{w}$ | + | − | − |
| $\underline{s} < s < \overline{s}$ | $= MC_K$ | $\lambda = 1$ | ? | ? | ? | + | + | ? |
| $s < \underline{s}$ | $< MC_K$ | $0 < \lambda < 1$ | 0 | $> 0$ | $> \dfrac{MC_K}{w}$ | + | + | + |

*AJ Region*

**Proposition 9.1:** *If the profit and constraint curves intersect in a rising portion of the constraint curve, $\bar{s} \leqq s \leqq s^M$, then the usual AJ propositions hold: the fair return exceeds the marginal cost of capital, the Lagrange multiplier lies between 0 and 1, operation off the production frontier is unprofitable, the demand curve is elastic at the solution point, the firm is too capital intensive in its resource allocation, and as s is lowered profit decreases but capital and output increase.*

*Proof:* A rising cost of capital version of the AJ model is

$$\text{Maximize } \pi = R(L,K) - wL - r(K)K - x$$
$$L, K, x$$

$$\text{Subject to } \pi \leqq [s - r(K)]K$$

with Kuhn-Tucker conditions

$$\phi_L: \quad (R_L - w)(1 - \lambda) = 0 \tag{9.5}$$

$$\phi_K: \quad (R_K - MC_K)(1 - \lambda) + \lambda(s - MC_K) = 0 \tag{9.6}$$

$$\phi_x: \quad \lambda \leqq 1, \ x(1 - \lambda) = 0 \tag{9.7}$$

$$\phi_\lambda: \quad R(L,K) - wL - sK - x = 0. \tag{9.8}$$

If $\bar{s} < s < s^M$, so that $s > MC_K$, then $\lambda = 1$ would lead to a contradiction of the necessary condition (9.6). Thus, using (9.7), $\lambda < 1$. Also by (9.7), waste is then zero ($x = 0$). Equation (9.5) becomes $R_L = w$ so that demand is elastic ($R' > 0$). Dividing (9.5) by (9.6) we get the usual overcapitalization result, only now with $MC_K$ replacing the $r$ term in the numerator. Propositions 6.1, 6.2, and 6.4 about $\frac{dK}{ds}, \frac{d\pi}{ds}$, and $\frac{dq}{ds}$ go through precisely as in the previous analysis (see Chapter 6).

*End of Proof*

It is noteworthy that these are not the results we would obtain by assuming a rising cost of labor model (such as is suggested in footnote d) instead of a rising cost of capital model, that is

$$\text{Maximize } R(L,K) - w(L)L - rK - x$$
$$L, K, x$$

$$\text{Subject to } R(L,K) - w(L)L - x = sK.$$

In this case, the first-order conditions on labor and capital are

$$(1 - \lambda)(R_L - MC_L) = 0$$
$$(1 - \lambda)(R_K - r) + \lambda(s - r) = 0.$$

It is readily seen that $\lambda < 1$ always holds so that the comparative statics properties are similar qualitatively to those in the AJ model where, however, the marginal cost of labor $MC_L$ replaces the constant cost $w$.

*Interior Region*

*Proposition 9.2: If the maximum of the rising cost of capital constraint ceiling occurs in the interior of the profit region, $\underline{s} < s < \bar{s}$, then: the fair return equals the marginal cost of capital, the Lagrangian multiplier equals 1, the firm's best quantity of capital and its maximal profit are known (and decrease as s decreases), but there is an indeterminacy in the output level and resource allocation-waste combination that will be used to absorb the slack.*

*Proof:* If $\underline{s} < s < \bar{s}$, then $K$ is fixed by the condition $s = MC_K$ at some specific value, say, $K^0$. Equation (9.6) can no longer be used to rule out the $\lambda = 1$ case. Indeed, if $\lambda \neq 1$, then (9.5) and (9.6) require the monopoly values of $L$ and $K$, and thus will not in general be compatible with the $s = MC_K$ condition. Therefore, $\lambda = 1$.[h] When $\lambda = 1$, the usual rule for the allocation of labor, $R_L = w$, no longer necessarily holds, nor does the rule that operation off the production frontier is nonoptimal. Any combination of $L$ and $x$ which along with $K^0$ satisfies (9.8) can satisfy the system. Because of this indeterminacy in the firm's selection of $L$ and $x$, the resource allocation decision and the output decision cannot be derived, nor can we determine how much of the $K^0$ is productive and how much might be rate base padding. The comparative statics result $\frac{dK}{ds} > 0$ follows from the rising marginal cost of capital curve, and the $s = MC_K$ condition. The $\frac{d\pi}{ds} > 0$ result is obtained from $\frac{d\pi}{ds} = (s - MC_K)\frac{dK}{ds} + K$ which is positive when $s = MC_K$.

*End of Proof*

The existence of the region of fair returns over which the Lagrangian multiplier is one is perhaps the most intriguing analytical property of the

---

[h]Notice that the Chapter 3 graphical interpretation of the $\lambda = 1$ case agrees with that which we have here. However, the variable on the horizontal axis is capital (not output as in Chapter 3). Hence, if the constraint ceiling is shifted upward by one dollar, the firm will not change its use of capital in the slightest (though the adjustment in quantity of labor may be expected to result in an adjustment in output).

rising-cost-of-capital model. The point, of course, is that in this case the firm's output is limited effectively not by regulation but by the rising cost of funds. Thus, we are left with an interior maximum, despite the presence of regulation. Since there is an interior maximum, the model cannot of itself fix a unique $L$, $q$, or $x$, and the firm's flexibility in its decisions is evident.

The flexibility can provide the firm with a cushion against increases in some of the cost parameters. If there are lags in price adjustments, then the firm can rid itself of any waste or padding during the lag period (at least up to the limit of the available slack) and maintain profit at or near the maximum permitted level. This flexibility may be beneficial from society's viewpoint as well, since it may prevent a deterioration in quality of service such as might otherwise occur in response to cost increases.

Another interesting analytical property that holds for the range $\underline{s} < s < \overline{s}$ concerns the character of the indeterminacy. Some of the firm's decisions are determinate (the total amount of capital and the total achievable profit), but in other decisions the firm is offered a fair amount of flexibility. We see there can be justification for the traditional argument that rate-of-return regulation does not bind the firm totally, but that the leeway open to the firm is of a specific variety.

The leeway means that there is apt to be no optimal fair return in a rising cost of capital model. One result from Chapter 7 was that in the presence of regulatory lag, the regulator's optimal course of action was to set the fair rate equal to the firm's cost of capital. However, in a rising-cost-of-capital model there is no unique cost-of-capital figure. Hence, the earlier rule no longer works.

An obvious alternative is to select $s = \overline{s}$ as the optimal fair return, since that is the value yielding highest capital usage. However, at $s = \overline{s}$, the firm finds it profitable to adopt an overly capital intensive technology. By lowering the fair return to $s_2$ of Figure 9-2 say, the firm may find that a reduced use of capital is optimal and that profit is lower; on the other hand, if the firm has a secondary objective such as maximization of output, the firm may misallocate less and end up producing more output, as it may at point $\overline{L}_2 K_2^0$ in Figure 9-2. Hence, if one could be sure that the firm would respond to the indeterminacy by acting in the most socially beneficial way, then it would appear that $s = s_2$ can be a better choice than $s = \overline{s}$. However, if the firm responds in some other way, as well it might, then the $s = \overline{s}$ decision may be the better one.

It is noteworthy that there is an apparent lack of symmetry between the effects on the analysis of a downward graduation in the fair return as $K$ is increased, as against a gradual rise in the cost of capital as the use of $K$ is expanded. In Chapter 6, we showed that the use of fair rate-of-return function $\sigma(K)$ instead of fixed value $s$ had absolutely no effect on the AJ expansion path. However, in this chapter we have obtained a very different result. The difference is attributable in part to the fact that $r(K)$ appears in the profit function whereas $\sigma(K)$ does not (see, for instance, Chapters 6 and 8). However, if the graduated fair return function had been permitted to have a crest of the sort depicted in Figure 9-3, then there would have been a region of indeterminacy just as we have here.

*Low Return Regions*

*Proposition 9.3:* In a rising cost of capital model, if the profit curve intersects the falling portion of the constraint ceiling curve, $s < \underline{s}$, then: the fair return is lower than the marginal cost of capital but greater than the average cost of capital, the Lagrange multiplier lies between 0 and 1, marginal revenue is positive and waste is zero, the firm adopts an overly labor intensive technology using less capital than the unregulated monopolist, and output, capital, and profit all go down as s is reduced.

*Proof:* If $s < \underline{s}$, so that $s < MC_K$, then $\lambda = 1$ produces a contradiction in Equation (9.6) so that $0 < \lambda < 1$. Therefore, by the usual reasoning, waste is zero from (9.7) and demand is elastic from (9.5). The adoption of an overly labor intensive technology follows because of the change in sign in (9.6) since $s < MC_K$. We then combine $\dfrac{dK}{ds} = \dfrac{K}{R_K - s}$ with $R_K - s = \dfrac{(MC_K - s)}{1 - \lambda}$, which is positive. Thus, $\dfrac{dK}{ds} > 0$, and $\dfrac{d\pi}{ds} = \dfrac{K(R_K - MC_K)}{R_K - s} > 0$. The output result is obtained from

$$\frac{dq}{ds} = \frac{dL}{ds} q_L + \frac{dK}{ds} q_K = \frac{R'(-q_L q_{LK} + q_K q_{LL})K}{R_{LL}(R_K - s)} > 0$$

if capital is not an inferior input (see proof of Proposition 6.4).

*End of Proof*

# 10 Peak-Load Pricing Under Regulatory Constraint[a]

## Introduction and Summary

In both the general regulatory model and the AJ model, it has been assumed that the demand for the utility's services is uniform over time. In reality, of course, the demand for electricity or telecommunications varies over time of day and/or according to the season of the year. Some periods are busy with demand pressing on the productive capacity of the firm; other periods are off-peak with demand insufficient to utilize the capacity fully. In this chapter, we present a way of incorporating peak-load pricing into a model of regulatory constraint.

The peak-load model is analyzed for both the symmetric markup-on-cost constraint described in Chapters 3 and 4 and for the rate-of-return constraint. In the return-on-cost case, as might be expected, regulation leads to the same percentage decrease in marginal revenue for the peak as for the off-peak period. In contrast, the return-on-investment constraint does contribute a distortion in the treatment of peak as opposed to off-peak users.

In particular, for a simple version of the model, the price reductions brought about by rate-of-return regulation are received entirely by the peak users. Capacity is expanded from the profit-maximizing level toward (and perhaps even past) the welfare-maximizing level. Rate-of-return regulation thus provides an advantage in that it dampens the monopolistic tendency to restrict output, but it also entails the disadvantage that off-peak users may not share in the price reductions.

The parallel with the Averch-Johnson model is obvious. In that model, capacity is assumed to be fully utilized at all times: the incentive to employ more capital thus takes the form of substituting capital for labor along an isoquant. Under peak-load pricing, the additional capital does not appear in the form of an inefficient capital-labor ratio. Rather, the AJ effect shows up as an incentive to lower prices to the peak users whose demand presses on capacity rather than to off-peak users.

## Traditional Approach to Peak-Load Pricing

### Description of the Problem

Figure 10-1 depicts several aspects of the peak-load pricing problem. Figure 10-1a shows that when price does not vary with time, the demand pattern

---
[a]Much of the material in this chapter is taken from Bailey (1972a).

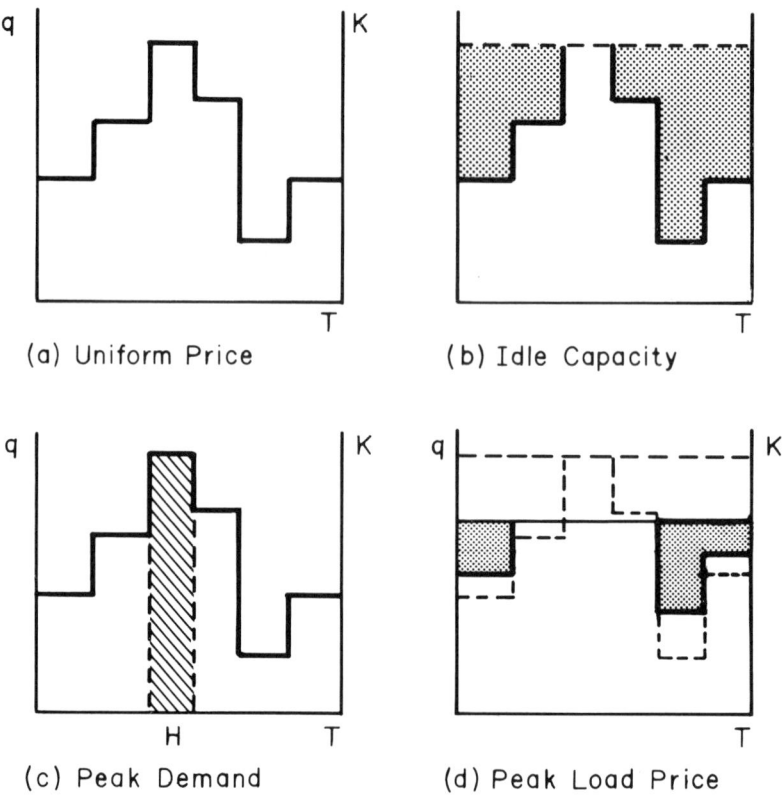

Figure 10-1. Typical Load Curve with Peak and Off-Peak Periods.

which occurs is characterized by peaks and hollows. Figure 10-1b reflects the assumption that the industries in question are required to provide a level of capacity sufficient to meet demand in peak periods. The reason for such a requirement is partly technical; if demand for electric service overloads the capacity, the result can be a brownout or blackout for all customers. The reason is also partly institutional in that the companies involved are often operating under public franchise to provide service to any person requesting it. By tailoring capacity to the peak periods, however, firms may be left with rather substantial amounts of idle capacity over the time period (Figure 10-1b, shaded area). The firms then wish to minimize or cut down this shaded area in some way.

Peak-load pricing involves the institution of different prices in different time intervals. In a peak period, such as $H$ in Figure 10-1c, one sets a relatively high price, thereby discouraging use, whereas in an off-peak period one sets a comparatively low price, thereby encouraging demand. The new pricing scheme thus serves to smooth the pattern of demand. A second reason which makes the setting of different prices for different periods appealing is that the user of the service in the interval marked $H$ is not only incurring expenses to the firm in the form of operating or energy costs but that user is also pressing on capacity, and hence requiring the firm to incur an additional capacity cost as well. Thus, efficiency in resource use requires that such a customer compensate the firm for both types of costs. On the other hand, a customer in a period of off-peak demand causes marginal expenses only in the form of operating costs, and hence it is appropriate that no marginal capacity costs be imputed to him.

The result of adoption of the more flexible pricing structure is shown in Figure 10-1d. Two effects are immediately apparent. First, the amount of unused capacity is reduced, that is, the shaded area is smaller than that in Figure 10-1b. In addition, the smoothing out of the load has meant that the capacity requirements of the firm have been reduced; the size of the reduction is indicated by the difference between the dashed and solid horizontal lines in Figure 10-1d. Of course, one has no way of predicting how large this reduction is in any particular firm unless one examines the relevant data. However, the experience of the French electric industry indicates that such savings can be substantial.[b]

The general principles of peak-load pricing can be summarized as follows:

(i) Set prices by the hour or hours of the day (or seasons of the year) in accordance with the pattern of demand.
(ii) Charge high prices when consumption tends to rise above the level of the capacity, while filling in any dips by charging low rates. After efficient pricing, the load curve is horizontal for peak periods and has dips during the off-peak intervals.
(iii) No responsibility for capacity costs is imputed at the margin to those customers whose demand does not press upon capacity.

Principle (i) quite specifically excludes certain other pricing schemes. One particularly natural scheme which suggests itself would be to charge users differentially depending on their volume of usage; for instance, business customers might be quoted a different rate from residential customers. Principle (i) has ruled out this alternative, however, and states rather that any customer in a particular hour be charged the same per unit rate regardless of how much he consumes.

Principle (iii) has not spelled out in detail how the marginal capacity or power costs should be allocated among the various peak users (those in the horizontal section of the load curve). The issue arises because it seems appropriate that a

---

[b]See Boiteux (1949), translated in 1960. The U.S. electric industry has been slower to adopt peak-load pricing and this has been cited by Shepherd and Gies as a "most glaring instance of inefficient pricing" (1966), p. 265n. See also Nelson (1964) and Davidson (1955).

user in period $H$ (see Figure 10-1c) be charged more for capacity than one in period $H - 1$ or $H + 1$, since the period $H$ demand was pressing on capacity initially. An analysis of the pricing for the joint peak case is given in Steiner.[1]

*Welfare Maximization Objective*

Many of the early theoretical treatments of peak-load pricing were provided by French economists.[c] These economists worked for nationalized industries, and hence were interested in studying models in which the firm's objective was to maximize social welfare rather than profit. Subsequently, most of the literature in the United States also considered this case.[d] These models consider a firm which faces a cyclic demand for its product or service. The cycle is assumed to be decomposable into $n$ segments and within each segment the demand $q_i$ associated with a given price $p_i$ takes on a constant value which is known with certainty.[e] The level of demand in each segment is taken to depend on the rate charged in that segment, and usually is assumed not to depend on the rates charged in other segments. The index of welfare is usually taken to be the sum of producer's plus consumer's surplus so that the model is

$$\text{Maximize } W = \sum_{i=1}^{n} \int_0^{q_i} p_i(q_i')dq_i' - H(q_1, \ldots, q_n) - rcK$$

$$\text{Subject to } q_i \leq K, i = 1, \ldots, n.$$

The costs are thus considered to be separable into two categories: operating expenses $H(q_1, \ldots, q_n)$ which depend on the total volume of load in each period, and capacity costs which depend only on the peak-period load. The plant is assumed to be infinitely divisible, so that expansion of the capacity $K$ can take place in units that are as small as one wishes. The marginal cost of a unit of capacity is denoted $rc$ and is assumed to be constant. The expression $rcK$ can be interpreted either as costs of expanded capacity or as capital costs, with the attendant implication that to purchase twice as many units of capacity the firm will have to raise twice as much capital. The constraint restricts the amount supplied by the firm in any period to its capacity.

The mathematical form of the capacity constraint is perhaps overly restrictive, particularly when combined with the assumed proportionality between capital and capacity. In essence, the constraint relates maximum output to

---

[c] See the summary by Drèze (1964).

[d] In particular, see Houthakker (1951), Steiner (1957), Hirshleifer (1958), Williamson (1966), Turvey (1968), and Littlechild (1970).

[e] An article by Brown and Johnson (1969) includes stochastic demand for this standard case of a welfare-maximizing firm.

capacity in a linear rather than a nonlinear way. A doubling of capacity (and hence of total capacity costs) permits at most a doubling of output in a peak period. However, for technologies such as those existing in telephone transmission or electricity generation, more than twice as much output can be produced if expenditures are doubled. In order to accommodate such cases, we either can replace the constraint by one such as

$$q_i \leq K^b, b > 1,$$

in which doubling $K$ more than doubles the maximum load that can be handled, or else we can use a nonlinear relation between investment and capacity, say $rcI(K)$ instead of $rcK$ with a unit of investment still taken to have a constant cost $rc$. Still another possibility suggested by both Riley[2] and Currie[3] is that a labor-requirements function be used for operating or maintenance expense, so that we have $wH(q_1,\ldots q_n,K)$ instead of $H(q_1,\ldots,q_n)$. We shall follow tradition in abiding by the usual capacity constraint, but will mention briefly what occurs when the form $H(q_1,\ldots,q_n,K)$ is adopted.

An alternative version of the objective function can be given for the interdependent demand case by using the notion of a line integral.[4] Social welfare then becomes

$$W = \sum_{i=1}^{n} \oint_0^q p_i(q')dq' - H(q) - rcK,$$

where $q$ is now a vector rather than a scalar. In order for the line integral method to "work," that is, to give price $p_i$ in the necessary condition, the problem must satisfy the so-called integrability conditions $\partial p_i/\partial q_j = \partial p_j/\partial q_i$, all $i$ and $j$. These conditions follow from the assumption that demand curves are of the compensated rather than ordinary variety, that is, if all income effects can be safely ignored. This seems a reasonable supposition in the public utility case, since any individual's expenditure on telephone or electric service is ordinarily a small fraction of a person's total budget.

The analysis is performed by using the Kuhn-Tucker technique. The Kuhn-Tucker conditions are

$$p_i - H_i - \mu_i = 0, \ i = 1,\ldots,n, \tag{10.1}$$

$$\sum_{i=1}^{n} \mu_i = cr, \tag{10.2}$$

$$K - q_i \geq 0, \ \mu_i(K - q_i) = 0, \ i = 1,\ldots,n. \tag{10.3}$$

The $\mu_i$ are the Lagrangian multipliers, and give the marginal profit contribution of an addition to capacity in period $i$; $\mu_i$ can also be interpreted as the value ("shadow" or "accounting" price) of capacity in period $i$. All of the output variables $q_i$ and the capacity $K$ are assumed to be positive.

Equation (10.1) states that the opportunity cost or accounting loss per unit of output in period $i$ must equal zero, where an opportunity cost occurs when the inputs used in providing a service during one period would be more profitably utilized in the provision of service in some other period. This condition means essentially that price is equated to the relevant marginal costs for each period. Equation (10.2) contains the statement about capacity, namely, that the opportunity cost of expanding capacity must be zero. Equation (10.3) gives information about peak or off-peak loads in any period. It says, in effect, that either the imputed cost of capacity in a particular period is zero, or else that capacity is fully utilized in the period (that is, that the level of capacity is equal to the demand in the period). Thus, if the demand is off-peak, so that there is partial underutilization of the total capacity available, there will be no imputation or responsibility for marginal capacity costs to users during the period. During peak periods, of course, there will be capacity costs imputed at the margin.

To analyze (10.1)-(10.3), we note that for the off-peak periods (denoted with $i$) the appropriate pricing policy is $p_i = H_i$. This follows because off-peak means $q_i < K$ in Equation (10.3), and hence $\mu_i = 0$. For the peak periods (denoted by $j$), $K = q_j$. Then Equation (10.3) no longer requires $\mu_j$ to be zero, so that $p_j = H_j + \mu_j$ and

$$\sum_j \mu_j = rc.$$

Thus, a welfare-maximizing firm sets price in an off-peak period equal to the marginal cost of the operating expense in the period. During peak periods, price not only covers the operating expense, but over all peak periods price is set just high enough to compensate for the marginal cost of increasing capacity. In addition, if marginal cost equals average cost (constant returns to scale), then the solution also has the property that total costs are exactly covered by revenues.

The economic rationale underlying the optimality of these results is that any increase in demand during peak periods requires the firm to expand capacity, and therefore is more expensive (has a higher cost associated with it) than increases in demand which occur during periods when there is excess capacity. Thus, each type of demand is charged enough to compensate exactly for the increased cost associated with satisfaction of that demand.

A somewhat more compact version of the results appears in the first row of Table 10-1. Here all peak periods have been summed together and Equations (10.1) and (10.2) combined to obtain $\Sigma p_j = \Sigma H_j + rc$. Similarly, non-peak periods are summed to obtain $\Sigma p_i = \Sigma H_i$.

**Table 10-1**
**Peak and Off-Peak Pricing Rules**

|  | Offpeak | Peak |
|---|---|---|
| Welfare maximizer | $\Sigma p_i = \Sigma H_i$ | $\Sigma p_j = \Sigma H_j + rc$ |
| Unregulated monopoly | $\Sigma R_i = \Sigma H_i$ | $\Sigma R_j = \Sigma H_j + rc$ |
| Rate-of-return regulation | $\Sigma R_i = \Sigma H_i$ | $\Sigma R_j = \Sigma H_j + rc - \frac{\lambda}{1-\lambda}(s-r)c$ |
| Return-on-cost regulation | $\Sigma R_i = g^* \Sigma H_i$ | $\Sigma R_j = g^*(\Sigma H_j + rc)$ |

A graphical interpretation for the two-period case is given in Figure 10-2. The demand curves in the two periods are noted $D_1$ and $D_2$. The expense costs are assumed to be constant at an amount $H$ per unit of output. The intersection point $A$ of the $H + cr$ curve with the demand curve gives peak price and output with output equaling capacity. The intersection point $B$ of the $H$ curve with the demand curve gives off-peak price and output. In this case, then, period $D_2$ is peak and period $D_1$ is off-peak. A joint peak would obtain if the capacity cost were instead at the level $(rc)^*$. This happens because point $C$ at which $p_2 = H + (rc)^*$ cannot determine capacity, since the off-peak rule $p_1 = H$ would entail a capacity (point $B$) larger than that at $C$. A reversal of the peak obtains if the expense cost were at a level $H^*$. Here the peak is determined by $p_i = H^* + rc$ (point $F$ on demand curve $D_1$) and the off-peak by $p_2 = H^*$ (point $E$).

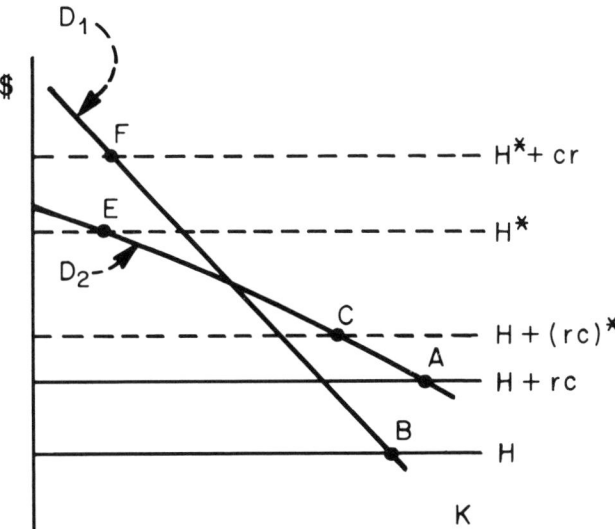

**Figure 10-2.** Peak and Off-Peak Pricing in a Two-Period Model.

## Peak-Load Pricing under Profit Objective

*Peak-Load Problem for Unregulated Monopoly*

The model for the profit-maximizing monopoly firm differs from the former model only in the fact that revenue replaces surplus in the objective function. That is, the firm will

$$\underset{q_1,\ldots,q_n,K}{\text{Maximize}} \; R(q_1,\ldots,q_n) - H(q_1,\ldots,q_n) - rcK$$

Subject to $q_i \leqq K, i = 1,\ldots,n$.

Revenue (sales) are determined by multiplying the price in each period by respective demands and summing over all periods. In the independent demand case

$$R(q_1,\ldots,q_n) = \sum_{i=1}^{n} p_i(q_i) q_i$$

and in the interdependent demand case

$$R(q_1,\ldots,q_n) = \sum_{i=1}^{n} p_i(q_1,\ldots,q_n) q_i.$$

In taking the first-order conditions, we use the term $R_i$ to denote marginal revenue. Marginal revenue can be expressed (in the most general case) as

$$R_i = p_i + q_i \partial p_i / \partial q_i + \sum_{j \neq i} q_j \partial p_j / \partial q_i, \tag{10.4}$$

and includes terms involving its own price effect and all cross effects with other periods. The relationship

$$R_i < p_i, \tag{10.5}$$

holds when only the own effect is considered (the independent demand case) since $\partial p_i / \partial q_i < 0$ (quantity demanded in period $i$ decreases when price in period $i$ increases, other things being equal). However, when interdependent demands are considered, the relationship (10.5) may not always hold. The own effect is still negative, but it may be swamped by positive cross effects which arise because an increase in price in an adjacent period shifts demand to the present period. The supposition ordinarily made in this chapter is that (10.5) holds.

The Kuhn-Tucker conditions for the profit-maximizing model are shown in Table 10-1 to be parallel in overall form to those already obtained. The only difference is that marginal revenue replaces price in the firm's decisionmaking process. The unregulated monopolist equates marginal revenue to marginal operating cost for the off-peak users, and to the sum of marginal operating and marginal capacity costs for the peak users.[f] Figure 10-3 illustrates the results for the case with two periods, no cross-elasticity of demand, and linear costs. The monopoly pricing serves to lower capacity from the $K^W$ level in the social welfare maximization case to the smaller level $K^M$ and to raise prices from $(\overline{p}^W, \underline{p}^W)$ to $(\overline{p}^M, \underline{p}^M)$.

The profit-maximizer's price exceeds rather than equals the appropriate marginal cost. When regulation is imposed, there will in theory be price reductions with the firm's output moving closer to the welfare-maximizing level. The interesting question is to determine whether all users benefit equally from these price reductions, or whether the method of regulation can introduce distortions as between peak and off-peak users.[g]

*Rate-of-Return Regulation*

For the peak-load pricing model, the rate-of-return constraint is

$$R(q_1,\ldots,q_n) - H(q_1,\ldots,q_n) \leqq scK.$$

*Proposition 10.1: The firm constrained to earn at most a fair return on its capital investment sets off-peak rates using the monopoly rule that marginal revenue equals marginal cost, but the new rule for peak users is that marginal revenue is less than marginal cost. As the fair rate of return is lowered, the reduction in rates to the peak users becomes larger, resulting in greater increases in capacity, but its utilization is not as efficient as it would be if the off-peak users were also benefiting from lower prices.*

---

[f]The pricing rules for the monopoly firm turn out to be related closely to those obtained when the welfare maximizing firm is subject to the stipulation that the firm at least break even in its operation, $\pi \geq 0$. Such a model has been studied by Boiteux (1956), Baumol and Bradford (1970), and Mohring (1970) and is particularly applicable to a firm facing decreasing average costs, since in such a case the unconstrained welfare maximizer would incur losses. To draw the parallel, the results for the off-peak period are derived, assuming demands are independent. The unregulated profit maximizer's rule is that $(p_i - H_i)/(p_i) = e_i$, where $e_i = -(\partial p_i/\partial q_i)(q_i/p_i)$ = demand elasticity of price. The welfare maximizer who breaks even follows a rule which differs only by a factor of proportionality $(p_i - H_i)/(p_i) = \lambda e_i$, where $\lambda$ is the Lagrange multiplier of the breakeven constraint. See also Bailey and White (1973), where it is shown that a two-part tariff can provide an efficient way of breaking even in a decreasing average cost industry.

[g]Pressman (1970) has come close to studying this problem, since he includes a constraint that profits lie below some fixed dollar amount. This would be a form of regulatory constraint if profits were the objective of the firm in his model. However, since Pressman uses the standard social welfare objective function, his constraint is not active in the case usually considered to be of interest, namely, that where the public utility firm has decreasing average costs in its production.

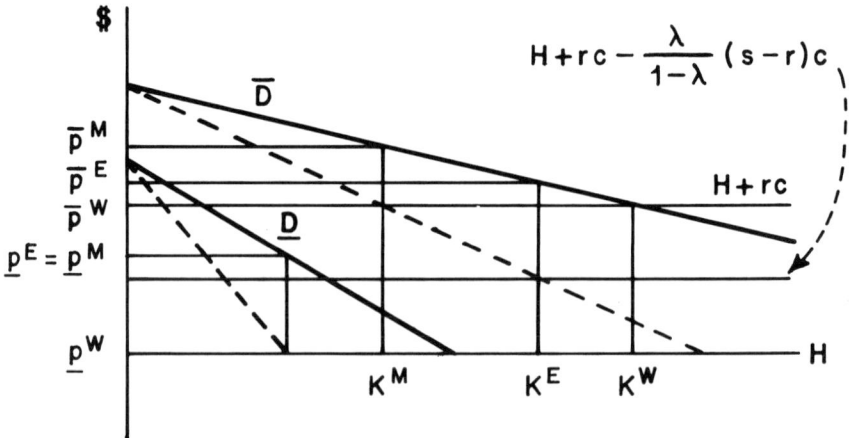

**Figure 10-3.** Peak-Load Pricing and Rate-of-Return Regulation.

*Proof:* The model is

$$\text{Maximize } \pi = R(q_1, \ldots, q_n) - H(q_1, \ldots, q_n) - rc(K + K^*)$$
$$q_1, \ldots, q_n, K, K^*$$

Subject to $q_i \leqq K$, $i = 1, \ldots, n$

$$\pi \leqq (s - r)c(K + K^*)$$

with $K^* =$ padding of capital. The Kuhn-Tucker conditions are

$$(1 - \lambda)R_i - (1 - \lambda)H_i - \mu_i = 0, \; i = 1, \ldots, n \qquad (10.6)$$

$$\sum_{i=1}^{n} \mu_i = rc - \lambda sc \qquad (10.7)$$

$$-rc + \lambda sc \leqq 0, \quad K^*c(\lambda s - r) = 0 \qquad (10.8)$$

$$K - q_i \geqq 0 \; \mu_i(K - q_i) = 0, \; i = 1, \ldots, n \qquad (10.9)$$

$$\pi = (s - r)c(K + K^*). \qquad (10.10)$$

By (10.8), $\lambda \leqq \frac{r}{s}$. When $\lambda = \frac{r}{s}$ then (10.7) becomes $\sum_{i=1}^{n} \mu_i = 0$, so that the imputed cost of expanding capacity is zero. This is equivalent to having redundant capacity become worthwhile, since as (10.8) then shows, $K^* \geqq 0$.

When $\lambda < \frac{r}{s}$, the imputed cost of expanding capacity is positive but less than the actual cost of the additional capacity as can be seen from (10.7).

The pricing rule for the off-peak users is obtained by summing the first-order conditions over off-peak periods

$$\Sigma R_i = \Sigma H_i \qquad (10.11)$$

and is identical with that of the unregulated monopoly (Table 10-1). For peak periods, we sum over all peak periods in (10.6), and substitute (10.7) in the result thereby eliminating $\mu$, to obtain

$$\Sigma R_j = \Sigma H_j + rc - \frac{\lambda}{1-\lambda}(s-r)c. \qquad (10.12)$$

Marginal revenue is now equated to the marginal operating cost plus a marginal capacity cost which is lower than the actual cost of expanding capacity. Figure 10-3 illustrates rules (10.11) and (10.12) for the case of linear costs and no cross-elasticities, and shows that regulation serves to expand capacity from $K^M$ to $K^E$ without changing off-peak price or quantity in the slightest.

To show more formally that capacity expands as regulation is tightened, use the comparative statics technique in the region where $\lambda < \frac{r}{s}$ so that $K^* = 0$.[h] Then we have from (10.9) and (10.10)

$$dK - dq_j = 0, \text{ all } j \text{ in peak periods} \qquad (10.13)$$

and

$$scdK - \sum_{i=1}^{n}(R_i - H_i)dq_i + cKds = 0. \qquad (10.14)$$

Equation (10.11) can be used to eliminate the middle terms in Equation (10.14) for off-peak periods. For peak periods, Equation (10.14) is used to rewrite (10.14) as

$$scdK - \Sigma(R_j - H_j)dK + cKds, \text{ all } j \text{ in peak periods.} \qquad (10.15)$$

Then Equation (10.13) is substituted into (10.17) to yield

---

[h]$K^* > 0$ only when $\lambda = \frac{r}{s}$. Then (10.7) becomes $\sum_{i=1}^{n} \mu_i = 0$, so that the marginal revenue from an expansion of output cannot even cover operating expenses. This is a circumstance under which it is best to expand using unproductive capital.

$$\frac{dK}{ds} = \frac{-cK}{(s-r)c(1+\frac{\lambda}{1-\lambda})} < 0.$$

*End of Proof*

Proposition 10.1 thus verifies the Wellisz[5] result that a regulated firm sets the off-peak prices according to the monopolistic rule. In peak periods, there is an alteration in the pricing rule as regulation is imposed. Intuitively, because constrained profits increase with the level of capacity, the firm passes on the benefits of regulation to those users whose increased demand will cause an increase in capacity.

Wellisz also suggests that the proceeds of monopolistic off-peak prices may be applied to cover peak-load costs, so that the capacity is expanded beyond the social welfare level.[6] In terms of Figure 10-3, this would mean that $K^E$ might be to the right of $K^W$. This idea has been clarified considerably in Bailey and White, who show for a simple two-period model such as is displayed in Figure 10-3 that

the crucial variables determining whether or not the peak capacity exceeds the welfare-maximizing level are the size of the offpeak surplus and the margin between $s$ and $r$. As the margin between $s$ and $r$ is reduced, the constrained level of profits declines, and it becomes more likely that the off-peak surplus will have to be absorbed by an expansion of peak period capacity and consequent peak period deficits.[7]

When cross-elasticities of demand are included, some change in off-peak price, $\underline{p}^E$, is to be expected along with the change in $\overline{p}^E$. The graphical results will be suggestive but not exact. Cross-elasticities will also play a role in the determination of whether or not $K^E > K^W$.

It should be emphasized that there are differences between the Averch-Johnson and the Wellisz effects. In both models, the differential between the fair return and the cost of capital gives the firm an incentive to increase its rate base, but the Averch-Johnson model requires the firm always to utilize its capacity to the fullest extent. Whatever the firm's decision about expansion of capacity, it can be shown that the firm has an incentive to substitute capital for labor and hence produce its output using a nonminimal-cost technology.

In the model presented here and in the Wellisz model, the assumption that capacity is fully utilized is relaxed. Although it is found that the firm increases its rate base by increasing capacity, there is no implication in the peak-load-pricing models that the firm has an incentive to substitute capital for labor in technology. The differences between the Averch-Johnson and Wellisz results can best be summarized thus: in the former model, the firm always adopts an overly capital intensive technology and, except in the case where capital is an inferior input, produces an output larger than that of the unconstrained profit-maximizing monopolist; in the latter model, the firm increases its capacity beyond the monopoly level, but does not utilize capacity as efficiently as it could.

A much closer tie between the two models can be obtained if the labor-requirements function $wH(q_1,\ldots,q_n,K)$ replaces $H(q_1,\ldots,q_n)$, as was suggested by Riley and Currie.[8] In this case, there will still be a distortion in rate structure between peak and off-peak users, but there will also be an Averch-Johnson bias between labor and capital.

*Markup-on-Cost Regulation*

Under the method of regulation which limits the firm's markup on cost, the constraint is $R(q_1,\ldots,q_n) \leq (1+g)[C(q_1,\ldots,q_n) + rcK]$, where $g$ is the markup on both operating and capacity expenses.

*Proposition 10.2: A firm which is constrained to earn no more than a fair return on costs will reduce marginal revenues from peak and off-peak periods by the same percentage amount.*

*Proof:* The model is

$$\text{Maximize } \pi = R(q_1,\ldots,q_n) - H(q_1,\ldots,q_n) - rcK - x$$
$$q_1,\ldots,q_n, K, x$$

$$\text{Subject to } q_i \leq K, \ i = 1,\ldots,n$$

$$\pi \leq g(H(q_1,\ldots,q_n) + rcK + x)$$

with Kuhn-Tucker conditions

$$(1-\lambda)R_i - (1-\lambda)H_i - \mu_i + \lambda g H_i = 0, \ i = 1,\ldots,n \quad (10.16)$$

$$\sum_{i=1}^{n} \mu_i - rc + \lambda grc = 0 \quad (10.17)$$

$$-1 + \lambda(1+g) \leq 0, \ x\left(\lambda - \frac{1}{1+g}\right) = 0 \quad (10.18)$$

$$K - q_i \geq 0 \ \mu_i(K - q_i) = 0, \ i = 1,\ldots,n \quad (10.19)$$

$$\pi = g(H(q_1,\ldots,q_n) + rcK + x). \quad (10.20)$$

Equation (10.16) shows that the firm's optimal policy requires equating marginal revenues to something less than the marginal costs. The reduction is caused by a term which reflects the interaction effect between operating expenses and the regulatory constraint. Equation (10.17) shows that in the regulatory situation the imputed cost of expanding capacity adds up to something less than the actual cost of expanding capacity. Hence, the imputed level of both operating costs and capacity costs is lowered.

Summing over off-peak periods, we obtain

$$\Sigma R_i = \Sigma (H_i - \frac{\lambda}{1-\lambda} gH_i) = g*\Sigma H_i$$

where $m* = \dfrac{1-\lambda(1+g)}{1-\lambda} < 1$. For peak periods

$$\Sigma R_j = g*[\Sigma H_j + rc].$$

Thus, as Table 10-1 shows, this method involves a proportional lowering of marginal revenues during peak and off-peak periods from the levels which occur in the case of the unregulated monopoly.

*End of Proof*

Unlike rate-of-return regulation, both peak and off-peak prices will be lower if we use the simple version of the model portrayed in Figure 10-3. Furthermore, the anomaly whereby $K^E > K^W$ can not show up in such a model. Thus, the particular form of the regulatory constraint does, at least in theory, have a substantial effect on the distribution of price reductions between peak and off-peak users.

# Summary

# 11 Some Theorems About Regulatory Constraint

Some of the propositions about regulatory constraint that we have encountered agree with the standard folklore while other results that we have arrived at are surprising and rather paradoxical. It seems appropriate to end with a brief summary of some of the more important conclusions from each of these two classes.

A classical instance where economic theory confirms a priori intuition occurs in the Averch-Johnson model of rate-of-return regulation. In this model a profit-maximizing firm is subject to a constraint that profit not exceed a positive fraction of its rate base. The folklore is unanimous in arriving at the conclusion that such a situation gives the firm an incentive to maximize this rate base. However, exactly what such a maximization entails had not been thoroughly understood. The Averch-Johnson proof demonstrated that the selection of an overly capital intensive technology is one decision that appears attractive to the firm. We have extended this result to show that capital-labor substitution is more profitable than padding the rate base or than paying an inflated price for capital equipment. Furthermore, while regulation may be successful in encouraging a firm to increase output as the level of fair return is lowered, regulation cannot succeed in giving the firm an incentive to move past the revenue-maximizing level of output.

Some other results from the AJ model are also intuitive. One of these asserts that delays in price adjustments can partially offset the firm's tendency to misallocate resources: the firm can gain profits during the interval of regulatory lag by adopting a technology that comes closer to minimizing costs. Another says that an AJ effect can show up in a model of peak-load pricing. Since peak users press on capacity whereas off-peak users do not, the return-on-capital constraint gives the firm an incentive to lower prices to the peak rather than the off-peak customer.

Not all the results of the Averch-Johnson model are in line with intuition, however. For instance, if the market cost of capital increases, the expectation is that the dollar amount of capital borrowed decreases since capital has become more expensive. The counterintuitive outcome reported here is that no change in factor usage or in output takes places. Another argument from the folklore that we have overturned is that the regulated firm automatically passes on cost increases to its customers. When the market cost of capital or wage rate or acquisition cost of capital go up, we have shown that the firm bears a substantial part of the cost increase through a reduction in its profitability.

One of the least satisfactory aspects of the Averch-Johnson model is that there is no slack or "elbow room" in the firm's decisions, yet such flexibility seems to occur in reality. Slack may exist because the firm has an objective other than profit, or as we explain here, it may exist because the per unit cost of capital rises as more capital is used by the firm. While capital and profit remain uniquely determined in a rising-cost-of-capital model, there exists a range of fair returns over which the labor and output and waste levels are indeterminate. Thus, the firm has some flexibility which it can use to increase output, thereby perhaps operating in an inelastic region of the revenue curve rather than always remaining in the elastic region as in the AJ model. It can also use the slack to protect its profit position during periods of rising costs. Over this same range of fair returns, the firm's most profitable policy is to cut back on capital usage (rather than expand on it as in the AJ model) as the fair rate is lowered. This effect may explain why regulated firms might in actuality often appear reluctant to adopt overly capital intensive methods of operation.

The return-on-cost (or any symmetric) method of regulation provides an excellent example of theory arriving at an insight that has been ignored in the previous literature. The folklore on return-on-cost regulation is unmistakable. It states that if a fair profit is somehow guaranteed and if the firm is not rewarded with increased profits when it increases its efficiency, then the firm most probably lapses into inefficient methods of production. No distinction is drawn between the productive (output-increasing) methods of increasing costs and the wasteful methods, and it is for this reason that the folklore turns out to be misleading in its answer.

We have shown that any method of increasing costs which also increases revenues is strictly preferred by a constrained profit maximizer to a method of increasing costs in which revenues remain unchanged. Thus, whenever demand is elastic so that output increases result in revenue increases, output-increasing activities are more profitable than is operation off the production frontier. Once the revenue-maximizing output has been reached, the firm's most profitable response to tighter regulation is to remain at this output and to absorb any remaining slack through wasteful activity. Only by detecting some or all of the waste and disallowing it from the cost base can the regulator encourage production in the inelastic region of the revenue curve.

In retrospect, the distinction that the theory draws between the benefits of productive and purely wasteful activity seems reasonable, and the importance of the revenue effect undeniable. Yet, in previous work, there had been virtually no recognition that such an effect could exist.

As a final example, we cite the usual supposition that a profit constraint averaged over all markets leads to various perverse subsidizations of one market by another. We have shown here that although such behavior is possible, nevertheless for many models of regulatory constraint, it is not optimal. Instead, the regulated firm has an incentive to adopt the same ratio rule between products as is adopted by a revenue-maximizing firm subject to its own internal profit constraint.

In sum, the theory has served to sharpen our understanding of behavior patterns that may arise when a monopoly firm is subject to regulatory constraint. We have been able to pinpoint characteristics that were not previously understood, and to suggest a number of results that are capable of empirical testing. While we make no pretense of having offered a theory which is directly relevant to regulatory proceedings, our propositions do treat in a systematic fashion at least some of the issues which arise in such proceedings. By first understanding which issues are important within the framework of simple models, perhaps we shall eventually be able to build a structure that captures more completely the essential features of the regulatory process.

**Notes**

# Notes

### Preface

1. Bailey and Coleman (1971).
2. Bailey and Finch (1973).
3. Bailey (1972a).

### Chapter 1
### An Analytic Approach to Regulation

1. Averch and Johnson (1962).
2. Wilson (1971).
3. Galbraith (1958), p. 116.
4. Samuelson (1972), p. 253.

### Chapter 2
### Formulation of Model and Method of Solution

1. Williamson (1964), p. 40.
2. Phillips (1969), p. 183.
3. Garfield and Lovejoy (1964), p. 133.
4. Furubotn and Pejovich (1972), p. 1153.
5. Williamson (1964) and Zajac (1972).
6. Takayama (1969).

### Chapter 3
### Operation off the Production Frontier

1. Wilcox (1966), p. 835.
2. Kahn (1971), p. 48.
3. Cross (1970), p. 239
4. Leibenstein (1966), p. 413.
5. Williamson (1964).

### Chapter 4
### Symmetric and Asymmetric Constraints

1. Averch and Johnson (1972), p. 1052.
2. Kafoglis (1971).

3. Baumol (1970), p. 353.
4. Dayan (1972).


## Chapter 5
## Averch-Johnson Model

1. Averch and Johnson (1962), p. 1058.
2. Westfield (1965).
3. Zajac (1970).
4. Hughes (1968), p. 74.
5. Westfield (1971), p. 217.
6. Johnson (1973), p. 91.
7. Vinod (1972).
8. Corey (1971), pp. 361-2.


## Chapter 6
## Fair Rate of Return

1. Klevorick (1971a).
2. Takayama (1969); Tasch (1968).
3. Baumol and Klevorick (1970); Tasch (1968).
4. Ibid.
5. Baumol and Klevorick (1970).
6. Hicks (1946), p. 95.
7. Scherer (1970), pp. 552-5.
8. Lie (1973).
9. Klevorick (1966).
10. Dansby (1973).
11. Sheshinkski (1971).
12. Klevorick (1971).


## Chapter 8
## Comparative Statics Analysis of
## AJ Model

1. Westfield (1965), p. 441.
2. Ibid.
3. Ibid., p. 440.
4. Emery (1973), p. 329.
5. Ibid., p. 336.

6. Dayan (1972).
7. Emery (1973).
8. McNicol (1973).

## Chapter 9
## Rising Cost of Capital

1. Baumol (1967), p. 88.
2. Bower (1965) and Shepherd (1966).
3. Fisher and Kaysen (1962), p. 86.
4. Bower (1965), pp. 31-2.

## Chapter 10
## Peak-Load Pricing under Profit Objective

1. Steiner (1957).
2. Riley (1972).
3. Currie (1973).
4. Pressman (1971).
5. Wellisz (1963).
6. Ibid., p. 41.
7. Bailey and White (1974).
8. Riley (1972) and Currie (1973).

# References

# References

Alchian, Armen, and R. Kessel (1962) "Competition, Monopoly, and the Pursuit of Money," in National Bureau of Economic Research, *Aspects of Labor Economics*. Princeton: Princeton University Press, pp. 157-75.

Archer, Stephen H., and LeRoy G. Faerber (1966) "Firm Size and the Cost of Externally Secured Equity Capital," *Journal of Finance* 21 (March): 69-83.

Arrow, Kenneth J., L. Hurwicz, and H. Uzawa (1961) "Constraint Qualifications in Maximization Problems," *Naval Research Logistics Quarterly* 8 (Jan.): 175-91.

Aten, Robert (1973) "Property Taxation in a Regulated Industry," manuscript.

Atkinson, A.B., and L. Waverman (1973) "Resource Allocation and the Regulated Firm: Comment," *Bell Journal of Economics and Management Science* 4 (Spring): 283-7.

Averch, Harvey, and Leland L. Johnson (1962) "Behavior of the Firm under Regulatory Constraint," *American Economic Review* 52 (Dec.): 1053-69.

Azariadis, Costas, Kalman J. Cohen, and Alfredo Porcar (1972) "A Partial Utility Approach to the Theory of the Firm," *Southern Economic Journal* 38 (April): 485-94.

Bailey, Elizabeth E. (1972) "Regulation Limiting Return on Cost," *Proceedings of the 11th Annual Conference on Public Utility Valuation and the Rate Making Process*, Iowa State University, May, 154-87.

_____ (1972a) "Peak Load Pricing under Regulatory Constraint," *Journal of Political Economy* 80 (July/August): 662-79.

_____ (1972b) "Innovation and Regulation," manuscript, revised Nov.

_____ (1973) "Resource Allocation and the Regulated Firm: Comment on the Comments," *Bell Journal of Economics and Management Science* 4 (Spring): 288-92.

_____ , and John C. Malone (1970) "Resource Allocation and the Regulated Firm," *Bell Journal of Economics and Mangement Science* 1 (Spring): 129-42.

_____ , and Roger D. Coleman (1970) "Discussion of Klevorick's Graduated Fair Return," Bell Laboratories Technical Memorandum, July.

_____ , and Roger D. Coleman (1971) "The Effect of Lagged Regulation in an Averch-Johnson Model," *Bell Journal of Economics and Management Science* 2 (Spring): 278-92.

_____ , and T. Austin Finch (1973) "Rate of Return Regulation and a Rising Cost of Capital," Paper presented at the University of Chicago Seminar, "The Economics of Regulated Public Utilities," June.

_____ , and Lawrence J. White (1974) "Reversals in Peak and Offpeak Prices," *Bell Journal of Economics and Management Science* 5 (Spring): (forthcoming).

Baumol, William J. (1967) *Business Behavior, Value and Growth*, rev. ed. New York: Harcourt, Brace & World.

Baumol, William J. (1970) "The Firm with Inelastic Demands," *Induction Growth and Trade: Essays in Honour of Sir Roy Harrod*, edited by W.A. Ellis, M.F.A. Scott, J.N. Wolfe. Oxford: Clarendon Press.

_____(1970a) "Reasonable Rules for Rate Regulation: Plausible Policies for an Imperfect World," P.W. MacAvoy, ed., *The Crisis of the Regulatory Commissions*. New York: W.W. Norton, 187-206. Also in A. Phillips and O.E. Williamson, eds. (1968) *Prices: Issues in Theory, Practice and Public Policy*. Philadelphia, Pa.

_____(1972) *Economic Theory and Operations Analysis*, 3rd ed. Englewood Cliffs, N.J.: Prentice-Hall.

_____, and David F. Bradford (1970) "Optimal Departures from Marginal Cost Pricing," *American Economic Review* 60 (June): 265-83.

_____, Otto Eckstein, and Alfred E. Kahn (1970) "Competition and Monopoly in Telecommunications Services," AT&T, Nov.

_____, and Alvin K. Klevorick (1970) "Input Choices and Rate-of-Return Regulation: An Overview of the Discussion," *Bell Journal of Economics and Management Science* 1 (Autumn): 162-90.

_____, and Burton G. Malkiel (1967) "The Firm's Optimal Debt Equity Combination and the Cost of Capital," *Quarterly Journal Of Economics* 81 (Nov.): 547-78.

_____, and Alfred G. Walton (1973) "Full Costing Competition, and Regulatory Practice," *Yale Law Journal* 82 (March): 639-55.

Bear, D.V.T. (1965) "Inferior Inputs and the Theory of the Firm," *Journal of Political Economy* 73 (June): 287-89.

_____(1972) "A Further Note on Factor Inferiority," *Southern Economic Journal* 38 (Jan.): 409-13.

Bergson, Abram (1972) "Optimal Pricing for a Public Enterprise," *Quarterly Journal of Economics* 86 (Nov.): 519-44.

Bilas, Richard A., and Fred A. Massey (1972) "A Note on Factor Inferiority," *Southern Economic Journal* 38 (Jan.): 407-8.

Boiteux, Marcel (1949) "La tarification des demandes en point: application de la théorie de la vente au coût marginal," *Revue Générale de l'Electricité* 58 (August): 321-40; translated as "Peak-Load Pricing," *Journal Business* 33 (April 1960): 157-79.

_____, (1956) "Sur la Gestion des Monopoles Publics Astreints à l'Équilbre Budgetaire," *Econometrica* 24 (Jan.): 22-40; translated as "On the Management of Public Monopolies Subject to Budgetary Constraints," *Journal of Economic Theory* 3 (Sept. 1971): 219-40.

Bonbright, James C. (1961) *Principles of Public Utilities Rates*. New York: Columbia University Press.

Bower, Richard S. (1965) "Rising Capital Cost versus Regulatory Restraint," *Public Utilities Fortnightly*, March 4, 31-3.

Breyer, Stephen G., and Paul W. MacAvoy (1972) *The Effects of the Federal*

*Power Commission: A Legal-Economic Assessment*, Brookings Institution, manuscript, May.

Brown, Gardner, Jr., and M. Bruce Johnson (1969) "Public Utility Pricing and Output Under Risk," *American Economic Review* 59 (March): 119-28.

Christensen, L., D. Jorgenson, and L. Lau (1970) "Conjugate Duality and the Transcendental Logarithmic Production Function," Paper Presented at the Second World Congress of the Econometric Society, Cambridge, Eng., Sept.

Corey, Gordon R. (1971) "The Averch and Johnson Proposition: A Critical Analysis," *Bell Journal of Economics and Management Science* 2 (Spring): 358-73.

Courville, Leon (1974) "Overcapitalization in Regulated Industries: The Electric Utility Case," *Bell Journal of Economics and Management Science* 5 (Spring): (in press).

Cross, John G. (1970) "Incentive Pricing and Utility Regulation," *Quarterly Journal of Economics* 84 (May): 236-53.

Currie, Kent A. (1973) "Peak-Load Pricing under Regulatory Constraint: Comment," manuscript.

Dansby, Robert E. (1973) "Effects of Depreciation on the Behavior of Regulated Firms," manuscript.

Davidson, Ralph K. (1955) *Price Discrimination in Selling Gas and Electricity*. Baltimore: Johns Hopkins Press.

Davis, Eric (1973) "A Dynamic Model of the Regulated Firm with a Price Adjustment Mechanism," *Bell Journal of Economics and Management Science* 4 (Spring): 270-82.

Dayan, David (1972) "Vertical Integration and Monopoly Regulation," Ph.D. Dissertation, Princeton University, Dec.

_____ (1973) "Taxation, Market Structure and Monopoly Regulation," manuscript.

Dorfman, Robert, and Peter O. Steiner (1954) "Optimal Advertising and Optimal Quality," *American Economic Review* 44 (Dec.): 826-36.

Dreze, J.A. (1964) "Some Postwar Contributions of French Economists to Theory and Public Policy," *American Economic Review* 54 (June, Supp.): 1-64.

Edelson, Noel M. (1971) "Resource Allocation and the Regulated Firm: A Reply to Bailey and Malone," *Bell Journal of Economics and Management Science* 2 (Spring): 374-8.

Erickson, E., R.M. Spann, and R. Ciliano (1973) "Fossil Fuel Demand," Decision Sciences Corporation.

El Hodiri, Mohamed, and Akira Takayama (1973) "Behavior of the Firm under Regulatory Constraint: Clarifications," *American Economic Review* 63 (March): 235-7.

Emery, E. David (1973) "Regulated Utilities and Equipment Manufacturers' Conspiracies in the Electric Power Industry," *Bell Journal of Economics and Management Science* 4 (Spring): 322-37.

Faulhaber, Gerald R. (1972) "Competition and the Dynamics of Growth," Paper presented at the Dartmouth College Seminar on Problems of Regulation and Public Utilities, Aug.

———— (1972a) "On Subsidization: Some Observations and Tentative Conclusions," Paper Presented at the Office of Telecommunications Policy Conference on Communication Policy Research, Washington, D.C., Nov.

Feldstein, Martin S. (1972) "Equity and Efficiency in Public Sector Pricing: The Optimal Two-Part Tariff," *Quarterly Journal of Economics* 86 (May): 175-87.

Ferguson, C.E. (1971) *The Neoclassical Theory of Production and Distribution*. Cambridge, Eng.: The University Press.

Finch, T. Austin (1972) "The Effect of a Rising Cost of Capital in the Averch-Johnson Model," Unpublished Undergraduate Dissertation, Princeton University, April.

Fisher, Franklin M., and Carl Kaysen (1962) *A Study in Econometrics: The Demand for Electricity in the United States*. Amsterdam: North Holland Publishing Co.

Furubotn, Eirik G., and Svetozar Pejovich (1972) "Property Rights and Economic Theory: A Survey of Recent Literature," *Journal of Economic Literature* 10 (Dec.): 1137-62.

Galbraith, John K. (1958) *The Affluent Society*. New York: Mentor Books.

Garfield, Paul J., and Wallace F. Lovejoy (1964) *Public Utility Economics*. Englewood Cliffs, N.J.: Prentice-Hall.

Greene, Julian M. (1971) "An Empirical Analysis of Rate-of-Return Regulation and its Effect on Investment in Steam-Electric Generation," Ph.D. Dissertation, University of Minnesota.

Harberger, Arnold (1954) "Monopoly and Resource Allocation," *American Economic Review* 44 (May): 770-87.

Haring, Joseph E., and Joseph F. Humphrey, eds. (1971) *Utility Regulation during Inflation*. Los Angeles: Occidental College.

Hicks, John R. (1946) *Value and Capital*. London: Oxford University Press, 2nd ed.

Hirshleifer, Jack (1958) "Peak Loads and Efficient Pricing: Comment," *Quarterly Journal of Economics* 72 (August): 451-62.

Houthakker, H.S. (1951) "Electricity Tariffs in Theory and Practice," *Economic Journal* 61 (March): 1-25.

Hughes, William R. (1972) "Comments" in H.M. Trebing, ed., *Performance Under Regulation*. East Lansing: Michigan State University.

Irwin, Manley R. (1971) *Telecommunications Industry: Integration vs Competition*. New York: Praeger.

Johnson, Leland L. (1973) "Behavior of the Firm under Regulatory Constraint: A Reassessment," *American Economic Review* 63 (May): 90-7.

Jordan, William A. (1972) "Producer Protection, Prior Market Structure, and

the Effects of Government Regulation," *Journal of Law and Economics* 15 (April): 151-76.
Jorgenson, Dale W. (1965) "Anticipations and Investment Behavior," in J.S. Duesenberry, G. Fromm, L.R. Klein, and E. Kuh, eds., *The Brookings Quarterly Econometric Model of the United States*. Chicago and Amsterdam: Rand McNally and North-Holland, pp. 35-94.
Joskow, Paul (1972) "The Determination of the Allowed Rate of Return in a Formal Regulatory Proceeding," *Bell Journal of Economics and Management Science* 3 (Autumn): 632-44.
_____ (1973) "Pricing Decisions of Regulated Firms: A Behavioral Approach," *Bell Journal of Economics and Management Science* 4 (Spring): 118-40.
Kafoglis, Milton Z. (1969) "Output of the Restrained Firm," *American Economic Review* 59 (Sept.): 553-9.
_____ (1971) "Comment" in Harry M. Trebing, ed., *Essays on Public Utility Pricing and Regulation*. East Lansing: Michigan State University.
Kahn, Alfred E. (1968) "The Graduated Fair Return: Comment," *American Economic Review* 58 (March): 170-3.
_____ (1970-71) *The Economics of Regulation*, Vol. I and Vol. II. New York: John Wiley & Sons.
Klevorick, Alvin K. (1966) "The Graduated Fair Return: A Regulatory Proposal," *American Economic Review* 56 (June): 477-84.
_____ (1971) "The 'Optimal' Fair Rate of Return," *Bell Journal of Economics and Management Science* 2 (Spring): 122-53.
_____ (1971a) " 'The Graduated Fair Return' A Further Comment," *American Economic Review* 61 (Sept.): 727-9.
_____ (1973) "The Behavior of a Firm Subject to Stochastic Regulatory Review," *Bell Journal of Economics and Management Science* 4 (Spring): 57-88.
Kuh, Edwin, and John R. Meyer (1963) "Investment, Liquidity, and Monetary Policy," in *Impacts of Monetary Policy*. Englewood Cliffs, N.J.: Prentice-Hall.
Kuhn, Harold W., and A.W. Tucker (1950) "Nonlinear Programming" in Jerzy Neyman, ed., *Proceedings of the Second Berkeley Symposium on Mathematical Statistics and Probability*. Berkeley, 481-92. Reprinted in Peter Newman, ed., *Readings in Mathematical Economics*, Vol. I. Baltimore: Johns Hopkins Press, 1968, pp. 3-14.
Leibenstein, Harvey (1966) "Allocative Efficiency vs. 'X-efficiency,' " *American Economic Review* 56 (June): 392-415.
Levhari, David, and Yoram Peles (1973) "Market Structure, Quality, and Durability," *Bell Journal of Economics and Management Science* 4 (Spring): 235-48.
Lewis, Ben W. (1966) "Emphasis and Misemphasis in Regulatory Policy," in

W.G. Shepherd and T.G. Gies, eds., *Utility Regulation: New Directions in Theory and Policy*. New York: Random House, pp. 212-49.

Lie, Kyu Uck (1973) "On the Relative Distortion in the Averch-Johnson Model: Note," manuscript.

Lindenberg, Eric B. (1973) "The Effect of Demand and Output Elasticity Parameters in Two-Factor Models of Firm Behavior," Paper Presented at the Western Economic Association Meeting, Claremont, California, Aug.

Littlechild, S.C. (1970) "Peak-Load Pricing of Telephone Calls," *Bell Journal of Economics and Management Science* 1 (Autumn): 191-210.

Loehman, Edna, and Andrew Whinston (1971) "A New Theory of Pricing and Decision Making for Public Investment," *Bell Journal of Economics and Management Science* 2 (Autumn): 606-25.

MacAvoy, Paul W., ed. (1970) *The Crisis of the Regulatory Commissions*. New York: W.W. Norton.

———— and Roger Noll (1973) "Relative Prices on Regulated Transactions of the Natural Gas Pipelines," *Bell Journal of Economics and Management Science* 4 (Spring): 212-34.

Machlup, Fritz (1967) "Theories of the Firm: Marginalist, Behavioral, Managerial," *American Economic Review* 57 (March): 1-33.

Mangasarian, Olvi L. (1969) *Nonlinear Programming*. New York: McGraw Hill, especially p. 102.

Manne, Alan S. (1952) "Multiple Purpose Public Enterprises—Criteria for Pricing," *Economica* 19: 322-26.

McCall, John (1970) "The Simple Economics of Incentive Contracting," *American Economic Review* 60 (Dec.): 837-46.

McNicol, David L. (1973) "The Comparative Statics Properties of the Theory of the Regulated Firm," *Bell Journal of Economics and Management Science* 4 (Autumn).

Meyer, John R., and Mahlon R. Straszheim (1971) *Pricing and Project Evaluation*. Washington, D.C.: The Brookings Institution.

Miller, Merton H., and Franco Modigliani (1966) "Some Estimates of the Cost of Capital to the Electric Utility Industry, 1954-57," *American Economic Review* 56 (June): 333-91.

Modigliani, Franco, and Merton H. Miller (1958) "The Cost of Capital, Corporation Finance, and the Theory of Investment," *American Economic Review* 48 (June): 261-97.

Mohring, Herbert (1970) "The Peak Load Problem with Increasing Returns and Pricing Constraints," *American Economic Review* 60 (Sept.): 693-705.

Moore, Thomas G. (1970) "The Effectiveness of Regulation of Electric Utility Prices," *Southern Economic Journal* 36 (April): 365-75.

Myers, Stewart C. (1973) "A Simple Model of Firm Behavior Under Regulation and Uncertainty," *Bell Journal of Economics and Management Science* 4 (Spring): 304-15.

Nadiri, M. Ishaq (1972) "Aggregate and Sectoral Investment Behavior," *Brookings Papers on Economic Activity*. Washington, D.C.: The Brookings Institution, Oct.

Needham, Douglas (1969) *Economic Analysis and Industrial Structure*. New York: Holt, Rinehart and Winston.

Nelson, James R., ed. (1964) *Marginal Cost Pricing in Practice*. Englewood Cliffs, N.J.: Prentice-Hall.

⎯⎯⎯ (1972) "Discussion of Johnson and Shepherd Papers," Presented at the American Economic Association Meeting, Toronto, Dec.

Oi, Walter Y. (1971) "A Disneyland Dilemma: Two-Part Tariffs for a Mickey Mouse Monopoly," *Quarterly Journal of Economics* 85 (February): 77-96.

Peacock, Alan T., and Charles K. Rowley (1972) "Welfare Economics and the Public Regulation of Natural Monopoly," *Journal of Public Economics* 1 (Aug.): 227-44.

Peles, Yoram, and Jerome L. Stein (1973) "Rate of Return Regulation Will Not Necessarily Increase the Scale of Plant," manuscript.

Perrakis, Stylianos, and Izzet Sahin (1972) "Resource Allocation and Scale of Operations in a Monopoly Firm: A Dynamic Analysis," *International Economic Review* 13 (June): 399-407.

Phillips, Almarin, and Oliver E. Williamson, eds. (1968) *Prices: Issues in Theory, Practice and Public Policy*. Philadelphia, Pa.

Phillips, Charles F., Jr. (1969) *The Economics of Regulation*. Homewood, Ill.: Irwin.

Posner, Richard A. (1971) "Taxation by Regulation," *Bell Journal of Economics and Management Science* 2 (Spring): 22-50.

Pressman, Israel (1971) "Peak Load Pricing," *Bell Journal of Economics and Management Science* 2 (Spring): 22-50.

⎯⎯⎯, and Arthur Carol (1971) "Behavior of the Firm under Regulatory Constraint: Note," *American Economic Review* 61 (March): 210-2.

⎯⎯⎯, and Arthur Carol (1973) "Behavior of the Firm under Regulatory Constraint: Reply," *American Economic Review* 63 (March): 238.

Rees, R. (1968) "Second Best Rules for Public Enterprise Pricing," *Economica* 35 (Aug.): 260-73.

⎯⎯⎯ (1973) "A Reconsideration of the Expense Preference Theory of the Firm," *Economica* (forthcoming).

Ricardo, David (1971 edition) *Principles of Political Economy and Taxation*. Baltimore, Md.: Penguin Books, Inc.

Riley, John G. (1972) "Peak Load Pricing under Regulatory Constraint: Comment," manuscript.

Rosoff, Peter (1969) "The Application of Traditional Theory to a Regulated Firm," *Business Economics* 14 (Jan.): 77-81.

⎯⎯⎯ (1971) "Economics and Regulation," *Public Utility Law*, Annual Report Section.

Rosse, James N. (1972) "Product Quality and Regulatory Constraint," Paper presented at The Office of Telecommunications Policy Conference on Communications Policy Research, Nov.

Samuelson, Paul A. (1947) *Foundations of Economic Analysis*. Cambridge, Mass.: Harvard University Press.

_____ (1972) "Maximum Principles in Analytical Economics," *American Economic Review* 62 (June): 249-62.

Scherer, Frederic M. (1970) *Industrial Market Structure and Economic Performance*. Chicago: Rand McNally.

Schmalensee, Richard (1972) *The Economics of Advertising*. Amsterdam: North-Holland Publishing Co.

Shepherd, William G. (1966) "Regulatory Constraints and Public Utility Investment," *Land Economics* 42 (Aug.): 348-54.

_____, and T.G. Gies, eds. (1966) *Utility Regulation: New Directions in Theory and Policy*. New York: Random House.

Sheshinski, Eytan (1971) "Welfare Aspects of a Regulatory Constraint: Note," *American Economic Review* 61 (March): 175-8.

Smith, Adam (1937 edition) *The Wealth of Nations*. New York: The Modern Library edition.

Spann, Robert M. (1973) "Rate of Return Regulation and Efficiency in Production: An Empirical Test of the Averch-Johnson Thesis," *Bell Journal of Economics and Management Science* 5 (Spring): (in press).

Stein, Jerome L., and George H. Borts (1972) "Behavior of the Firm under Regulatory Constraint," *American Economic Review* 52 (Dec.): 964-70.

Steiner, Peter O. (1957) "Peak Loads and Efficient Pricing," *Quarterly Journal of Economics* 71 (Nov.) 585-610.

Stigler, George J. (1971) "The Theory of Economic Regulation," *Bell Journal of Economics and Management Science* 2 (Spring): 3-21.

_____, and Claire Friedland (1962) "What Can Regulator's Regulate? The Case of Electricity," *Journal of Law and Economics* 5 (Oct.): 1-16.

Tasch, Philip (1968) "A Review of Some Recent Literature on the Theory of the Regulated Firm," Bell Laboratories Technical Memorandum, Sept.

Takayama, Akira (1969) "Behavior of the Firm under Regulatory Constraint," *American Economic Review* 59 (June): 255-60.

Trebing, Harry M., ed. (1968) *Performance under Regulation*. East Lansing: Michigan State University.

_____, ed. (1971) *Essays on Public Utility Pricing and Regulation*. East Lansing: Michigan State University.

Turvey, Ralph, ed. (1968) *Public Enterprise*. Baltimore, Md.: Penguin Books.

Vinod, H.D. (1972) "Non-Homogeneous Production Functions, and Applications to Telecommunications," *Bell Journal of Economics and Management Science* 3 (Autumn): 531-43.

Wein, Harold W. (1968) "Fair Rate of Return and Incentives—Some General Considerations," with comments by Carl A. Conrad and William R. Hughes in H.M. Trebing, ed. *Performance Under Regulation*. East Lansing: Michigan State University.

Wellisz, Stanislaw H. (1963) "Regulation of Natural Gas Pipeline Companies: An Economic Analysis," *Journal of Political Economy* 71 (Feb.): 30-43.

Westfield, Fred M. (1965) "Regulation and Conspiracy," *American Economic Review* 55 (June): 424-43.

_____(1971) "Methodology of Evaluating Economic Regulation," *American Economic Review* 61 (May): 211-17.

_____(1971a) "Innovation and Monopoly Regulation," in William M. Capron, ed. *Technological Change in Regulated Industries*. Washington, D.C.: The Brookings Institution, pp. 13-43.

Weston, J. Fred, and Eugene F. Brigham (1972) *Managerial Finance*. New York: Holt, Rinehart and Winston, 4th ed.

White, Lawrence J. (1972) "Quality Variation when Prices are Regulated," *Bell Journal of Economics and Management Science* 3 (Autumn): 425-36.

Wichers, C. Robert (1971) "The Graduated Fair Return: Comment," *American Economic Review* 61 (Sept.): 725-6.

Wilcox, Clair (1966) *Public Policies Toward Business*. Homewood, Ill.: Irwin, 3rd ed.

Williamson, Oliver E. (1964) *The Economics of Discretionary Behavior: Managerial Objectives in a Theory of the Firm*. Englewood Cliffs, N.J.: Prentice-Hall.

_____(1966) "Peak-Load Pricing and Optimal Capacity Under Indivisibility Constraints," *American Economic Review* 56 (Sept.): 910-27.

_____(1970) *Corporate Control and Business Behavior*. Englewood Cliffs, N.J.: Prentice-Hall.

_____(1971) "The Vertical Integration of Production: Market Failure Considerations," *American Economic Review* 61 (May): 112-23, and Comments by Roland N. McKean, 124-7.

Wilson, George W. (1972) "The Theory of Peak Load Pricing: A Final Note," *Bell Journal of Economics and Management Science* 3 (Spring): 307-10.

Wilson, J. (1970) "Residential and Industrial Demand for Electricity: An Empirical Analysis," Ph.D. Dissertation, Cornell University.

Wilson, James Q. (1971) "The Dead Hand of Regulation," *The Public Interest* 25 (Fall): 39-58.

Wilson, John W. (1972) "Rate of Return Regulation under Changing Economic Conditions," *Public Utilities Fortnightly* 90 (July 6): 16-21.

Yoon, Segi (1973) "Effects of Escalator Clauses on Rate of Return for the Regulated Firm," Ph.D. Dissertation, New York University, June.

Zajac, Edward E. (1970) "A Geometric Treatment of Averch-Johnson's Behavior of the Firm Model," *American Economic Review* 60 (March): 117-25.

Zajac, Edward E. (1972) "Note on 'Gold Plating' or 'Rate Base Padding,' " *Bell Journal of Economics and Management Science* 3 (Spring): 311-5.

———— (1972a) "Lagrange Multiplier Values at Constrained Optima," *Journal of Economic Theory* 4 (April): 125-31.

———— (1972b) "Some General Theorems on Resource Allocation and Waste," Letter Written to Mrs. E.E. Bailey.

———— (1972c) "Some Preliminary Thoughts on Subsidization," Paper presented at the Office of Telecommunications Policy Conference on Communication Policy Research, Washington, D.C., Nov.

# Index

# Index

Advertising 11, 13, 30, 51, 83
AJ effect (See overly capital intensive technology, Misallocation of resources
Alchian, Armen 37n
Archer, Stephen H. 140n
Arrow, Kenneth J. 16, 16n, 18
Aten, Robert 99n
Atkinson A.B. 83n
Automatic adjustment clause 136f
Averch, Harvey 3, 4, 22, 25, 26n, 53, 65, 72, 74n, 78, 80, 84, 88, 95, 111, 139, 166, 171f
Averch-Johnson (AJ) model 3, 4, 22, 25, 53, Part II, 171f
Azariadis, Costas 69n

Bailey, Elizabeth E. 26n, 31n, 33n, 35n, 38n, 50n, 57n, 74n, 76n, 83n, 84, 99n, 111n, 123n, 139n, 155n, 163n, 166
Baumol, William J. 16n, 26n, 44n, 50n, 51, 51n, 69n, 74n, 80n, 83n, 93, 94n, 97n, 102n, 108, 111n, 139, 140n, 163n
Bear, D.V.T. 92n
Bender, Craig 96n
Bergson, Abram 50n
Boiteux, Marcel 157n, 163n
Bonbright, James C. 111n
bordered Hessian 26, 80
Borts, George H. 94, 94n
Bower, Richard S. 140, 145, 145n
Bradford, David F. 69n, 163n
Breyer, Stephen G. 58n
Brigham, Eugene F. 140n
Brown, Gardner 158n

Capacity (See Capital, Excess capacity, Rate Base)
Capital
  acquisition cost of 65, 66, 68, 125f, 132ff, 140, 171
  enlargement 118f, 121
  fixed versus circulating 102f
  input to production 10, 14, 43, 51, 61, Part II
  market cost of 65, 66, 68, 74, 82, 87, 125-32, 171
  marginal physical product of 75f, 95, 125
  marginal revenue product of 89, 140
  rising cost of 5, 22, 139-153, 172
  user cost of 130
Capital-labor ratio 59, 94, 95, 155
Carol, Arthur 74n
Christensen, L. 79n
Ciliano, R. 75n
Cohen, Kalman J. 69n
Coleman, Roger D. 76n, 99n, 111n
Collusion with equipment suppliers 6, 125, 133f
Comparative statics analysis
  on acquisition cost of capital 68, 125f, 132-134
  on market cost of capital 4, 68, 125-132
  on rate of return 87-93, 126, 147-9, 165f
  on wage rate 126, 135-7
  on taxes 126
Competitive output 108f
Complements
  in production of output 91ff
  in production of revenue 91, 127
Concavity
  definition of 18n
  in regulatory models 16, 18, 20, 28, 74
  of revenue 80
Conspiracy (see Collusion)
Constraint
  active 20, 22, 25
  asymmetric 4, 14, 41, 43, 52-7, 86, 103f, 145
  binding 20, 83, 83n
  ceiling 9, 20, 24f, 28, 30, 33, 56, 88, 97, 103
  curve (ray, plane, surface) 19, 28, 31, 47f, 53ff, 70, 90, 100, 112, 118, 122, 127, 132f, 135ff, 142-9
  qualification 15f, 18
  symmetric 4, 14, 41-52, 58, 86, 103f, 145, 155
  tightness of 18, 27, 45, 51, 90, 92, 95, 99, 108, 125, 127, 148, 165

Constraint *(Cont.)*
  zero-profit (breakeven) 21, 37, 50n, 69, 111, 122, 163
Consumers surplus 38, 158, 161
Convexity
  definition of 18n
  of the feasible region 18, 22, 80f
Corey, Gordon R. 79, 79n, 126n
Cost (see also Capital, Acquisition Cost of; Capital, Market Cost of; Capital, Rising Cost of; Capital, User Cost of; Joint-cost; Minimum-cost technology; Opportunity Cost; Wasteful cost)
  decreasing average 88, 106, 108, 163
  marginal 13, 29f, 49f, 105, 107f, 163
  of capacity in peak-load pricing model 157-60, 167ff
  of production 9, 24, 35, 66, 73
  operating costs in peak-load pricing model 157-60, 167
Cost-plus Regulation (see Regulation, Return on cost method of)
Courville, Leon 77n
Cross, John G. 35, 35n, 36
Cross-elasticity of demand 30, 162, 165f
Cross-subsidization 4, 50, 50n, 172
Currie, Kent A. 159, 159n, 167, 167n
Customer charge 38f

Dansby, Robert E. 68n, 99
Davidson, Ralph K. 157n
Davis, Eric 67n
Dayan, David 26n, 75n, 76n, 99n, 125n, 126n, 134, 134n
Debt/equity structure 67, 130, 140n
Demand function (See also Elastic Region of Revenue Curve; Inelastic Region of Revenue Curve) 10, 66, 156f
Depreciation policy 68, 88, 99
Discount rate 68, 113f
Divestiture 61
Dorfman, Robert 51n
Dreze, J.A. 158n
Economies of scale (See also Costs, Decreasing Average) 79n, 159
Eckstein, Otto 50n
Edelson, Noel M. 43n, 76n, 83n

Efficiency
  exchange 87f, 108f
  production (or allocative) 23, 32, 34, 41, 65, 77f, 82f, 87f, 104f, 108f, 122, 137
Elastic region of revenue curve 4, 23, 31ff, 37, 41, 49, 74, 75n, 82, 139, 145, 150, 153, 172
El Hodiri, Mohamed 26n
Emery, E. David 76n, 126n, 133f, 134n
Empirical (or testable) hypotheses 5, 66, 75, 78, 129, 134
Entry 3
Environmental aspects of regulation 79
Erickson, Edward 75n
Excess capacity 76, 79n, 119, 160, 164
Expansion Path
  AJ 66, 88, 95-8, 104, 108, 113, 125, 152
  efficient (or minimum cost) 32, 93, 95f, 113, 122f, 130, 141
  in rising cost of capital model 141
  invariance property of 56, 79-101
  of revenue-maximizing firm 31-7, 42ff, 51, 56, 59, 83, 96f
  of true investment model 101-4
  under asymmetric regulation 55f
  under operating ratio method of regulation 59f
  under symmetric regulation 32, 44f, 48f
Expense preference Theory of the Firm 10, 37

Factors of production (See Capital; Inferiority of factors; Labor)
Faerber, LeRoy G. 140n
Fair rate of return on capital 4, 14f, 35n, 66, 68f, 74, 83, 87-109, 125-132, 139, 141, 147ff, 171
  optimal value of 4, 36f, 87, 104-9
Fair value adjustment 68, 134
Faulhaber, Gerald R. 50n, 79n
Feasible region (See also Convexity of feasible region) 16, 19, 22, 80
Feldstein, Martin 33n, 38n
Ferguson, C.E. 92n
Financial instruments (See Debt-equity structure)
Finch, Austin 139n

Firm (See Multi-stage firm; Profit-maximizing firm; Output-maximizing firm; Revenue-maximizing firm)
First-order conditions (See necessary conditions)
Fisher, Franklin M. 75n
Friedland, Claire 79n
Full-cost pricing 36
Furubotn, Eirik G. 12, 12n

Galbraith, John K. 3n
Garfield, Paul J. 12, 12n, 61n
General equilibrium model 87f, 107ff
Gies, T.G. 157n
Goldplating (see padding of the rate base)
Graduated Fair Return (see regulation, graduated return method of)
Gratzer, Frank 125n
Greene, Julian M. 79n

Harberger, Arnold 37n
Haring, Joseph E. 137n
Hicks, Sir John R. 93, 93n, 137
Hirshleifer, Jack 158n
Houthakker, H.S. 158n
Hughes, William R. 76
Humphrey, Joseph F. 137n
Hurwicz, L. 16, 16n, 18

Inefficiency in Production (see also Misallocation of Resources; Overly Capital Intensive Operation; Overly Labor Intensive Operation; Padding of the Rate Base; Wasteful Activity) 4, 13, 33, 37, 79, 83, 87, 98, 104f, 108, 131, 145, 155, 163, 167
Inelastic Region of Revenue Curve 23, 33f, 49ff, 66, 139, 145, 172
Inferiority of Factors 87, 92-4, 126, 133, 153, 166
Inflationary periods 130f, 137
Interest Rate (see Discount rate; Capital, Market cost of)
Investment (see Capital)
Irwin, Manley R. 61n
Isoconstraint Contour 59f
Isocost Line 12, 77-81, 93, 97, 141
Isoprofit Contour 46-9, 55, 59f, 70ff, 77f, 78n, 82n, 95f, 98, 101, 146

Isoquant 12, 51, 77f, 78n, 79, 82, 93, 95ff, 117, 122, 141
Isorate-of-return Contour 66, 70ff, 80ff, 101, 128
Isorevenue Curve 48, 51
Isowelfare Contour 108f

Johnson, Leland L. 1, 3, 4, 22, 25, 26n, 53, 65, 72, 74n, 78n, 80, 88, 93, 95, 111, 139, 166, 171f
Johnson, M. Bruce 158n
Joint Costs 30, 66, 84
Jordon, William A. 3, 79n
Jorgenson, Dale W. 79n, 130n
Joskow, Paul 67n

Kahn, Alfred E. 23, 23n, 50n, 59n, 61n, 99n, 126n
Kafoglis, Milton Z. 35n, 50, 50n
Kaysen, Carl 75n
Kessel, R. 37n
Klevorick, Alvin K. 10n, 26n, 67n, 74n, 80n, 83n, 85n, 88n, 93, 94n, 97n, 98, 99n, 107
Knightian Region III 134
Kuh, Edwin 130n
Kuhn, Harold 9, 15, 16n, 18ff, 24, 42, 54, 60, 73, 80, 84, 150, 159, 163, 164, 167
Kuhn-Tucker Conditions 9, 15-20, 24, 42, 54, 60, 73, 80, 84, 150, 159, 163, 164, 167

Labor
  diminishing returns to 80, 92
  input to production 10, 22, 43, 51, 61, Part II
  marginal physical product of 75, 95, 133f
  marginal revenue product of 75
  rising cost of 151, 150f
Labor-requirement function 10, 85, 136, 159, 167
Lag (See Regulation, Lagged)
Lagrangian
  function 15-19, 24, 42, 60, 73, 77n, 80, 84f
  multiplier 15, 18, 23-8, 43n, 73f, 77n, 150-3, 160, 163n
Lau, L. 79n
Leibenstein, Harvey 37
Levhari, David 51n

Lewis, Ben W. 111n
Lie, Kyu Uck 58n, 78n, 95, 125n
Lindenberg, Eric B. 91n, 105n
Line Integral 159
Littlechild, S.C. 158n
Loehman, Edna 50n
Lovejoy, Wallace F. 12, 12n, 61n

MacAvoy, Paul W. 3n, 33n, 58, 58n, 79n
Machlup, Fritz 52n
Malkiel, Burton G. 140n
Malone, John C. 26n, 31n, 50n, 74n, 83n, 84
Managerial staff or enoluments 11, 37f, 51, 83
Mangasarian, Olvi L. 16, 16n
Manne, Alan S. 50n
Marginal cost (see cost, marginal)
Marginal revenue (see revenue, marginal)
Market structure 61
Markup (see regulation, return on cost method of)
McCall, John 35n
McNicol, David L. 83n, 85n, 125n, 136
Meyer, John R. 130n, 137n
Miller, Merton H. 140n
Minimum-cost technology 23, 31, 33, 37, 41, 66, 77n, 78, 108, 113, 118, 123, 145, 171
Minimum-return requirement 83
Misallocation of resources (See also Overly Capital Intensive Technology; Overly Labor Intensive Technology) 4, 12f, 41, 51, 53, 56f, 66, 76f, 81, 83f, 87, 94f, 99, 103, 112, 116, 119, 121, 130, 139
Modigliani, Franco 140n
Mohring, Herbert 163n
Monetary policy 125, 130
Monopoly firm (see profit-maximizing firm)
Monopsonist 67
Moore, Thomas G. 79n
Myers, Stewart C. 67n

Nadiri, M. Ishaq 130n
Necessary conditions
  for constrained maximum 18, 24f,
  28, 44, 58f, 85, 88
  for cost-minimization 77n
  for profit-maximization 11, 44
Needham, Douglas 61n
Nelson, James R. 80n, 157n
Noll, Roger 33n, 58, 58n, 79n
Nonminimum cost activity (see Inefficiency, Wasteful activity)

Off-peak price (see Peak-load Pricing)
Oi, Walter 33n, 38n
Operation off the Production Frontier, 4, 9-14, 23ff, 28-37, 41ff, 51, 53, 65, 72f, 75, 80, 83, 139, 150f, 172
Opportunity cost 87, 108, 160
Oram, Gibb 70n
Output
  maximization of 81-3, 145
Overcapitalization (see Overly Capital Intensive Technology)
Overly Capital Intensive Technology 5, 13, 65, 76, 78f, 81, 96, 111, 113ff, 117, 119-22, 130, 134, 145, 148, 150ff, 166, 171f
Overly Labor Intensive Technology 13, 66, 80-3, 145, 153

Padding of the rate base 3, 10f, 25, 74, 76, 83, 134, 139, 151, 164, 171
Pareto-optimality 22
Partial equilibrium model 3, 87, 100, 104-7, 137
Peacock, Alan T. 69n
Peak-load pricing 5, 22, 57, 155-68, 171
Pejovich, Svetozar 12, 12n
Peles, Yoram 51n, 112n
Perrakis, Stylianos 67n
Phillips, Charles S. Jr. 12n, 61n, 111n
Porcar, Alfredo 69n
Posner, Richard A. 50n
Present value of firm 67f, 113
Pressman, Israel 74n, 163n
Price (see also Peak-Load Pricing; Tariffs, two-part)
  adjustment 67, 112, 116, 123, 171
  discrimination 33, 50
  structure 67n, 79, 168
Production (see also Efficiency, Production; Minimum-cost Techno-

logy; Operation off the Production Frontier)
   function 10, 66, 91n, 92, 93n, 95, 120
   possibility locus 108
Productive variables 9ff, 14, 21, 24f, 28, 31, 33, 41, 43, 47, 51, 56
Profit
   attainable 9, 19, 22
   ceiling level of permitted profit 4, 9, 14f, 22, 26, 30-3, 36, 38, 41ff, 47, 51, 53, 68f, 96, 142f
   hill or surface 19, 22, 26ff, 31, 46ff, 53, 55, 69-71, 74, 90, 98, 100, 101, 127, 132f, 137, 143-49
   maximizing firm 33, 37, 44, 54, 65, 69, 74, 93, 95, 126, 161ff

Quality 11, 13, 30, 46, 51, 57, 83, 149, 152

Rate base (see also padding of the rate base) 35, 66, 72, 118, 171
Rate of Return (see fair rate of return; regulation, rate of return method of)
Ratio rule 45, 50, 53, 66, 85, 172
Rees, R. 12n, 50n, 52n
Regulation
   asymmetric (see asymmetric constraint)
   graduated return method of 56, 88, 98f, 152f
   lagged 5, 111-123, 137, 152
   limiting return per-unit output 34
   of multi-stage firm 60f
   operating ratio method of 21, 35n, 59f
   rate-of-return method of 4, 14, 30, 38, 53, 59, Part II
   return on cost method of 34-9, 41, 43, 58, 167f
   symmetric (see symmetric constraint)
Regulatory Lag (see regulation, lagged)
Resource Allocation (see also misallocation of resources) 43n, 53, 65, 82f, 94f, 144f, 151ff
Revenue (see also expansion path of revenue-maximizing firm)

marginal 11, 13, 29-34, 44f, 49f, 74f, 83, 153ff, 163, 167
maximizing firm 41, 44, 46, 49, 50, 66, 69, 82ff, 86, 97, 171ff
Ricardo, David 102n
Riley, John G. 159, 159n, 167, 167n
risk 87n, 140n
Rosoff, Peter 80n
Rosse, James N. 30n
Rowley, Charles K. 69n

Saddle value problem 17f
Sahin, Izzet 67n
Samuelson, P.A. 3n
Scherer, Frederic M. 94
Schmalensee, Richard 51n
Second-best solution 106
Second-order conditions (see Bordered Hessian)
Shapiro, Perry 73n
Shepherd, William G. 148n, 157n
Sheshinski, Eytan 87, 87n, 107
Sign information (see Comparative Statics)
Smith, Adam 102n
Spann, Robert M. 75n, 79, 79n
Stein, Jerome L. 94, 94n, 112n
Steiner, Peter O. 51n, 158, 158n
Stigler, George J. 37n, 79n
Straszheim, Mahlon R. 137n
Substitutes
   in production 76, 91, 93
   in production of revenue 91
Sufficiency condition (see also Bordered Hessian) 18f, 22, 80

Takayama, Akira 18, 26n, 74n
Tariff, two-part 33, 38, 58, 163n
Tasch, Philip 89n, 91n, 93n, 125n
Tax
   corporate profit 99-101, 125
   property 99-102, 125
Technological charge 123, 136f
Trebing, Harry M. 126n
Tucker, A.W. 9, 15, 16n, 18ff, 24, 42, 54, 60, 73, 80, 84, 150, 159, 163f, 167
Turnover period of fixed or circulating capital 102-4
Turvey, Ralph 158n

Uncertainty 87, 158

Undercapitalization (see Overly Labor Intensive Technology)
Usage Charge 87
Uzawa, H. 16, 16n, 18

Vinod, H.D. 80

Wage rate 5, 66, 68, 135f
Walton, Alfred G. 50n
Waste (see also wasteful activity)
   detection of 26, 33f
   utility of 38
Wasteful activity 5, 9, 12ff, 23ff, 29-38, 52, 72, 75, 76, 88, 146, 150ff, 172
Waverman, L. 83n
Wein, Harold W. 76, 111n
Welfare
   implications 36, 57
   maximization 13, 22, 69, 105-9, 158-61, 163, 166

Wellisz, Stanislaw H. 166, 166n
Westfield, Fred M. 43n, 67, 74n, 76, 125, 133f, 137f
Weston, J. Fred 140n
Whinston, Andrew 50n
White, Lawrence J. 33n, 38n, 51n, 57n, 163n, 166
Wichers, C. Robert 99n
Wilcox, Clair 23, 23n
Williamson, Oliver E. 10, 37, 52, 52n, 61n, 158n
Wilson J. 75n
Wilson, James Q. 3n
Wilson, John W. 59n

X-inefficiency 37, 72

Yoon, Segi 136n

Zajac, Edward E. 26n, 31n, 43n, 50n, 69, 74n, 76n

## About the Author

**Elizabeth E. Bailey** is supervisor of the Economic Analysis Group at Bell Telephone Laboratories and adjunct assistant professor of Economics at New York University. She received the B.A. in economics from Radcliffe College, the M.S. in mathematics and computer science from Stevens Institute of Technology and the Ph.D. in economics from Princeton University. She is the author of numerous articles on the effects and theory of regulatory constraint.